Swimming Pools
How to Plan, Maintain & Enjoy

HPBooks

Contents

Planning Your Swimming Pool 5
    Where to Begin 7
    Know the Rules 8
    How to Pick a Site 9
    Including a Spa 14
    Indoor and Enclosed Pools 15
    Money-Saving Ideas 16

Choosing a Pool 19
    Size and Shape 19
    Design Considerations 21
    Concrete Pools 23
    Vinyl-Lined Pools 25
    Fiberglass Pools 27
    Finishing Touches 29

Before You Build 33
    Who Can Help You 33
    Being Your Own Contractor 35
    Finding Qualified Help 36
    Competitive Bids 37
    Negotiating a Contract 38
    How to Avoid Trouble 41

Selecting Pool Equipment 43
    How to Size Equipment 44
    Choosing a Pump 44
    Choosing a Filter 48
    Choosing a Heater 50
    Surface Skimmers 53
    Equipment Controls 54
    Pool Accessories 55

Solar Heating & Energy-Saving Ideas 59
    Why Buy Solar? 59
    Solar Pool Systems 60
    Active Solar Systems 61
    Using Passive Solar Energy 66
    Small Steps Mean Big Savings 72

How Pools Are Built 75
    The Basic Steps 76
    Preparing the Site 77
    Sprayed-Concrete Pools 80
    Vinyl-Lined Pools 84
    One-Piece Fiberglass Pools 89
    Fiberglass-Sidewall Pools 89
    Adding Coping 91
    Adding the Deck 92
    Setting Up Support Equipment 95

Published by HPBooks
A division of Price Stern Sloan, Inc.
360 N. La Cienega Boulevard
Los Angeles, CA 90048
ISBN: 0-89586-280-8
Library of Congress Catalog Card Number: 84-81028
©1984 HPBooks, Inc.
Printed in U.S.A.
9 8 7 6 5 4

Cover Photograph:
Large boulders and used brick are major design elements of this free-form concrete pool. Dark bottom increases natural heat gain from sun. Short waterfall links pool to spa in background. *Pool Design: Mark Sutter, AIA, Encino, CA. Pool Contractor: Walter Harrington, Reseda, CA. Landscape Contractor: Sequoia Landscape Inc., Granada Hills, CA. Photo by Richard Fish.*

- **Above-Ground Pools** ... 97
  - Choosing a Site ... 98
  - Choosing a Pool ... 98
  - Choosing Support Equipment ... 100
  - Accessories ... 100
  - How to Install Your Pool ... 101
- **Pool Landscaping** ... 105
  - Landscaping Elements ... 106
  - Contouring ... 106
  - Plantings ... 107
  - Rocks ... 108
  - Fences, Walls and Screens ... 108
  - Decks and Patios ... 111
  - Walks ... 111
  - Lighting ... 112
  - Pool Buildings ... 113
- **Pool Care & Repair** ... 117
  - Maintaining Water Quality ... 118
  - pH Testing ... 119
  - Working with Chlorine ... 122
  - Troubleshooting ... 124
  - Water Chemistry Glossary ... 126
  - Equipment Maintenance ... 127
  - Pool Repair ... 134
  - Opening Your Pool ... 134
  - Closing Your Pool ... 136
  - Pool Maintenance Tools ... 138
- **Swimming for Fitness** ... 141
  - Lap Pools ... 141
  - Jet Pools ... 143
  - Swimming for Health ... 144
  - Aqua Dynamics ... 146
  - Swimming While Pregnant ... 146
  - Fitness and Fun for Children ... 146
- **Pool Safety** ... 149
  - Rules of Safety ... 149
  - Rescue Equipment and Techniques ... 152
  - Pool Alarms ... 153
  - Pool Fences ... 154
  - Pool Covers ... 154
  - Looking After Children ... 154
  - Emergency Treatment ... 156
- **Index** ... 158
- **Acknowledgments** ... 160

NOTICE: The information in this book is true and complete to the best of our knowledge. All recommendations are made without guarantees on the part of the author or Price Stern Sloan. The author and publisher disclaim all liability incurred with the use of this information.

Landscaping elements are carefully combined to create a naturalistic setting for this pool and attached spa. Flagstone deck harmonizes with informal plantings. Waterfall doubles as a pool slide. Design: Wise Pool Co. Inc, Conroe, TX.

CHAPTER 1

Planning Your Swimming Pool

Private swimming pools, once a luxury of the wealthy, are now affordable by the average homeowner. Improvements in pool materials, equipment and water chemistry have produced economical pools that provide a safe, clean place to swim. Today's residential pools are easier to maintain and have fewer repair problems than the pools of 30 years ago. Almost 2 million in-ground residential pools and an equal number of above-ground pools are in use across the United States.

Swimming pools are available for every need and budget. For those who want a pool immediately, a full-size vinyl-lined or fiberglass pool can be installed in 2 weeks or so. Above-ground pools, which can be installed in a few days, have evolved from the backyard plastic wading pool to rival in-ground pools in size and depth. Sprayed-concrete pools can be virtually any size or shape, offering the homeowner unlimited design options.

The Purpose of This Book—This book provides essential information for planning and installing a residential pool. It will help you choose a suitable pool, negotiate a contract with a reputable pool builder and take you step-by-step through the stages of installation. It also provides details on how to select support equipment and pool accessories. This information can help you avoid costly mistakes.

Photos and illustrations offer ideas you may want to include when building and landscaping your pool. Design and landscaping advice will help you save time and money, and create a pleasant, relaxing place to swim. Building a pool represents a major financial investment. A knowledgeable investment will return good value and provide years of enjoyment.

If you already own a pool, this book includes valuable information on maintaining the pool and its equipment and selecting new equipment and accessories. It has many design and landscaping ideas you can use to improve the appearance of your present pool.

This book does not provide construction details necessary to build your own in-ground swimming pool. Building a sprayed-concrete (gunite or shotcrete) pool requires special skills, experience and equipment not readily available to the average homeowner.

Though assembling a vinyl-lined pool can be done by a competent do-it-yourselfer, the labor involved is often a small percentage of the pool's total cost. One-piece fiberglass pools are easily installed, but require heavy equipment to lift the shell into place.

Excavation, plumbing and electrical work for all pools is best left to experienced pool builders. In short, you'll save little money by making a pool a complete do-it-yourself project. But you can do certain construction-related jobs to cut costs. These are discussed on pages 16-17. You can also take on landscaping and other pool-related projects to create the total pool environment. See pages 105-115.

Many above-ground pools, discussed in detail on pages 96-103, can be installed by the do-it-yourselfer. Pool kits usually include complete installation instructions. These pools offer a practical, lower-cost alternative to the traditional in-ground pool.

WHY OWN A POOL?

Building a pool is often an emotional decision. Once you decide you really want a pool, it isn't difficult to find many reasons for taking the plunge. Although you should carefully consider your reasons, rationalizing shouldn't be necessary. There are many legitimate reasons to build. A few of them are discussed here.

Lap pools are used primarily for physical fitness and competitive training. Most occupy less space than conventional pools. This one is designed to fit a steep hillside lot. For more on lap pools, see pages 141-142. Design: 20th Century Pools, Buena Vista, CA.

In recent years, the cost of single-family homes has increased rapidly in proportion to average family incomes. Average mortgage rates are also higher than they were when private homes were more widely affordable. The result is that homeowners are moving less frequently and investing more in home improvements. A new in-ground swimming pool is one investment that increases the value of a home.

A private pool provides a home-oriented center for family fun, exercise, relaxation and entertainment. It's available every day, all day during the swimming season.

An increase in two-income families has also had its effect. Two working adults in the same family who find it difficult to schedule vacation days at the same time spend more vacations at home. Two-income families are more likely to have high enough combined incomes to afford a pool.

Traveling will always be expensive. Stay-at-home savings can add up quickly to offset the cost of a pool. A pool need be no more expensive than a modest recreational vehicle or boat.

Continuing interest in physical fitness has led to greater interest in swimming. A private lap pool has tremendous appeal to a swimmer who has to fit exercise periods to the schedule of the nearest public pool.

Conventional pools can be designed to permit lap swimming. A pool designed specifically for lap swimming occupies less space than a conventional pool and is cheaper to operate. A typical lap pool is shown above. Swimming provides a safe, effective form of aerobic exercise. For more on lap pools and swimming for fitness, see pages 140-147.

NEW POOL IDEAS

Increasing energy costs and the need to conserve water have led to significant changes in how pools are designed, built and maintained. A number of energy-saving devices, including solar-heating systems and pool covers, are available to reduce operating costs. In the past few years, heaters, pumps and filters have become more energy-efficient.

Pool Care—Pool maintenance will always be required of the pool owner. The time and effort involved can be greatly reduced by adding recently developed automatic pool-cleaning systems, pool-chemical feeders and automated pool covers. Modern pool-support systems can include state-of-the-art electronic controls and programmable monitors for convenience and ease of operation.

Vinyl-Lined Pools—Technical improvements in vinyl-lined pool materials have increased pool life. Vinyl liners are treated with ultraviolet ray inhibitors to help prevent deterioration. Some suppliers now guarantee liners for 15 years. Vinyl liners are precisely cut to fit a wide variety of pool shapes—some liners are even designed by computer. New techniques have strengthened liner seams. Pool shells that support the liner are sturdier and available in a wide variety of shapes and sizes. For more on vinyl-lined pools, see pages 25-27.

Fiberglass Pools—Fiberglass construction techniques have also been improved. New fiberglass pools are stronger and more resistant to blistering. Resins used to bond fiberglass layers actually harden over a

6 Planning Your Swimming Pool

Interest in small, shallow pools is partially due to increased interest in energy and water conservation. They're also less expensive to build, operate and maintain than larger pools with deep ends. A pool like this one can be an attractive feature in a small yard. *Design: Ken Nelson Aquatech Pools, Shrewsbury, NJ.*

period of years, increasing the structural strength of the pool. New fiberglass pools are guaranteed for at least 15 years and can last many years longer with proper care. See pages 27-29.

Above-Ground Pools—These have come a long way since the days of the large, round plastic wading pools. Above-ground pools now come in several shapes—rectangular, oval, octagonal, and, of course, round. Pool size and depth are equivalent to average-size in-ground pools. Some above-ground pools are installed partially in-ground to provide a deep end for diving. Most have integral support equipment, with optional heaters.

Pool sidewalls are aluminum, fiberglass, wood or galvanized steel. On some types, the walls are insulated to prevent heat loss. Wall panels come in many attractive patterns and colors. Some above-ground pools include wood decks and safety rails. For more on above-ground pools, see pages 96-103.

Support Equipment—Pumps, filters and heaters are more efficient, easier to maintain, last longer and use less energy. The development of quiet, two-speed pump motors has greatly reduced energy use. Better-designed combustion chambers and coil configurations have made gas-fired pool heaters more efficient. Pilot lights on many gas heaters have been replaced with electric-spark ignition systems to cut gas use. Pumps and filters made of corrosion-resistant, high-impact plastics extend the life of the equipment. For more on support equipment, see pages 42-57.

Solar Heating—These systems are gaining wider acceptance. Existing pool heaters are being replaced or supplemented by active solar systems. Rooftop solar collectors have become a common sight in California and the Southwest. Solar-heated pools are cost-effective in many other parts of the country as well. Several states offer tax credits for installing solar systems or for replacing gas or electric pool heaters with solar.

Solar, thermal and insulated pool blankets and covers are more widely used to reduce water and chemical evaporation and heat loss. Solar blankets help capture heat during periods of bright sunshine. Thermal and insulated blankets help retain heat. Pools with black or other dark-color bottoms improve heat gain from direct sunlight.

Shallow Pools—Many people prefer shallow pools for several reasons. They require less energy to heat and take less water to fill. A depth of 3-1/2 to 4 feet is all that is required for most pool activities. The only advantage to a deeper pool is to permit diving. You'll find details on solar heating and other energy-saving ideas on pages 58-73.

These and many other options may make pool selection seem confusing. But if you carefully evaluate all the options, you have a better chance of installing a pool perfectly matched to your needs and budget. The chapter, *Choosing a Pool,* starting on page 19, includes all the information you need to choose a suitable in-ground pool. Details on choosing and installing an above-ground pool are on pages 96-103.

WHERE TO BEGIN

When you begin seriously planning a pool, you will collect information from many sources—pool dealers and designers, lending institutions, your local building department, utility companies and friends with pools. Buy a good notebook and a few folders to hold pool literature.

You will save time and frustration if your records are well organized from the beginning. You'll probably refer to your records frequently during planning and construction. You will also want to keep warranties for the pool's support equipment and accessories. Once your pool is completed, equipment problems covered by warranty usually must be resolved directly with the equipment manufacturer, not the pool builder.

The first step in planning a pool is to check with your local building department to make sure there are no ordinances, zoning laws or code restrictions that prohibit a pool on your property. Codes may also dictate the type of pool you can build and its location on the property. In most localities, you can check building codes at the local library.

If you employ an architect, landscape architect, landscape designer or pool contractor to do the entire job, this preliminary work will be one of his or her responsibilities. The designer or pool company that installs your pool will also be responsible for securing building permits and scheduling building inspections as work progresses. Finding capable help is discussed on pages 32-41.

KNOW THE RULES

Most pool builders are familiar with local regulations and can tell you what local restrictions will affect you. Their business depends on satisfying local requirements.

Many of your building decisions will be influenced by property setback distances, fence requirements, easements and other rules and regulations. These are contained in zoning laws, ordinances, deed restrictions or covenants.

Most restrictions that apply to the pool also apply to pool buildings and related structures. You may have to go through several local agencies to get permission to build your pool.

There are no clear definitions of the terms *ordinance, zoning law, code, deed restriction* or *covenant*. What each covers may differ from state to state or from one community to another. For instance, setback requirements in one area may be included in a zoning law, while they are covered in building codes or covenants in another area.

Ordinances and zoning laws are usually legislated by local or state governments for the mutual protection of property owners and residents of a community. They prevent types of construction or establishment of businesses that are out of character with surrounding properties or considered unsuited to a specific area.

Building codes adopted by local governments have been created to guarantee safety and call for minimum standards for materials, workmanship and construction. Codes are often exacting and written in great detail. Although local codes for building, plumbing and electrical work are based on regional master codes, they will vary slightly from one community to the next.

Deed restrictions are usually inherited from the previous property owner. When you take title to a piece of property, the deed may contain restrictions on how the property is to be used. When you agree to buy property, it is assumed you accept the existing restrictions.

Covenants are most often adopted by a community, neighborhood, homeowner's association or similar group. They serve the same basic purpose as ordinances and zoning laws.

The Appeal—If your investigation uncovers restrictions that prevent you from building the type of pool you wish, almost all ordinances or zoning laws, building codes and deed restrictions include information on how to file an appeal. Restrictions are normally written to prevent inappropriate use of property. Requests for a waiver or zoning variance for residential property improvement, including pools, are usually made to a local zoning board.

You may be required to take formal steps to get a zoning variance. You may have to file a written appeal, post notices, then appear at an open hearing where individuals both supporting and opposing the changes can be heard. You have a better chance of success if you get advance approval or support from your immediate neighbors. Obtaining a waiver of a deed restriction or local covenant may require no more than a simple request to a neighborhood association or other local group. Make sure you get the waiver in writing.

If you can't get your plans approved any other way, you can make a formal appeal through the courts. If you believe strongly enough that existing rules or restrictions are unjust, you have the right to challenge them. This action can involve a good deal of

This pool is located far enough from house to provide seclusion, yet can be seen from back windows. Locate your pool to suit your family's lifestyle and activities. *Design: Aqua-Rama of Atlanta, Marietta, GA.*

8 Planning Your Swimming Pool

time, filing fees and the expense of legal counsel.

WATER USE

Some communities have water-use restrictions that determine how and when you may fill your pool and how you may dispose of pool waste water. This may determine what type of pool filter you can use.

If you're not allowed to drain pool waste water into the community sewer system, you may need to install a dry well. Diatomaceous earth (DE) filters may be required to have separation tanks to trap waste solids, preventing them from entering the sewers. See pages 43-57 for information on how to select a filter and other pool support equipment. If it becomes necessary to empty the pool, you may have to have the water pumped out and removed by truck.

Some areas have restrictions on filling pools from the city water supply. Standard residential pools have capacities of 15,000 to 30,000 gallons of water. It may be necessary to truck in water to fill a new pool.

UTILITIES

Restrictions on energy use tend to fluctuate, depending on the current energy situation. During past shortages, some areas have restricted or curtailed use of natural gas for pool heating. This is one reason why some states offer tax incentives to install solar-heating systems.

Where natural gas is available, check with the gas company to make sure there is enough line pressure to your property. Gas-fired heaters need a main-line gas pressure of 5 inches water column pressure (wcp) delivered to the heater for efficient operation. This figure must be factored into the demand of other gas appliances in your house to determine if service is of adequate capacity.

The utility company can also tell if you have sufficient electrical power to install an electric pool heater. You'll have to install an additional, separate circuit for a heat pump or an electric-resistance heater. These appliances usually require 240-volt service. The circuit capacity must equal or exceed the amperage specified for the heater. Have an electrician or the utility company check to see if the main service entrance box has the capacity to handle the additional load.

Before you decide where to put your pool in the yard, check with local utility companies to locate existing underground phone cables and utility lines—gas, water, electric and sewer. If you use a septic tank for waste disposal, locate the tank and leach field. Determine what underground utilities may be relocated and at what cost.

Consider what complications may be caused by overhead utility lines during construction. Overhead lines may have to be temporarily moved to permit equipment access. Codes prohibit overhead electrical lines above the completed pool—these or the pool must be relocated. Find out how much cooperation you might expect from the telephone company or local utility company in relocating the lines.

Once you know what restrictions will apply, you can consider potential pool sites on your property.

HOW TO PICK A SITE

Almost every yard has several possible sites for a swimming pool. Each site will have a unique combination of elements that must be considered to determine if it is suitable. In some cases, the site will have to be modified to provide the right environment for a pool. This section covers the basic considerations for selecting a site and modifying it for a pool installation.

DRAWING A SITE PLAN

Begin by preparing a simple site plan. You'll need a pencil, a ruler or straightedge, a 50- or 100-foot tape measure and some graph paper. Choose graph paper with a *1/4-inch grid* (4 squares per lineal inch) or *1/8-inch grid* (8 squares per lineal inch). Measure your property boundaries to determine which scale and what size paper to use.

If you use a scale of 1/4 inch to the foot, it will take a sheet of paper at least 25 inches wide to scale a 100-foot-wide lot. A scale of 1/8 inch per foot reduces 100 feet to 12-1/2 inches of graph paper. The larger the scale, the more detail you will be able to include on the site plan. The site plan for an average-size suburban lot will usually fit on a 24x36" sheet of graph paper with a 1/4-inch grid. A typical site plan is shown below.

Helpful Aids—A *deed map, architect's drawings, landscape plan* or a *site survey* will save time, if they're available.

Deed maps or *assessor's parcel maps* are available from the city clerk's or county recorder's office, or the bank or title company that carries the loan

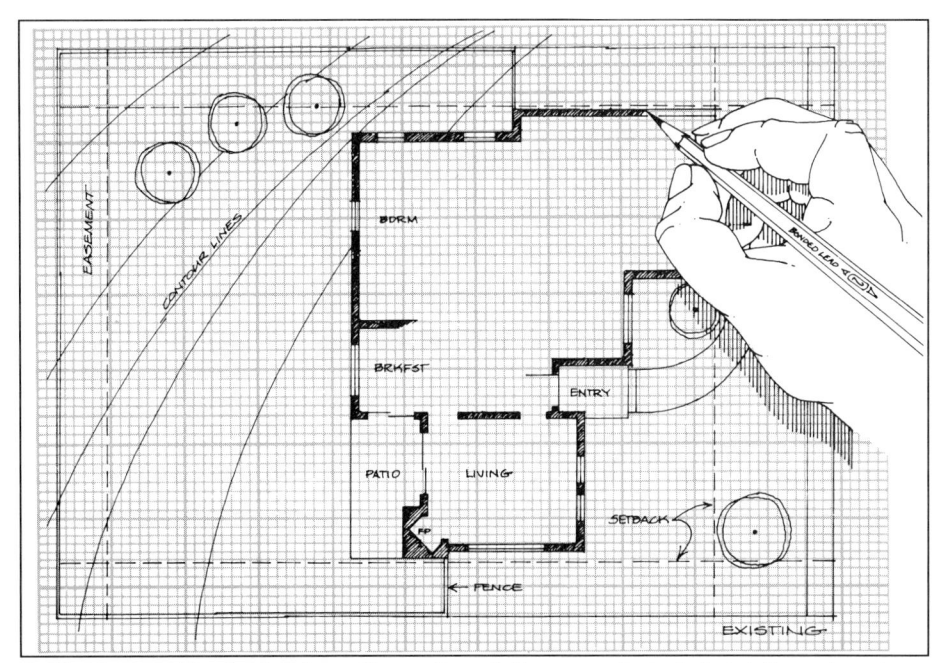

A site plan provides basic information on the existing property. Include lot dimensions, location of house and all other important features of the property. If the property is sloped, draw in rough contour lines.

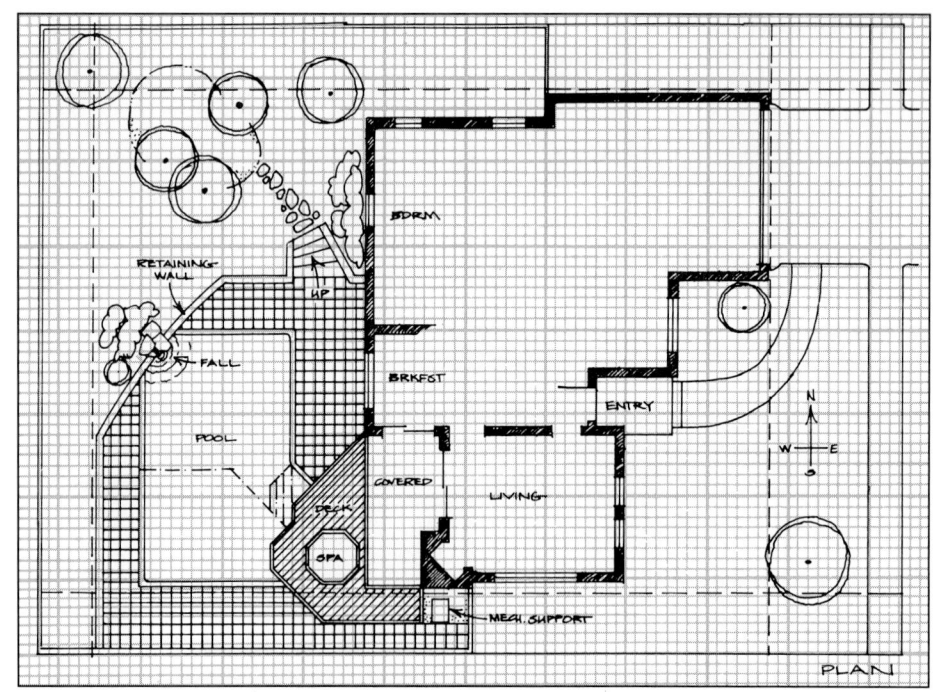

Completed plan shows location of pool, deck and other new structures and plantings. The entire plan should be drawn neatly and to scale. This is the best way to communicate your ideas to pool designers and installers.

on your home. These generally show overall lot dimensions, orientation to north and relationship to surrounding properties.

Site surveys and *architect's drawings* are often available from the original builder of the home, or the architect who designed it. These contain more detailed information than the deed map, including the basic location of the house on the property.

If a landscape architect or designer did the original landscape plan, a landscape map or master plan may be available. If this work was completed before you purchased your house, it would be worth the effort to trace the plans through the previous owner.

A landscape plan or site survey for uneven or sloping sites will often include *contour lines.* These show differences in elevation that indicate grade and drainage areas. This information will be necessary to determine pool design, and grading and drainage requirements around the pool area. If contour lines aren't included on your plans, hire a surveyor to make an accurate contour map. The surveyor will also be able to verify property lines.

What to Include—Begin by drawing the boundaries of your property. If there aren't existing walks, walls or fences to indicate the basic dimensions, refer to your deed map, site plan, or other documentation that includes a legal description of the property. If you're still not sure of your property boundaries, hire a surveyor to establish and mark them.

Next, locate the house and garage on the site by measuring from property lines. Don't rely on the house location indicated in your site plan or architect's drawings. The builder may not have located the house precisely as indicated on the plan.

Unless you're landscaping the entire property, it isn't necessary to produce a room-by-room drawing of the house. You only need to show rooms facing the pool, including sizes and locations of doors and windows.

Add all other existing permanent structures and major plantings, such as garden or patio structures, paved patio areas, trees, hedges, walks, fences and so forth.

Mark off setbacks and easements as required by code. Locate all underground utility lines—sewer, gas, water, cable TV, telephone and electric. Indicate depth below ground, if possible. The utility and phone companies can often provide this information. Also include any overhead utility lines on the property. If any lines will be above the completed pool, find a new pool location or plan to relocate utility lines.

Locate the septic tank and its leach field if your plumbing system has one. Local codes usually dictate how far the pool must be from a septic tank or leach field.

Locate water outlets and exterior electrical outlets. Indicate the locations of the gas meter and electrical-service entrance.

If the site has a gradual slope, draw in contour lines. You can determine slope by running a string from the top of the slope to the bottom and leveling the string. Measure the distance from the string to the ground at regular intervals. If the land is uneven or steeply sloped, hire a surveyor to prepare an accurate contour map, if you don't already have one.

Consider Site Access—In preparing your site plan, consider access for the pool builder. A backhoe and dump truck used for excavation both require an average of 8 to 10 feet side and overhead clearance. This may require removing one or more sections of fence or wall to provide access. Plan a path that does the least damage to the landscape and indicate it on your site plan. The path should avoid fragile walks or driveways not built to carry the weight of a loaded dump truck.

When considering access requirements, find out how the pool builder intends to remove excess earth. Some pool builders remove excess earth as excavating progresses. This saves cleanup time after the job has been completed and reduces damage to lawn and plants. The backhoe deposits dirt directly into a waiting dump truck. The truck carries it away. On sites with difficult access, some builders will use conveyor equipment to transfer dirt to a truck parked outside the property.

The completed site plan will show you feasible locations to install a pool. It will also help determine pool size and shape. A side yard area that is too narrow for a conventional rectangular pool may be ideal for a lap pool.

Sprayed-concrete (gunite or shotcrete) pools can be created to fit any space and are especially suitable for odd-shape lots. Vinyl-lined and fiberglass pools also come in a variety of shapes and sizes. The various types and shapes of pools available are discussed on pages 19-31. Details on types of above-ground pools start on page 99.

Get Your Ideas on Paper—You'll probably want to experiment with several different plans or ideas. When your original drawing of the existing

10   Planning Your Swimming Pool

landscape is complete, cover it with a tissue-paper overlay and sketch in various ideas. Translucent, lightweight tracing paper is available at art-supply or stationery stores.

In considering a site, sketch in general landscaping ideas, including pool structures, patio areas, decks, screens, fences, walls, walks, planting areas and lighting. See the chapter, *Pool Landscaping,* starting on page 105, for suggestions on landscaping. Look through photos in this book for specific ideas you may want to include. When you've arrived at a final plan, make a neat, accurate scale drawing to show prospective pool builders, designers and others you'll be working with. The drawing on page 10 is a finished plan for the site plan on page 9.

SITE EVALUATION

In addition to physical limitations, there are a number of other factors to consider. Sun, wind, foliage, noise, view and safety are the primary considerations. There may be no ideal location for your pool. The final choice will require establishing priorities to determine which conditions are the most important to you.

Sunshine—If possible, orient the pool to take full advantage of the sun. Maximum sunshine extends swimming hours each day and assures the longest possible swimming season. It also provides maximum natural solar heat gain to lower heating costs.

It's not difficult to track the path of the sun. Seasonal changes will affect shadow patterns. The high arc of the sun in early summer produces the most sunlight. In the Northern Hemisphere, the sun will be at its highest the third week of June. The house, neighboring buildings, fences and trees will cast longer shadows in early spring, late summer and fall. The longest shadows occur during winter months.

In the Northern Hemisphere, a southern exposure takes best advantage of the sun. In other words, a pool on the south side of a building or shade screen will receive more sunlight than one on the north side. A pool facing west will be slightly warmer than a pool facing east. A northern exposure is normally avoided except in hot climates where shade is desirable or where site limitations offer no alternative.

Sun and shade are important in choosing a pool location. Ideally, pool should receive maximum sunlight throughout the day. Nearby shade should be available to swimmers on hot days. This pool is located in a clearing among mature shade trees. Enough deck space has been provided for sunbathing. *Design: Barnett-Hendricks Pools Inc., Cherry Hill, NJ.*

Nearby shade is a convenience in hot climates. If there is no natural shade, a poolside cabana or gazebo can be a useful substitute. If your back yard is facing north and you want the pool to receive full sunlight, locate it to avoid the house shadow, if possible.

Reflected sunlight will also be a consideration. If the pool will include a diving board, orient the pool so the sun is at a diver's back during the hours the pool is most likely to be used.

Sunlight reflected off the pool into the house can be a distraction to those inside the house. Consider the pool location in relation to windows and glass doors. Pool glare can be controlled by fences, shrubbery and trees.

Wind Patterns—A gentle breeze can be a welcome relief on a hot day. Too much wind can be not only uncomfortable, but it robs the pool of heat and increases water and chemical evaporation. This increases operating costs. An ideal pool site is protected from strong winds.

Every pool site will have its own wind conditions. If the house, fences or other structures don't provide enough protection from prevailing

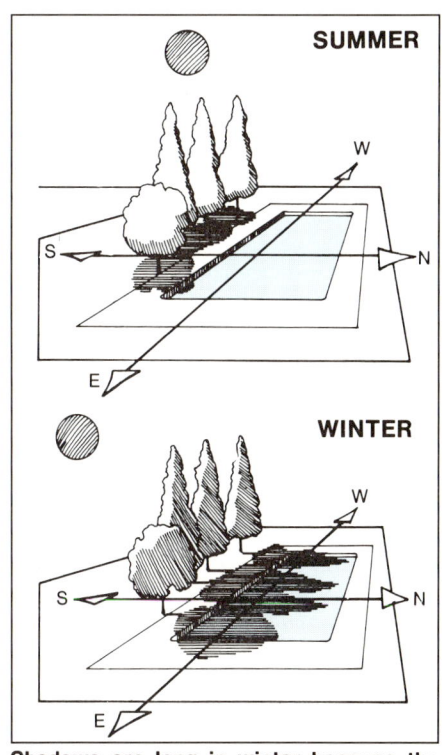

Shadows are long in winter because the sun is low in the southern sky. Trees and buildings cast more shade. In summer, sun is high in the sky and shadows are short. Trees and buildings cast less shade. Take this into account when locating the pool and planning shade screens.

Trees and shrubs offer privacy and are effective windbreaks. Here, deciduous and evergreen trees are artfully placed in a terraced patio. Larger trees outside fence block neighbor's view of pool. *Design: Stuart Bauer Pool Construction Co., Louisville, KY.*

winds, natural or artificial barriers will help. Wind screens, fences, hedges or trees are some of the devices used for wind protection. Specific types of fences and screens that make effective windbreaks are discussed on pages 109-110.

Homes situated near large bodies of water may be subjected to changing winds where morning breezes are reversed by evening. If this is the case where you live, determine at what hours of the day you'll most likely be using the pool, and note wind direction during those hours.

The house itself can be an effective windbreak. If breezes spill over the roof onto the potential pool area or sunning area, an overhead screen or roof addition may be necessary.

Learn about wind around your house by walking around potential pool sites at different times of the day during the swimming season. Ask neighbors, keeping in mind that winds around their houses may be different than around your own. Check the direction trees and shrubs lean.

A local meteorologist may be able to give you information on the direction of prevailing winds during the months you will be using your pool.

For more information on dealing with wind problems, see page 110.

Foliage—Natural growth enhances a pool's appearance. Strategically located trees provide shade. Bushes and hedges serve as windbreaks and provide privacy. If you choose to keep existing foliage, consider the prevailing winds so falling leaves won't blow into the pool. Note shadow patterns of trees at various times of the day.

Fruit trees or berry bushes may stain the pool deck and increase pool maintenance. Fruit and berries also attract insects and birds.

Trees located too close to the pool will drop leaves, which clog the skimmer and make maintenance more difficult. Tree roots are a potential problem as trees mature. Roots can damage the pool shell and support-equipment plumbing. Selecting and planting trees and other plants is discussed on page 108.

Safety—If possible, locate the pool so it can be seen from the most commonly used rooms in the house. Then you will be better able to spot intruders or unauthorized swimmers. When children are using the pool, poolside supervision is an essential safety precaution.

Plan on fencing around the pool. In most areas, pool fences are required. Local codes dictate the type of fence you can build—generally, tall and hard to climb. Gates to the pool area should be self-latching and self-locking. If a fence is built between the house and pool for safety, it should be wrought-iron, chain link or some other type of open design that won't obscure a view of the pool from the house. For more on safety requirements, see the chapter, *Pool Safety,* starting on page 149.

Privacy—It is more relaxing for family and guests to use the pool out of sight of neighbors or street traffic. You can achieve privacy by locating the pool where it can't be seen from outside your property.

Plan privacy screens or plant trees or tall shrubs to block the view of unwelcome spectators. See page 108 for more information on privacy screens.

View—If there is an appealing view from your property, you may want to situate the pool so you can enjoy the view from poolside. Hillside lots or waterfront locations offer the best view opportunities. It is possible to design a pool with a view while preserving privacy. Hillside pools facing an open area may be located above

12   Planning Your Swimming Pool

eye level or even rooftop level of neighbors below. Strategically placed trees, shrubs or fences can leave open view areas while blocking views of neighboring houses, sidewalks or busy traffic areas.

Noise—Natural growth works well to dissipate noise created by swimmers and children at play or sounds coming from neighboring yards or the street. Sound over water can be intensified. Enclosed patio areas and hard surfaces reflect and magnify sound within the patio area.

Solid enclosures block sound originating from outside the pool area. A thick, solid barrier extending above the noise source is most effective. Shrubs, grass and other foliage within an enclosed patio area will muffle reflected sound.

A noise problem may not be apparent before a pool is installed. You may have to add foliage, screens and sound-blocking structures later—if and when noise becomes a problem. Plants are not the most effective noise barriers. Hedges and plant screens will seem to reduce noise if they visually block its source. This is mainly psychological. Actual noise levels, measured in decibels, are only slightly reduced. Shrubs, ground covers and lawns will absorb noise better than a hard, reflective surface such as concrete. Natural earth berms with plantings on top are also effective noise reducers.

Soil Tests—In looking over your property for a suitable site, consider soil conditions. Excessive rock, seepage or damp soil, a high water table or other natural complications will make pool excavation more difficult, adding to the cost of the job. Excessive ground water can exert enough hydrostatic pressure to damage an in-ground pool.

If there is any question about soil conditions, have a formal test completed by a soils engineer. This test may be required before you will be issued a building permit. Problem soils are discussed in detail on pages 77-79.

Drainage—In your site plan, note any grading or contouring needed to assure adequate drainage. The object is to direct runoff away from the house and pool. Runoff can contaminate pool water and make it hard to keep water chemically balanced.

This spa is designed as part of the pool. It uses same water and support equipment. Spa overflow helps heat pool water. Design: J & J Aquatech Pools, Turlock, CA.

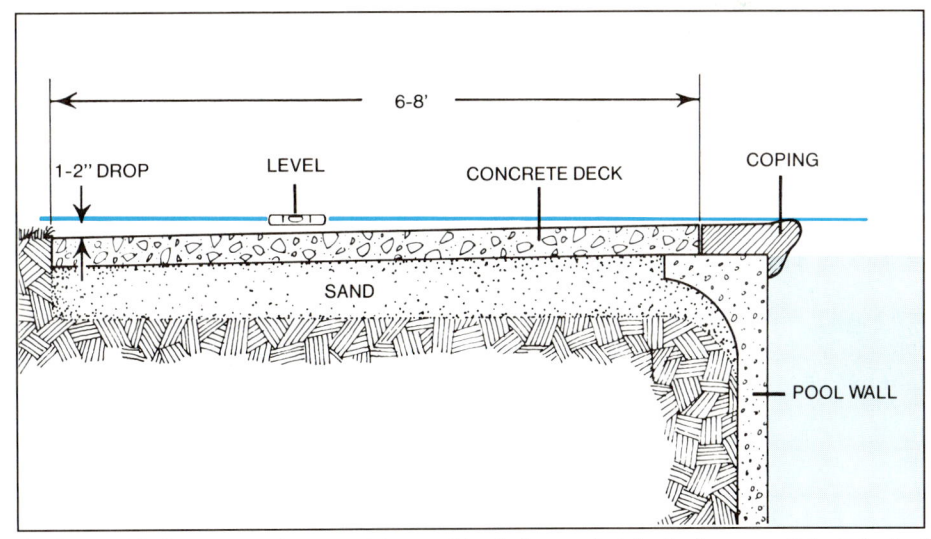

Deck should slope away from pool to provide drainage. A 1-inch slope per 6 to 8 feet of deck is adequate for most deck materials. Pool coping should be above deck level.

Design your pool so the coping around its edge is slightly higher than the surrounding pool deck. The deck should slope slightly away from the pool on all sides. For most masonry decks, the slope need not be much—about 1-inch drop for each 6 to 8 feet of horizontal run.

Only the slightest slope is necessary to drain water naturally from your property. Isolated low spots should be filled or recontoured to permit drainage. In enclosed areas where natural runoff is blocked, a deck drain or catch basin can be installed to drain accumulated water. The drain is connected to a pipe that leads to a lower spot on the property, or an underground dry well.

Subsurface water can be a more complex and expensive problem. You may already be aware of a high water table if you have a basement with moisture problems. A soil test is the best method of discovering how much of a problem subsurface water might be. Subsurface drainage may require a special, underground system around the pool to carry away excess water. Subsurface conditions may also deter-

A separate spa can relate to the pool in form and function. This sprayed-concrete spa is separate from pool but shares same angular design and support equipment. Design: Mark Berry, ASLA, Pasadena, CA.

mine what type of pool is most practical and dictate construction methods. This is discussed in greater detail in the chapter, *Choosing a Pool,* pages 19-31.

INCLUDING A SPA

Many new pool owners include a spa in their basic pool designs to enjoy both a vigorous swim and a relaxing hot-water soak. Whether you include a spa in your swimming pool plans is a matter of choice. Incorporating a spa into the pool design is less expensive than installing one separately, or adding a spa to the pool at a later date. Unless you have strong reasons for installing a spa away from the pool area, such as inside the house, it's best to include the spa as part of the pool installation.

There are as many spa designs as there are pool designs, perhaps more. Spas occupy little space and are less complicated to install. Complete information on spas and hot tubs can be found in the book by A. Cort Sinnes, *Spas & Hot Tubs,* published by HPBooks. It is an important reference for anyone considering a spa.

Spas designed to complement swimming pools are often built of the same materials as the pool. Sprayed-concrete spas are finished with a smooth lining of plaster or ceramic tile. Other spas are prefabricated units constructed of fiberglass with a gelcoat or acrylic interior coating. A hot tub is traditionally wood. Both usually include hydrotherapy devices such as hydrojets or air bubblers to agitate the water.

A spa will add to the pool's cost, but a pool and spa built at the same time will cost less than if each is built separately. They can share the same pump, filter and heater. Plumbing and wiring can be completed for both at the same time. Adding a spa after the deck has been completed and yard landscaped is possible, but costly. A spa designed to be a permanent part of the pool adds value to the home and can be an appealing bonus should you elect to sell in the future.

There are pool-support systems (pump, filter and heater) that have been designed specifically to handle the added demands of a spa. If you want to build away from the pool, a separate support system may be more practical. If your pool has a solar-heating system, a spa may need a booster heater of its own.

Spas are normally heated to a recommended maximum of 104F (40C) and are comfortable above 95F (35C). An average spa will hold between 400 and 800 gallons of water. The steps necessary to assure good water quality are similar to those needed to maintain a pool. Warmer spa water causes sanitizing chemicals to dissipate more quickly than they do in cooler pool water. Water quality must be tested more frequently.

If you have no immediate interest in a spa or simply can't work one into the budget, plan your pool so a spa can be added at a later date. Consider

14 Planning Your Swimming Pool

installing initial support equipment capable of taking care of both the pool and a spa. If you add a spa later, you will save money if the plumbing is already roughed in when the pool was built.

The key to a combined pool and spa is in the system of valves that regulate the flow of water through the filtration system. By diverting water flow through the system, it is possible for the pool and spa to be operated as independent units.

Some attached spas are physically separated from the pool. Others are built so spa overflows into the swimming pool. Another option is to build the spa as part of the pool itself, so spa and pool share the same body of water.

INDOOR AND ENCLOSED POOLS

Indoor or enclosed pools can extend the swimming season or make year-round swimming possible, even in cold climates.

Pool enclosures include air-supported plastic bubbles and metal frame structures covered by plastic or fiberglass. Conventional greenhouses can also be used to enclose pools. Enclosures can be temporary or permanent and added any time after the pool has been completed. They can be free-standing or attached to the house. Temporary enclosures can be removed during the summer and replaced in the fall for year-round swimming.

Pool enclosures help reduce heat loss and eliminate wind-accelerated water evaporation. If you intend to use some form of enclosure, a traditional rectangular pool is the most practical design. Most enclosures are designed to cover rectangular or round pools.

Indoor pools are either incorporated into the original house design or enclosed in a room addition. Designs for indoor pools are limited only by cost and the architect's creativity.

An indoor pool combines all the problems of building a new pool with the construction of a new home or room addition. The pool and enclosure are permanent additions to the home and require careful planning. Employing an architect or contractor with experience in building indoor pools will save time in sorting out the

Room additions for indoor pools must be carefully designed to match architecture and floor plan of house. South-facing location and large windows or skylights take best advantage of sun. This pool is enclosed in solarium-style addition. *Design: Barnett-Hendricks Pools Inc., Cherry Hill, NJ.*

Greenhouse-type enclosure provides maximum solar gain. This one is a custom-designed enclosure attached to the house. There are also a number of prefabricated greenhouses—attached and freestanding models—that can be used for pool enclosures. *Design: Aqua-Blue Aquatech Pools, Satellite Beach, FL.*

When planning your pool budget, decide how much you'll spend on pool surroundings. A well-designed and landscaped pool like this one can be more inviting than a larger pool with minimal landscaping. *Design: Galper/Baldon & Associates, Landscape Architects, Venice, CA.*

various zoning requirements and building codes and permits that will affect your plans. Using an experienced builder will also help prevent serious design and building errors.

Indoor and enclosed pools have the advantages of weather protection, privacy and an unlimited season for swimming and exercise. A well-designed indoor pool enclosure can double as a greenhouse or family recreation room. Attached indoor pools are best located with a southern or southwestern exposure. This provides the maximum natural heat gain, making the pool more economical to heat. Moisture, ventilation, heating and acoustical problems for indoor pools require special solutions that are best handled by a knowledgeable builder.

MONEY-SAVING IDEAS

In planning a new pool, the age-old rule, *you get what you pay for*, will almost always apply. A bargain pool may turn out to be no bargain at all. A properly designed and installed in-ground pool involves unavoidable costs for labor and materials. Special equipment and expertise is necessary to produce a quality pool.

The least expensive pool won't necessarily offer the best value. The lowest bid may not be the best deal. But there are opportunities to save money and reduce costs. Following are a few steps you can take to get a satisfactory pool at a fair price.

HOW MUCH SHOULD YOU INVEST?

Before you set your heart on a specific pool, take a realistic look at how much money you can afford to invest in the total project—pool, deck, fences, landscaping and pool buildings. If you intend to obtain a loan to finance your pool, check with local lending institutions to find out current interest rates and the maximum amount you can borrow. Shop for a loan.

Compare interest rates on loans available to you from savings and loan companies, credit unions or wherever else you may be able to obtain credit. If you are adding a pool to an existing home, you may have enough equity in the home to finance the pool through a *home-equity loan* from the bank that carries your present mortgage. The pool itself is considered an improvement. This is often an easy way to get a substantial loan for home improvements, but not always the least expensive way. Check other loan options available to you.

Find out what the bank considers a realistic investment in a pool in relation to the value of your home. What effect would the pool have on its resale value? If you sell your property, you'll recover a smaller percentage of the cost of an expensive pool added to a modest-size home. For maximum resale value, the pool should be in scale with the home and surrounding properties.

MAKE A BUDGET

Once you have determined how much you can afford to invest, decide how much money will be spent on the pool, its support equipment and accessories, and how much will be spent on landscaping around the pool. Landscape elements include patios and decks, fences and walls, pool buildings and plant materials.

Support Equipment—Don't stretch your budget to build a large pool of inferior quality. Settling for an undersize pump, filter and heater is false economy. What you initially save will be quickly lost in higher operating costs.

An undersize heater actually consumes more fuel to raise the water temperature the same number of degrees than a correctly sized one. Too small a filter requires frequent backwashing or cleaning and can increase both the cost of pool chemicals and time spent maintaining the pool. Become familiar with the information in the chapter *Selecting Pool Equipment,* pages 43-57, and the chapter, *Pool Care & Repair,* pages 117-139.

If your budget is limited, you'll be better off settling for a smaller pool of the best quality. If you can't afford to spend what is necessary for what you believe to be the ideal pool, spend your money on the pool, its support equipment, and the accessories that are most economical to install during pool construction. This would include underwater pool lights, the pool deck, safety lighting around the pool and plumbing and wiring for a future spa addition. Some of the accessories, landscaping and pool structures can wait.

Landscaping—A large, expensive pool in a bare, ugly yard won't be as pleasant to use as a modest-size pool in an attractive, comfortable environment. Include in your budget the necessary landscape elements, such as adequate deck space around the pool,

16   Planning Your Swimming Pool

One way to save money is to do pool-related structures and plantings yourself. If you were to build this pool, the builder could install the pool and surrounding concrete deck. You could add the wood deck, lawn, and pool house. *Design: Heldor, Morristown, NJ.*

safety fences, and screens or major plantings for shade, wind control and privacy. Add these when you build the pool. Less-important features can be added in the future, as budget allows.

When you've made your budget, contact pool designers or builders and let them know exactly how much money you have available for the pool. Ask what you can expect for your money.

You may already know what size, shape and type of pool you want, but you should be flexible. An experienced pool builder will be able to suggest economies in design and materials that can save you money without compromising quality.

HOLDING DOWN COSTS

From the date you decide to have a pool built on your property until you are enjoying your first splash in a completed pool, there will be many opportunities to save money. Don't hesitate to let your builder know you do have a budget and that you want to do everything possible to hold down costs without sacrificing quality in materials and workmanship.

While discussing costs and the construction contract, agree to take on some of the less-complicated work yourself. Include the specifics in the final contract. Pages 38-39 include useful information on negotiating a contract. Here are a few steps you can take to reduce costs:

Footwork—Take on some of the time-consuming tasks that have to be completed before building can begin. Obtain your own building permits. Work directly with the utility companies to locate and arrange for the relocation of utility lines, if necessary. These chores can be handled by your pool builder, but they take time. Your builder can legitimately charge you for these services.

Prepare the Site—Before the builder arrives to begin installation, do the preliminary work necessary to see that the contractor has access to the site and everything is ready for work to begin. You can remove fences or other obstacles that block access for construction equipment. You can remove or transplant trees and other plants.

The pool builder's goal is to get onto the site as quickly as possible, complete the work properly, get out and move on to the next job. This is how the builder makes a profit.

Discuss these details with the builder long before construction begins. If there are price concessions to be had, find out what they are. Have a clear understanding as to what you must do to earn the price break agreed upon. Include this information in the contract.

Off-Season—Offer to let the builder install your pool in the off-season, or agree to a longer construction period. A pool builder with a skilled crew wants to keep them as steadily employed as possible.

The builder may be willing to make price concessions if your job is scheduled during the off-season or can be given a lower priority and worked in and around other, more pressing projects. If you do agree to an extended installation time, still insist on a specific date for completion.

In cold climates, demand for pools is highest in the spring. Offer to have your pool installed in late summer or fall—or after your builder has taken care of other obligations. Your pool can be filled and ready for use first thing next spring.

In areas with mild winters, pool construction is often a year-round business. However, most people still want their pools installed in early spring, so they can enjoy them throughout the swimming season. Fall and early winter months are usually the slowest time for pool builders in these areas.

Cleanup—The pool builder should assume responsibility for removing excavated dirt and rock. This requires heavy equipment. Final light cleaning around the pool and grounds is a job you can agree to do yourself.

Landscaping—Depending on your skills, your budget and how much free time you have, you can handle many pool-related projects that are costly if completed by outside contractors.

A completed pool with a deck and safety fence can be used immediately. Plantings, patios, decks, steps, walks and pool structures can be do-it-yourself projects that can be completed over a period of time after the basic pool is in. For more information, see the chapter, *Pool Landscaping,* starting on page 105.

Shape and appearance help determine type of pool and deck you choose. This pool is but one of many design possibilities with sprayed-concrete pools. Brick is a versatile deck material. Sprayed-concrete pools are discussed on page 23. For more on pool decks, see page 92. *Design: Ken Nelson Aquatech Pools, Shrewsbury, NJ.*

18 Choosing a Pool

CHAPTER 2

Choosing a Pool

In recent years, pool materials have improved significantly in quality and durability. No specific type of pool is clearly superior to all others. All pool manufacturers and builders can make a good case for the types of pools they offer. All types can be installed in any part of the country if they're adequately reinforced to withstand local climatic and soil conditions.

Certain types of pools are more suitable to various parts of the country. Popularity is based largely on climate and regional conditions. Sprayed-concrete pools (gunite or shotcrete) are most common in warm climates—the South, Southwest and California. Because sprayed-concrete application is a highly specialized trade, these pools will naturally be found in warmer climates where spray-gun operators can stay employed all year long. Vinyl-lined pools are most common in the Midwest and Northeast where there is a short swimming season, short building season and sub-zero winter temperatures.

Fiberglass pools, which can be installed in any climate, are popular in areas where the manufacturer has the most effective dealer network. See page 27.

This chapter discusses points to consider in selecting pool size and shape. It provides details on the types of in-ground pools currently being installed. Above-ground pools are discussed on pages 97-103.

SIZE AND SHAPE

It is not difficult to design a multi-purpose pool that satisfies most family interests. Size is limited only by available space, your budget and how large a pool you are willing to heat and maintain.

Sprayed-concrete pools can be built in any size and shape. Shapes for poured-concrete pools and concrete-block pools are much more limited. Vinyl-lined pools are manufactured in a number of standard sizes and shapes, which vary from one manufacturer to another.

There are two basic types of fiberglass pools. One type is a one-piece, molded fiberglass shell. The other type consists of a pool shell with fiberglass sidewalls and a concrete bottom.

One-piece fiberglass pools are usually restricted to a small number of sizes and shapes because of the expensive, complex molds used in their manufacture. Ease of installation is the main advantage of these pools.

The fiberglass-sidewall, concrete-bottom type can be built in almost any size and shape using different combinations of sidewall panels. Some sidewall panels are flexible enough to be warped into a slight curve to make free-form pool shapes. Joints between sidewall panels are watertight, so no vinyl liner is required. Both types of fiberglass pools are discussed in detail on pages 27-29.

POOL SIZES

Perimeter dimensions, water surface area, and capacity in gallons are common ways of describing a pool's size. You have several logistical decisions to make in selecting the right pool size.

Fitting to the Landscape—Consider how well a new pool will fit into the overall landscape. How will it look in proportion to the size of your home and yard?

In sizing a pool, plan adequate space for the deck around it. A suitable deck has roughly the same number of square feet as the pool surface. Minimum deck width around any pool is 3 feet. Additional deck space is often added at one end or side to accommodate pool furniture for a lounging or sunning area. A diving board will also require additional deck space. See page 57.

The pool should fit comfortably into the total environment. A large pool in a small yard can be too

Choosing a Pool 19

COMMON POOL SHAPES

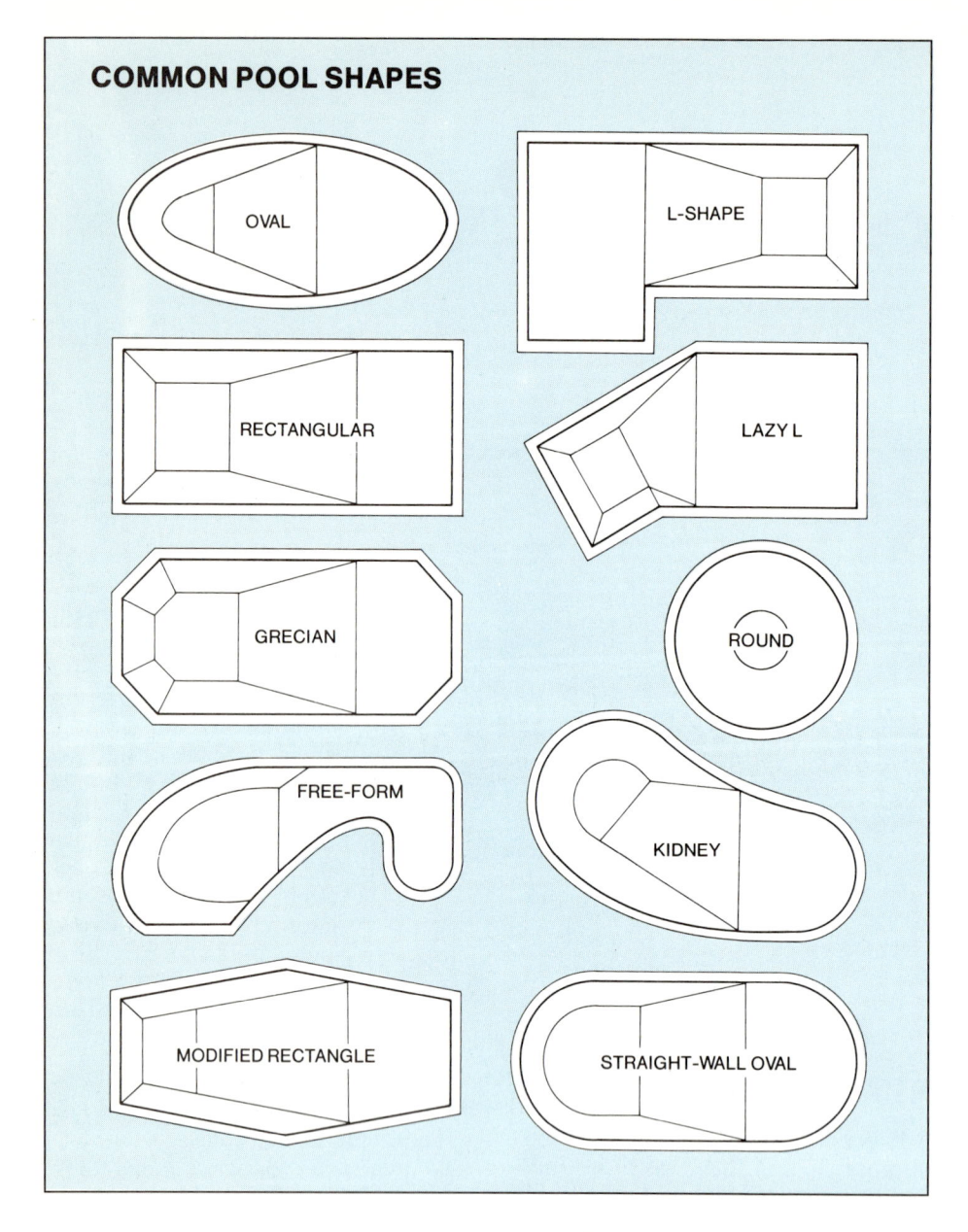

- OVAL
- RECTANGULAR
- GRECIAN
- FREE-FORM
- MODIFIED RECTANGLE
- L-SHAPE
- LAZY L
- ROUND
- KIDNEY
- STRAIGHT-WALL OVAL

dominant, especially if you plan to use the yard for other family activities. If you have an exceptionally large yard, an average-size pool can be blended in by using walls, flower beds, hedges and other landscaping tricks to break up space. For more information, see the chapter, *Pool Landscaping,* starting on page 105.

Budget—Building a pool, regardless of size, involves basic fixed costs. It costs the same to truck a backhoe to the site for a small pool as for an Olympic-size pool. So a pool twice as large won't necessarily cost twice as much. Building costs rise in decreasing proportion to pool size.

In figuring the cost of going from a minimum-size pool to a larger size, additional cost should be calculated as add-on costs. These are the additional costs for materials, labor and higher-capacity support equipment—pumps, filters and heaters—involved in a larger pool.

The real cost of a larger pool is the continuing expense of heating and pool chemicals. Maintenance costs are in direct proportion to pool size. Pool covers and other accessories will also be more expensive for larger-size pools.

Capacity—A 16x32' pool with a deep end for diving is considered a minimum comfortable size for all-around swimming activities. The practical minimum depth for swimming is 3-1/2 to 4 feet. The industry standard for figuring the number of people a pool can accommodate comfortably is 36 square feet of water surface area for each swimmer and 100 square feet for each diver.

A standard 16x32' pool—512 square feet—will accommodate 12 swimmers at one time or eight swimmers and two divers. This formula also works for determining the comfortable and safe capacity for an existing pool. See the chapter, *Pool Safety,* starting on page 149, for more information on using a pool safely.

Other Family Activities—A large pool in a small yard can dominate it. Not only is the pool visually out of scale with the surrounding landscape and structures, but it leaves little room for other activities.

Consider your family's lifestyle and leisure activities when selecting a pool size. If swimming and poolside lounging will be the primary activities, the pool can be a major element in the yard. If the yard will be used for other activities, plan pool size accordingly. People who frequently entertain outdoors may sacrifice actual pool space for a larger deck area or a spacious adjoining patio. This may include a large lanai or cabana, or a barbecue and outdoor-eating center.

Avid gardeners will have to balance pool size with garden space. Dogs or other large animals will need room. Also consider space required for storage areas and outbuildings.

If you have small children, you may want to use part of the yard for a play area. If so, allow sufficient space so the kids don't feel caged, but keep in mind that they'll soon outgrow the play yard, no matter what size it is. The play yard or pool should be sufficiently fenced so the children don't need constant supervision while playing. Children should not be left unattended in the pool area.

POOL SHAPE

You can build a sprayed-concrete pool in any shape you wish. Pools built in the shape of pianos, guitars and hearts reflect their owners' interests or personalities. Free-form shapes can be custom-fitted to odd-shape lots, or simulate a natural pond. Vinyl-lined pools and fiberglass-sidewall pools also offer a great variety of shapes.

Custom shapes require custom work and can add considerably to the cost. If home resale is a consideration, it may be hard to find a buyer who

Large boulders are integral to structure of this naturalistic pool. Sprayed-concrete—gunite or shotcrete—construction makes pools like this possible. *Design: Wildwood Pools, Fresno, CA.*

shares similar tastes in design.

The most commonly built pool in the U.S. today is the traditional rectangular pool with a deep end for diving. This basic pool has been found satisfactory because it's economical, permits diving, offers a shallow end for play or games and is suitable for lap swimming.

Rectangular pools are easy to landscape. Because most manual and automatic pool covers are designed for rectangular pools, you have a greater selection of covers if you install a rectangular pool.

Custom-designed free-form pools utilizing rock and other natural materials can be created for a natural-looking landscape. These pools are usually the most costly to build. Odd-shape pools are generally built to fit pie-shape, narrow or steeply sloping sites. In these special cases, unusual shapes can be effective and attractive.

Don't overlook the more traditional shapes—kidney, oval, Roman, L-shape and other common shapes. Most standard pool shapes are based on some combination of basic geometric forms—squares, rectangles or circles. These shapes fit well into most landscapes. Standard shapes offered by dealers are often less expensive than custom shapes of the same size. Some of the more traditional pool shapes are shown in the drawing on page 20.

DESIGN CONSIDERATIONS

Base the final decision of pool size, shape and depth on how you intend to use the pool. Not all pool owners have the same interests or anticipate the same use by family or friends.

Exercise—Swimming for exercise requires a lap pool, a rectangular pool or a custom pool designed to permit lap swimming. Length is more important than any other feature. Other requirements include a clear lane at least 8 feet wide with a minimum depth of 3-1/2 to 4 feet and parallel, vertical ends for making turns.

The length of the swimming lane will be limited by design and available space. A standard-length pool for competition swimming is 75 feet or 25 meters, normally too long for an average back yard. Selecting a length divisible into a standard competitive swimming distance makes the most satisfactory lap length. Ideal lengths are 37-1/2 feet or 50 feet. A length less than 37-1/2 feet permits too few strokes on each lap and requires too many turns to be effective for competitive training.

Another option in fitness pools is a small, narrow pool that produces a current for swimming in place. Although these pools aren't as suitable as lap pools for competitive training, they're a good exercise alternative where space is limited. These are called *jet pools*. One is shown on page 145. The chapter, *Swimming for Fitness,* starting on page 141, includes more information on using your pool for physical fitness.

Shallow Play Area—A family with children or frequent young visitors may prefer a pool with a large shallow end for play. The minimum depth

Choosing a Pool 21

Standard rectangular pools with deep end for diving are still popular for several reasons: They are easy to landscape and usually less expensive than custom-shaped pools of similar size. This 20x40' vinyl-lined pool accommodates a broad range of pool activities—lap swimming, diving, water sports and games, and just splashing around. *Design: Aqua-Rama of Atlanta, Marietta, GA.*

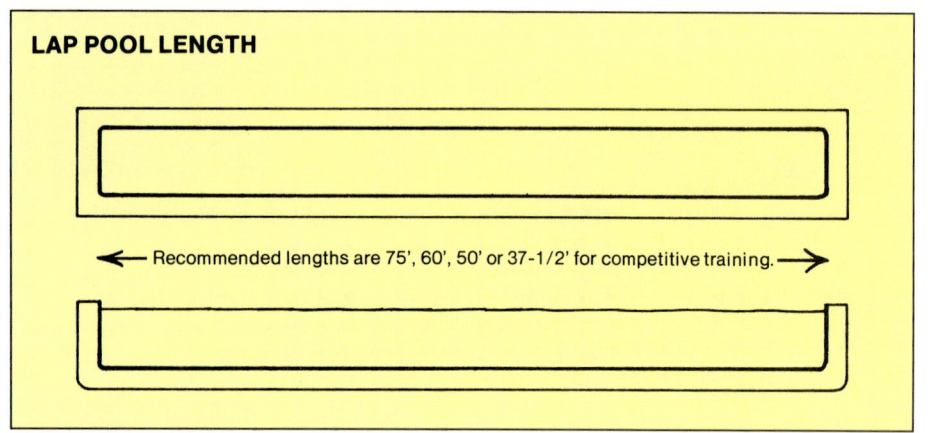

LAP POOL LENGTH

← Recommended lengths are 75', 60', 50' or 37-1/2' for competitive training. →

Length of lap pool should be even divisor of a standard swimming distance. 37-1/2 feet is considered the minimum desirable length for competitive training. These lengths are not required for simple fitness training and exercise.

recommended by the National Spa and Pool Institute (NSPI) is 33 inches.

A well-built pool will provide many years of service. Don't include a large shallow area only because there are young children in the family. Children can be taught to swim at an early age and may outgrow a shallow pool quickly. They may also become interested in diving as they grow older. As mentioned, a depth of 3-1/2 to 4 feet is suitable for swimming purposes.

As an alternative to a large shallow area in an in-ground pool, consider setting up a portable, inexpensive wading pool for toddlers.

Saving Energy—Over a period of years, the cost of heating and maintaining a pool can surpass the original cost of building it. Small, shallow pools use fewer chemicals, require less energy to heat and use smaller heaters and filtration systems. Solar-heating systems are also scaled down. For complete details on solar installations, see the chapter, *Solar Heating & Energy-Saving Ideas,* starting on page 59.

As a conservation measure, there has been an increase in the installation of pools 3 to 5 feet deep, with flat bottoms. A shallow pool holds less water, therefore requires less energy to heat and benefits from greater natural heat gain from the sun. The only disadvantage of a shallow pool is that it can't be used for diving.

Diving—The traditional pool is designed to include a deep end for a diving board. For many people, diving is one of the pleasures of owning a pool. A well-designed residential pool provides one of the safest opportunities for diving. Most diving accidents occur in the ocean or in lakes or ponds.

Pool manufacturers recommend a specific-size diving board for each of their pools. The NSPI has also set minimum standards for pool depths for diving. Exceeding the minimum-depth recommendations will provide an added margin of safety.

For an 8-foot board 20 inches above the water, the pool should be a minimum of 7 feet, 6 inches deep. Depth should be 8 feet for a 10-foot board, 26 inches above the water; 8 feet, 6 inches for a 12-foot board 30 inches above the water, and 9 feet for a 12-foot board 40 inches (1 meter) above the water.

Diving-board manufacturers will also recommend minimum pool widths and depths for specific boards they sell. For more details on choosing a diving board, see the chapter, *Selecting Pool Equipment,* pages 43-57.

Architecture and Landscape—The esthetic beauty of a pool can be just as important as the uses it will be put to. With careful planning, you can relate pool size and shape to the architectural design of the house and the landscape design.

Kidney-shaped and free-form pools fit best into natural or rustic settings. Classic Roman or Grecian shapes fit best in highly structured, formal landscapes. Pools based on squares and rectangles fit well into landscapes based on the same.

Pool shape may also be dictated by other major structural or natural elements on the property. For instance, a pool may be built to wrap around the corner of the house to take advantage of sunlight at different times of the day, or to create an effect when viewed from within the house. Or the shape may take advantage of a natural

22 Choosing a Pool

Pool shape should complement surrounding landscape and architecture. L-shaped pool and surrounding deck are precisely designed elements in overall scheme based on squares and rectangles. *Design: Ken Nelson Aquatech Pools, Shrewsbury, NJ.*

rock outcropping on the property, or a specimen tree that you wish to preserve. For more ideas, see the chapter, *Pool Landscaping,* starting on page 105.

WHAT TYPE OF POOL?

There are many types of in-ground pools being built today. Most are some variation of sprayed-concrete, vinyl-lined or fiberglass models. Each has advantages and disadvantages to consider before making a final choice. Quality of workmanship and materials will also vary within each of the three basic pool categories.

The complexity of installation and the materials used will affect the price of the pool. Support equipment, landscaping, pool buildings and other amenities will often exceed the basic cost of the pool itself.

Basic installation procedures for each major type of pool described here are included in the chapter, *How Pools Are Built,* starting on page 75.

CONCRETE POOLS

A well-built concrete pool is durable and will outlast most homes. Archeologists have discovered masonry pools thousands of years old, still intact.

Concrete is most commonly used for residential pools in warm and temperate climates. In colder climates where there is a deep frost line, concrete is used primarily for commercial pools. In colder climates, the walls must be considerably thicker and stronger, adding to the cost.

The interior of a concrete pool is troweled smooth and painted with a waterproof sealer or finished with a smooth coat of plaster.

Sprayed-concrete pools (gunite or shotcrete) are by far the most common concrete pools built today. Poured-concrete pools and pools with masonry-block walls are much less common, but are occasionally built in areas where other pool types aren't readily available.

Gunite and Shotcrete—Strength and flexibility are the primary assets of gunite or shotcrete construction. Gunite pools are formed by shooting an almost-dry mixture of hydrated cement and sand from a nozzle to cover a network of tied steel reinforcing bars (rebar). This forms a durable, seamless, one-piece shell. Shotcrete construction is almost identical, except shotcrete is premixed and pumped wet to the pool site. Complete installation details for sprayed-concrete pools start on page 80.

There are several advantages to building with sprayed-concrete. A pool can be created in almost any

Choosing a Pool 23

SPRAYED-CONCRETE POOL

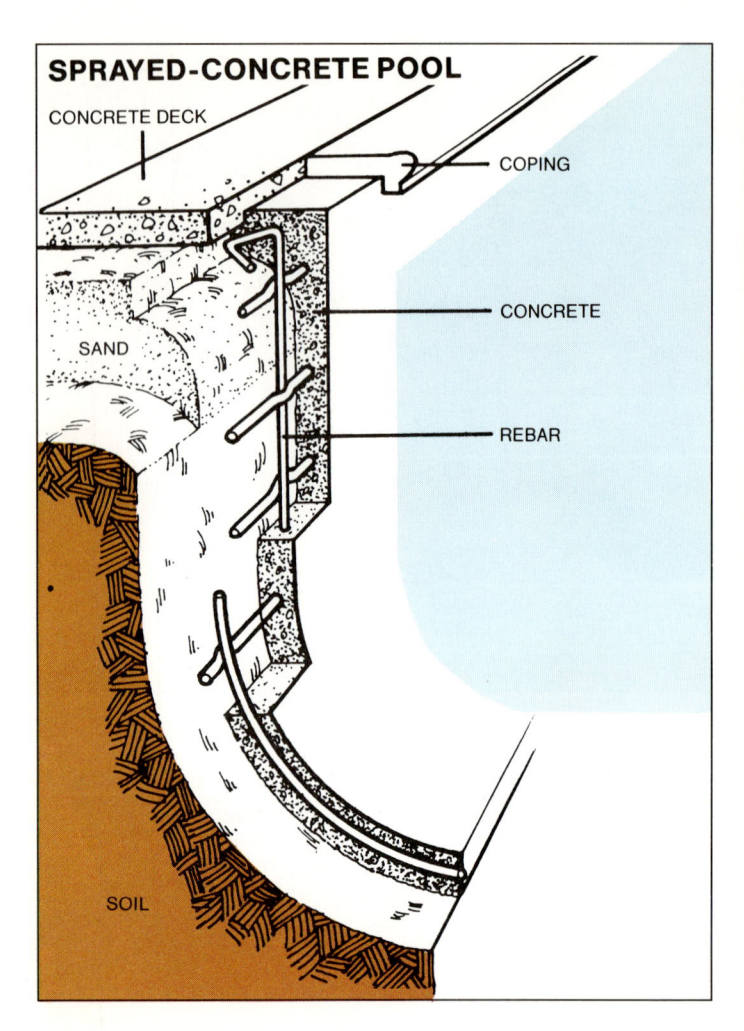

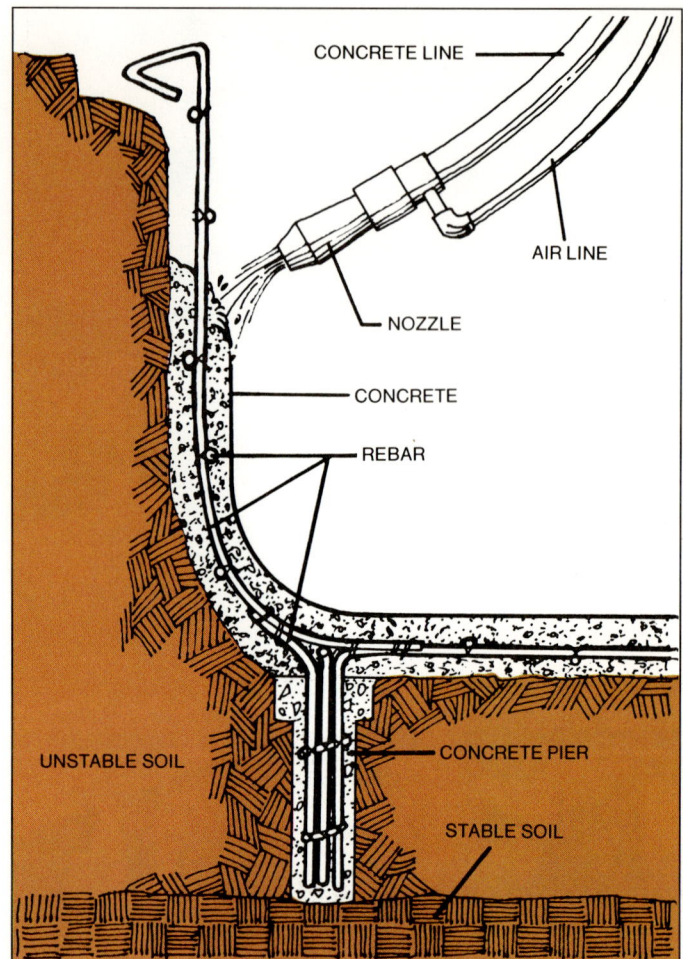

Labels on left diagram: CONCRETE DECK, COPING, CONCRETE, SAND, REBAR, SOIL

Labels on right diagram: CONCRETE LINE, AIR LINE, NOZZLE, CONCRETE, REBAR, UNSTABLE SOIL, CONCRETE PIER, STABLE SOIL

custom shape and can include a spa of the same materials and design. When building on loose fill or other unstable soil, a one-piece concrete shell can be supported by concrete piers set on stable soil or rock below the fill. See drawing above right.

Sprayed-concrete construction has a few disadvantages. It requires skilled workmanship and an experienced pool builder. The gunite or shotcrete must be sprayed evenly to assure uniform wall thickness of the pool shell. A custom gunite or shotcrete pool is usually more expensive than other common pools.

The painted or plastered surface is rougher and more porous than vinyl or fiberglass. As a result, a concrete pool may use more chemicals than a vinyl-lined or fiberglass pool, and the walls are harder to keep clean. Algae formation is also a problem. Until the plaster has cured and the pool is free of plaster dust and other debris, about 1 to 2 weeks, it will be hard to chemically balance the water.

Poured Concrete—This system is seldom used because it involves costly labor and complex forms, and limits design options. Poured-concrete pools are usually rectangular. They can be built in irregular shapes, but this requires expensive form work. Heavier equipment is needed to bring in materials. Access has to be provided for heavy transit-mix trucks.

A poured-concrete pool is an alternative to sprayed-concrete in areas where gunite or shotcrete is not available. But in many of these areas, poured-concrete pools have been mostly replaced by lighter, less-complicated, prefabricated pools.

Construction is similar to pouring walls for a commercial building. Forms are built to the thickness of the walls, rebar is placed, then the walls are poured. The floor of the pool is poured and tied into the walls with rebar. Pool walls are capped with a poured-concrete *bond beam*, which supports the coping and surrounding deck. Poured-concrete pools are either plastered or painted with a waterproof sealer.

Masonry Block—A pool with walls built of block is less complicated than a poured-concrete pool. Footings are poured for the walls, then the block walls erected. The walls are reinforced with rebar and the hollow cores of the block filled with concrete. Next, the pool floor is poured and finally the wall is topped with a poured-concrete bond beam.

The block walls are plastered to provide a smooth finish. This system can also be used to create a shell for a vinyl liner. Masonry-block pools are no longer common because better technology is available today.

Tiled Pools—Most concrete pools have a band of ceramic tile at the waterline—both for appearance and ease of maintenance. The glasslike surface of glazed tile is more resistant than concrete to stains from pool chemicals, minerals and algae. Tile is also easier to keep clean. Some fiberglass pools also can be tiled at the waterline.

Any part of the pool interior—or all of it—can be tiled. This includes

24   Choosing a Pool

Small mosaic tiles easily conform to curved steps and other curved surfaces of sprayed-concrete pools. To cover entire pool shell with tile would be extremely expensive. *Design: Mark Sutter, AIA, Encino, CA.*

Tile is often applied on pool walls that extend above the waterline. Elevated pool walls are called *raised bond beams.* Classic blue-and-white tile design combines with brick and wood to lend a formal appearance to pool and spa. If raised bond beams are used, a safety rope is required at the waterline. *Design: California Pools & Spas, Orange, CA.*

steps, sidewalls, and bottom. Tiles are often applied to raised sections of the bond beam on pools that have this feature.

Tiles 4x4" or larger are restricted to pools with straight, angular surfaces. Curved walls and bottoms of free-form pools are easily covered with small mosaic tiles. In most cases, tile is used sparingly as an accent—to tile an entire pool is extremely expensive. The photos here shows how striking tile can be. Other beautiful and unique examples of how tile is used on pools appear in photos throughout this book.

VINYL-LINED POOLS

These are pools with prefabricated walls that support a heavy vinyl liner. Vinyl-lined pools are gaining popularity for several reasons. Less technical skill is required to install a vinyl-lined pool than to build a gunite pool with a plastered interior shell. Individual wall sections from 2 to 8 feet long are bolted together to form the pool wall. Prefabricated steps and radiused corners speed up the building process. The initial cost is usually less than gunite construction, especially in cold climates.

A competent builder can install a complete vinyl-lined pool in 3 to 5 working days. Once the homeowner has decided on a style and shape, and selected a pump, filter, skimmer and heater, the order is forwarded to the factory. The pool is prepackaged on a pallet along with steps, ladders and all

Prefabricated vinyl-lined pools come in a variety of shapes and sizes. This one is a traditional kidney shape. Recent advances in materials and installation techniques have made these in-ground pools a desirable alternative to sprayed-concrete pools. *Design: Aqua-Rama of Atlanta, Marietta, GA.*

Choosing a Pool 25

VINYL-LINED POOL, FIBERGLASS WALLS

Labels: CONCRETE COPING AND DECK, SAND, VINYL LINER, WALL PANEL (PLASTIC OR FIBERGLASS), BRACES, CONCRETE, SAND, SOIL, ANCHOR PIN

VINYL-LINED POOL, METAL WALLS

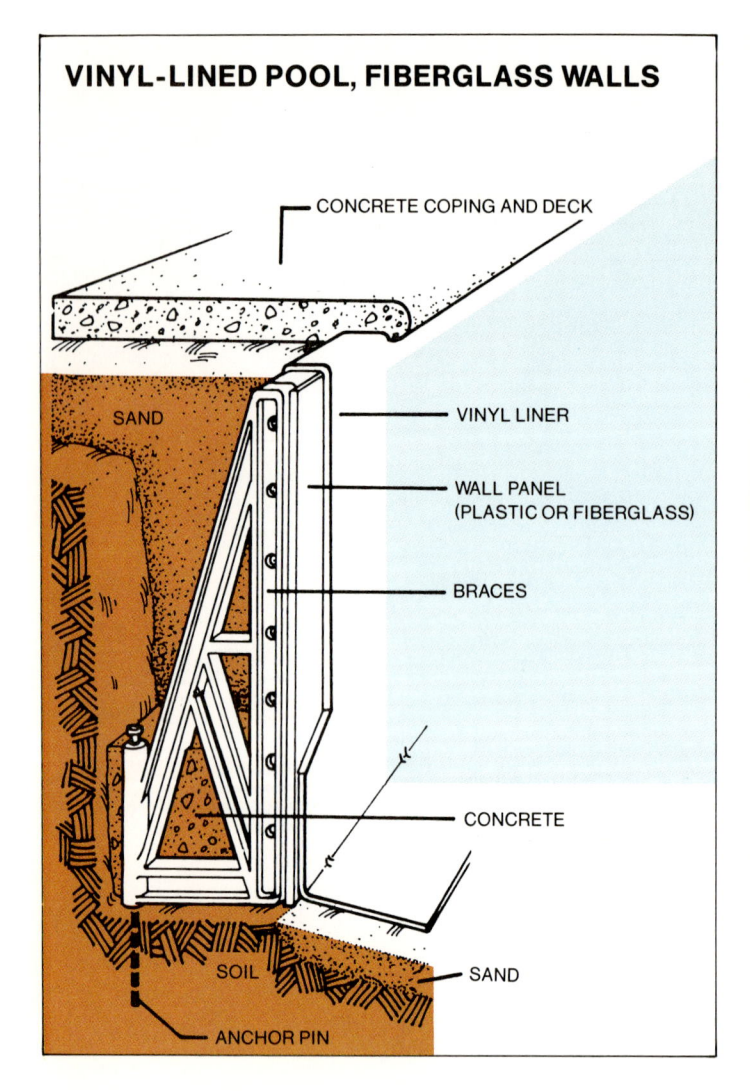

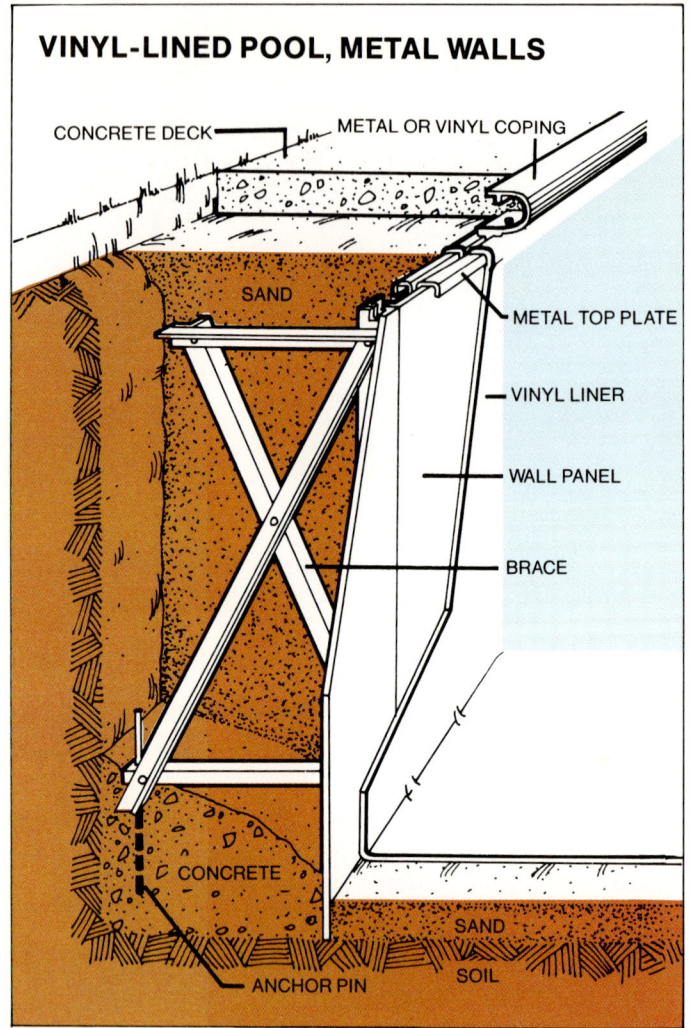

Labels: CONCRETE DECK, METAL OR VINYL COPING, SAND, METAL TOP PLATE, VINYL LINER, WALL PANEL, BRACE, CONCRETE, SAND, SOIL, ANCHOR PIN

support equipment, and delivered to the site. A complete pool can be carried on a light truck.

In recent years, major improvements have been made in the materials used in vinyl-lined pools. Increased longevity has helped this type of pool gain an increasing share of the residential-pool market.

Pool manufacturers can show prospective buyers a selection of standard pools illustrated in a color catalog. By using combinations of standard modular wall panels, almost any shape can be custom-designed.

Vinyl liners are also available in several colors and patterns. Choosing a pattern is similar to selecting wallpaper. What you choose is largely a matter of personal taste. The liner color should complement colors of other features around the pool—deck, pool buildings, fences, major plantings, or the house.

The most common patterns are pebble designs in white, blue and earthtones, or solid black and shades of blue, white and tan. Imitation tile patterns are also available. Liners can be designed combining any colors available from the manufacturer. It's possible to order a vinyl liner with blue or white sidewalls and a black bottom. Black absorbs sunlight and can help cut pool heating costs.

Dark colors tend to reflect images around the pool. Light colors will be less reflective and show more of the pool interior. A pebble or tile pattern will disguise debris or dirt on the pool bottom; solid colors will show dirt.

Sophisticated equipment makes it possible for the manufacturer to fabricate a liner to fit almost any size and shape pool. Ultraviolet inhibitors have made liners less susceptible to deterioration in sunlight and more resistant to alkalinity and common pool chemicals. Improvements have made to pool walls more resistant to corrosion. The result is longer pool life and longer warranties.

Pool suppliers offer varying warranties on pool walls—from 15 to 25 years. A few guarantee pool walls for as long as the pool is owned by the original buyer. The warranty for vinyl liners usually runs from 10 to 15 years or more.

Manufacturers are continually increasing the variety and styles of liners. This gives the homeowner more choices in colors, patterns and materials.

Most vinyl-lined pools are manufactured and installed in much the same way. The major difference from one pool to another is in material quality and in the choice of materials for wall panels. Don't overlook the pool dealer's reliability and reputation for follow-up service. For more information on choosing a reputable pool dealer, see pages 36-41.

Metal, plastic and wood are the most common materials for sidewalls. Each manufacturer can make a persuasive argument to support the use

26   Choosing a Pool

of a particular material. A few offer the homeowner the option of selecting from two or more materials. The major types of sidewalls are discussed here.

Metal Walls—Galvanized steel, stainless steel and aluminum are the most common metal wall panels produced for vinyl-lined pools. Over a period of years, metal panels have proven to a durable pool-wall material.

Proponents of galvanized steel cite its strength. Aluminum is valued as a corrosion-resistant metal. Stainless steel is strong and corrosion-resistant, but considerably more expensive than either aluminum or galvanized steel. A cross-section drawing of a vinyl-lined pool with metal walls is shown on page 26.

Plastic Walls—Fiberglass and various types of molded-plastic walls are becoming increasingly popular. They are completely corrosion-resistant. In some cases, they are slightly less expensive than metal panels.

The highest quality fiberglass panels are constructed by placing a gelcoat layer over a mold and covering it with layers of resin-impregnated fiberglass cloth. This forms a strong, laminated panel of consistent thickness.

An alternative method is spraying chopped-glass fibers mixed with resins over an acrylic- or gelcoat-covered mold. This is a system commonly used in fiberglass spa and boat-hull construction. Both types of fiberglass panels are usually strengthened with reinforcing steel.

Panels are also cast in a mold using polypropylene, a thermoplastic polymer. Fiberglass and polymer panels are structurally supported with either metal, plastic or fiberglass struts when erected on the site. The drawing on page 26 shows typical sidewall construction for fiberglass walls.

Wood Walls—Ordinary, untreated wood is subject to decay, fungi and termites. All wood panels used for pool walls should be pressure-treated with a wood preservative. Treated panels of 1/2-inch plywood and supporting wood struts are being used successfully to form walls for in-ground pools. Some early installations have been in the ground 20 years with little sign of deterioration.

In the pressure-treating process, chemicals are forced into the wood fibers under pressure, exceeding 100 pounds per square inch. The chemicals are fixed in the structure of the wood and will not wash out. Several pool manufacturers use pressure-treated wood panels as a standard material for in-ground, vinyl-lined pools.

Masonry Walls—Gunite, shotcrete or poured concrete shells don't require vinyl liners. Properly treated, they are completely waterproof. Porous masonry-block walls can accept a vinyl liner and need not be waterproof. Masonry walls have become rare since the development of prefabricated pool-wall panels of metal, plastic and wood.

FIBERGLASS POOLS

The technique for building fiberglass pools evolved from the construction process developed for fiberglass boat hulls. Some pools built in the late 1950s—when fiberglass construction was a new art—were flawed. Pool owners had problems with surface blistering, staining from pool chemicals, leaks, color fading and structural instability.

Improved materials, manufacturing processes and installation techniques have eliminated the early problems. Resins used in fiberglass construction harden and gain strength over a period of years. Long life and modest cost are two of the primary appeals of a fiberglass pool. Major fiberglass-pool manufacturers offer guarantees against structural failure for 25 years or more.

However, if pool maintenance is neglected, pool walls can spot or blister. This condition will only be in the gelcoat surface and won't affect pool strength or structure. The source of the problem can be corrected by bringing the water back into chemical balance.

Pool manufacturers no longer recommend repainting fiberglass. The original gelcoat finish applied under heat will always be harder than pool paint applied cold. Most manufacturers and pool suppliers offer a gelcoat conditioner that extends the life of the surface and helps prevent staining and color fading. Fiberglass repair kits are also available for making minor repairs to the pool shell. See the chapter, *Pool Care & Repair,* starting on page 117.

As mentioned, there are two major types of fiberglass pools currently being made. They are the one-piece, molded-fiberglass shell and the fiberglass-sidewall, concrete-bottom pool. Some vinyl-lined pools use fiberglass-sidewall construction, as previously discussed. Both types of fiberglass pools are equal in durability to other major pool types. Major manufacturers of both types include standard support equipment and fittings—pump and motor, filter, heat-

One-piece fiberglass pools are the closest thing to an "instant pool." Ease of installation and maintenance are major advantages. Correctly installed, they are as durable and long-lasting as any other in-ground pool. Shapes are limited. As this example shows, they can be an attractive addition to the yard. *Pool Design: Swim Factory, Marietta, GA.*

ONE-PIECE FIBERGLASS POOL

- CONCRETE DECK
- FLANGE SET IN CONCRETE BOND BEAM
- FIBERGLASS SHELL
- REBAR
- GRAVEL
- PEA GRAVEL (may be used instead of sand)
- SAND
- SOIL

FIBERGLASS-SIDEWALL POOL

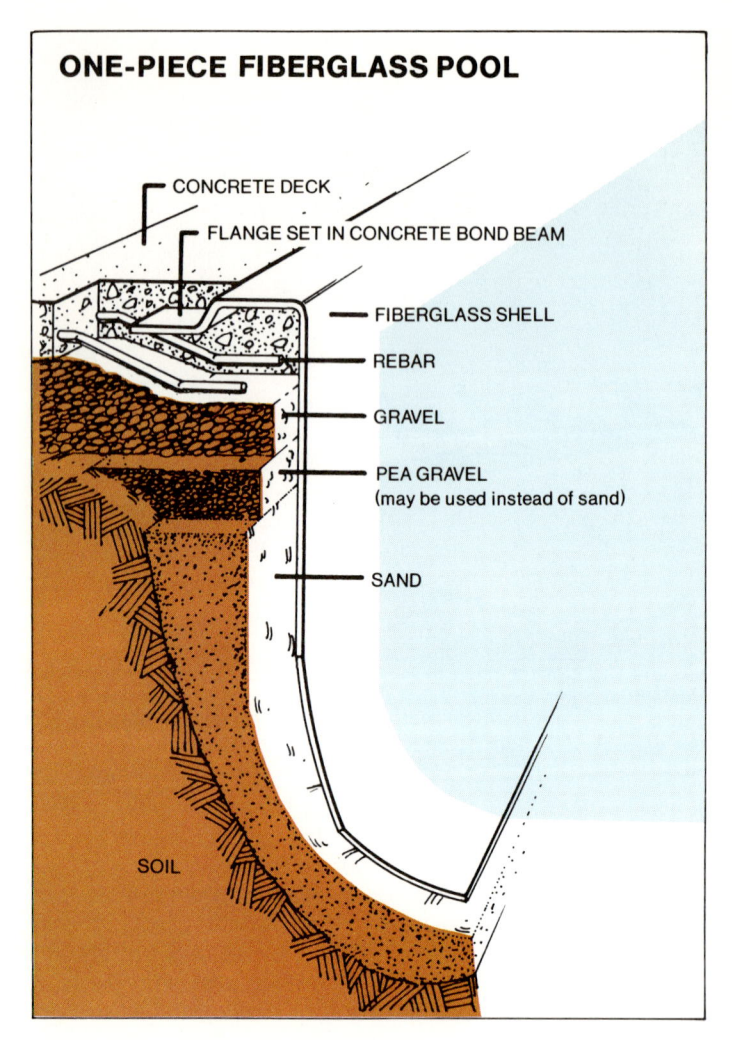

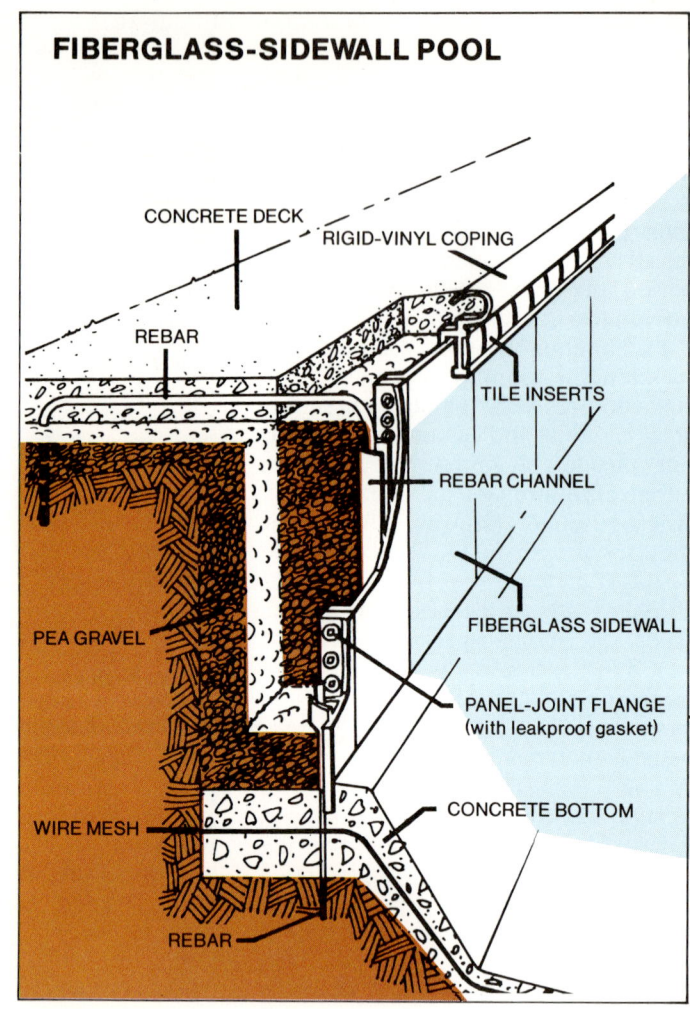

- CONCRETE DECK
- RIGID-VINYL COPING
- REBAR
- TILE INSERTS
- REBAR CHANNEL
- PEA GRAVEL
- FIBERGLASS SIDEWALL
- PANEL-JOINT FLANGE (with leakproof gasket)
- CONCRETE BOTTOM
- WIRE MESH
- REBAR

er, skimmer and drain and inlet fittings. They also offer optional accessories such as ladders, molded fiberglass steps, underwater lights, diving boards, pool vacuums and automatic chlorinators.

One-Piece Shells—Quality fiberglass pool shells are constructed by hand. An upside-down mold is coated with a layer of gelcoat that includes the color desired for the inside of the pool. Layers of resin-impregnated mat and coving are laid on to build the pool wall to a predetermined thickness.

When the resins have hardened, the finished pool is lifted off the mold. Shells used today are flexible and can absorb minor ground movement with no structural damage.

Molds are expensive so pool models offered by manufacturers are limited. You may have as few as five models or as many as a dozen to choose from. Because the shells are large, the cost of shipping to dealers and transportation to the pool site limit availability of these pools to locations near the manufacturer.

Colors are also limited. Some fiberglass-pool manufacturers are producing only white shells or recommend white as a finish that will retain its appearance for the longest time. Blue and aqua gelcoat finishes on these pools are still subject to fading over a period of years.

Pool lengths average about 30 to 32 feet. The largest models are about 42 feet. If the market for one-piece fiberglass pools expands, the number of available models should increase.

Installation is relatively easy. The pool shell is delivered to the site by large truck. A crane lifts the pool off the truck and into the sand-filled excavation. Plumbing is connected to the shell and the excavation is backfilled with sand. Support equipment is hooked up, pool deck and accessories are added, and the pool is ready to use. An experienced crew can install a ready-to-use pool in a week to 10 days.

Experience in installing these pools under a number of conditions has reduced problems with leaks and buckling of the shell. Greater care is taken in site preparation. Rocks and other objects that can wear on the pool shell are removed from the excavation. A thick bed of sand is placed in the bottom of the excavation. When the shell is positioned, sand backfill is tamped solidly into place.

The backfill process is the most critical step in one-piece shell installation. If any large voids or hollows are left under the shell, the weight of the water can crack the shell, causing a leak.

In areas with unstable soil or a high water table, experienced local installers will know how to provide adequate reinforcement and drainage to deal with these problems. The drawing above left shows a typical one-piece fiberglass-shell installation. For more details on how these pools are installed, see page 89.

Fiberglass-Sidewall Pools—These pools are similar in design to sidewall construction of vinyl-lined pools.

28 Choosing a Pool

Wall panels are approximately the same height as those used for vinyl-lined pools—slightly over 3 feet tall. The difference is that the fiberglass wall panels, when bolted together, are watertight and serve as the finished sidewall of the pool. Pool deck, pool bottom and hopper area, or deep end, are reinforced concrete. In tandem, these two materials form a strong, durable pool shell.

Early versions of these pools were prone to leaks at panel joints and buckling due to earth movement. Sophisticated manufacturing and construction techniques have greatly improved the structural stability of these pools. Many fiberglass-sidewall pools have been successfully installed in cold climates where frost heaving causes severe earth movement. Leaks and other structural problems with these pools are usually due to improper installation by inexperienced builders.

Flexible panels allow these pools to be constructed in almost any desired shape. Panels are bolted together. Vinyl gaskets between panels prevent leaks. On most types, an integral, prefabricated coping ties the panels into the concrete pool deck. The drawing on page 28 is a cross-section of a typical fiberglass-sidewall pool.

Fiberglass-sidewall, concrete-bottom pools have both the advantages and disadvantages of both materials. Because the concrete bottom is usually installed below the frost line, it is not as prone to cracking and chipping as are pools with concrete sidewalls. However, the concrete bottom must be sealed with a waterproof epoxy paint, and repainted every few years. Some epoxy coatings will last as long as 8 years without reapplication. Cleaning and maintenance difficulties are the same as for other concrete pools.

Fiberglass Spas—Fiberglass is the most common material used for building prefabricated spas. Many fiberglass pool manufacturers also make a line of spas. This means that it is relatively easy to find a matching spa for a fiberglass pool. Adding a spa to your pool is discussed on pages 14-15.

For more comprehensive information on spas and hot tubs, refer to the book, *Spas & Hot Tubs,* by A. Cort Sinnes, published by HPBooks. It is a complete guide for anyone considering a spa or hot tub installation.

Fiberglass-sidewall pools have nearly as many design possibilities as sprayed-concrete pools. The flexible sidewalls can be warped to almost any shape. Because sidewalls are waterproof, no liner is required. Pool bottom is poured concrete. This pool includes a fiberglass spa, offered by same manufacturer. Design: Hallmark Pools, Rolling Meadows, IL.

FINISHING TOUCHES

There are as many options in selecting pool deck, lighting, slides, diving boards and other pool accessories as there are in choosing a pool. When shopping, examine accessories for how well they combine appearance, function and safety.

POOL STEPS

Steps provide the easiest and safest way to enter and leave a pool. Most sprayed-concrete pools have steps built into the end wall or corner of the pool's shallow end. Steps are custom built to conform to the design of the pool. A ladder at the deep end is a convenience for divers. One-piece fiberglass pools have steps molded into the shell in the shallow end.

Buyers of vinyl-lined pools and fiberglass-sidewall pools have several options. Prefabricated steps and pool ladders of acrylic-coated fiberglass or molded plastic are available to tie into the wall structure as an optional panel. They come in several widths, styles and colors. These steps may be built into a corner panel or installed at any point on the wall in the shallow end.

Some prefabricated steps are designed to be added to a vinyl-lined pool after the vinyl liner has been put in place. Other types consist of prefabricated panels that are installed when the sidewalls are erected. A handrail that anchors into the pool deck is an available option for most step units.

POOL LIGHTS

Underwater lights and lights in the pool area are essential if the pool is to be used at night. Lighting also helps provide an attractive, safe atmosphere around the pool. It can be an effective part of the landscaping plan.

For underwater lights in a sprayed-concrete pool, the niche housing for the lights must be installed before concrete work begins. The housing is tied to the reinforcing steel and the conduit is attached. A single light located beneath the diving board and several feet below the surface is adequate for most pools. Irregularly-shaped pools may need more lights to illuminate all areas in the pool.

If you intend to use the pool at night, it should include one or more underwater lights and adequate lighting around the deck. Lighting can also be used for dramatic effect, as discussed on page 112. *Design: Whitaker Aquatech Pools, Tucson, AZ.*

Openings for lights in concrete and fiberglass pools are planned in the initial construction. For vinyl-lined pools, the light is added after the vinyl liner has been installed. A hole must be cut in the sidewall panel for the light niche. The light is screw-tightened on the panel. Gaskets on both sides of the pool wall seal the opening.

Lights in one-piece fiberglass pools can be added when the pool is ready to be lowered into place. They are attached in the same way lights are installed in a vinyl-lined pool.

Have underwater lights checked by the electrician responsible for wiring the pump motor and other pool accessories. The electrician should make sure the lights are correctly grounded and protected with ground-fault circuit interrupters (GFCIs). The lights and wiring must meet local electrical codes.

A dimmer switch will enable you to raise and lower the light level. The pool should be well illuminated when children are swimming. The light level can be lowered for adults using the pool or when softer light is more appropriate for entertaining by the pool.

To help prevent accidents, landscape lighting should adequately illuminate walkways, steps and the immediate area around the pool. Additional lighting may be added to highlight shrubs, flower beds, trees and fences. Experiment and use your imagination. Additional information on lighting is included on page 112.

POOL DECKS

The finished area immediately around the pool provides walking room for swimmers, a space for pool furniture, a sunning spot and a transition from pool to surrounding areas. There are many building materials for decks that are attractive and provide firm footing. The ideal surface is comfortable underfoot, but not slick. Most deck materials can be used with any type of pool.

Concrete is the most common deck material. It's easy to clean and is strong and durable. Ordinary concrete can be modified by adding coloring or using an exposed-aggregate finish. A lightly brushed surface can give concrete texture without being too harsh on bare feet.

As an option to a basic concrete surface, you can use a porous concrete-surfacing material that won't heat to uncomfortable temperatures even in the hottest sun. This material is applied like plaster over a concrete base. One popular brand is called *Kool Deck*. Sand and adobe are the most popular colors. See top photo on page 31.

Almost any type of masonry material can be used to make an attractive deck. Materials include brick, outdoor tile, flagstone, slate or other natural stone. There is also deck material that consists of aggregate stone set in epoxy. Materials can be blended to match or complement paved walks or patio areas near the pool.

Most masonry is easily washed with a hose and will resist pool chemicals splashed out of the pool. Soft or porous materials such as sandstone or unglazed tile may need a coating of sealant to prevent stains. Most masonry deck materials are set in a bed of reinforced concrete to form a strong, waterproof deck.

Plan for adequate water drainage from the deck. The deck should always slope away from the pool to prevent dirt from being washed back into it, and to keep runoff from spilling over into the pool.

DIVING BOARDS AND SLIDES

If you're planning a new pool, decide early if you want a diving board or slide. A pool with a diving board needs a deep end and sufficient deck space around and behind the board.

The amount of room necessary is usually surprising to anyone first considering a diving board. If deck space is limited, a shorter jump board can be installed. See photo on page 57.

Only about a quarter to a third of the board will actually extend out over the water. This means that a 12-foot board will need at least 8 feet from the edge of the pool to the end of the board and another 2 or 3 feet clearance behind the board for walking.

Slides also take up a lot of deck space. A slide can be used safely in 4 or 5 feet or water. A large, straight slide will need a deck 9 to 12 feet wide. Curved slides installed parallel to the pool edge require a much narrower deck—about 3 to 6 feet.

A pool with no diving board or slide need only be deep enough for swimming—3-1/2 to 4 feet. Specifications and additional information on diving boards and slides are included in the chapter, *Selecting Pool Equipment,* starting on page 43.

POOL BUILDINGS AND OTHER STRUCTURES

The pool's support equipment is one of the less-attractive features in the landscape. Unless it is behind a fence or otherwise hidden, you'll probably want to build an enclosure for it. The equipment will last longer if it is completely enclosed in a roofed structure. Such equipment sheds can be attractive, especially if they're part of a larger pool building.

Changing rooms, lanais, gazebos and pool houses are other structures to consider. For more on these, see pages 113-115.

Several manufacturers produce a concrete-surfacing material that adds color and texture to an ordinary concrete deck. The material shown here, called *Kool Deck*, is also cooler under bare feet than most other masonry materials, making it popular in hot climates. It is available in several earth-tone colors. *Photo courtesy of Mortex Mfg. Co., Tucson, AZ.*

Swim-up snack bar and sunken barbecue center are custom touches that must be planned when the pool is built. This is one of the many design features possible with sprayed-concrete pools. *Design: J.M. Smith, Landscape Architect, Woodland Hills, CA.*

Choosing a Pool 31

A pool is a major investment that should be enjoyed for a long time to come. For years of trouble-free operation, it must be carefully designed and correctly installed. *Design: Barnett-Hendricks Pools Inc., Cherry Hill, NJ.*

32 Before You Build

CHAPTER 3

Before You Build

For most homeowners, planning and building a swimming pool is a once-in-a-lifetime experience. How satisfying that experience will be depends on how well you plan. You probably won't have the opportunity to benefit from first-time mistakes.

Careful planning means more than picking the right pool and the right mix of components and accessories. It means finding qualified help to design and install the pool and its surroundings. Expertise comes on many levels.

You will have a choice of dealing with an architect or landscape architect, a landscape designer, a building contractor who specializes in pool installations, or a pool builder or dealer who installs pools exclusively.

Each will bring a specialized type of education, training, experience and creativity to the project. The scope and nature of your project will help determine who you hire to install the pool. No matter who you hire, reputation and a long list of satisfied customers mean more than a job title.

The information in this chapter will outline who is available to assist you in building your pool, how to find qualified help and how to negotiate a contract.

WHO CAN HELP YOU

If you are building a new home and are including an indoor or attached pool, you may want the help of a licensed architect with experience in pool design. If you're building an outdoor pool, a landscape architect can design it as part of an overall landscape project.

There are many qualified pool builders or pool dealers capable of installing your pool. Some have permanent crews to handle the work. Some dealers work with independent builders experienced in pool installation. A few offer additional design and building services for related pool work such as general landscaping, walls, fences, decks, walks, patios, cabanas, gazebos and other related structures.

ARCHITECTS

An architect can prepare plans and working drawings for the full project, or involve other experts experienced in pool design and building. Licensed architects are qualified by law to design swimming pools, but not all architects are pool designers.

If you want to include a indoor pool in a new home or add an attached or free-standing pool enclosure to your current home, a qualified architect can design both the structure and the pool. An architect can also assume responsibility for subcontracting the work and overseeing the project.

If you are designing a new home and hope to add a pool in the future, an architect can design a pool into the original house plans so it can be installed at a later date. It will cost relatively little to rough in pool plumbing, wiring and a natural gas line to the pool location when the house is built. This could save you a good deal of money when you do add your pool.

LANDSCAPE ARCHITECTS AND DESIGNERS

Outdoor projects can be handled by landscape architects and landscape designers qualified to design pools. Landscape architects with pool-design experience can provide many of the same services as an architect. Landscape designers may have the practical experience and skills to design pools, but they are usually not licensed by the state.

Landscape architects and designers are frequently given pool work because of their ability to design a pool as part of the total environment. They are capable of providing detailed site plans that include recommendations for contouring, plantings, walks, walls, fences, decks, lighting, patios and pool buildings.

Before You Build 33

Qualified landscape architects design a pool as part of the overall landscape. It's their responsibility to choose elements that work well together. Design considerations for this pool include shape of distant lake beyond owner's property. *Design: Galper/Baldon & Associates, Landscape Architects, Venice, CA.*

THE DESIGNER'S JOB

Depending on the terms of the contract, the architect or designer is usually responsible for securing the necessary permits and finding a qualified pool builder. The designer's responsibilities also include seeing that the pool is completed according to specifications in the contract.

Architects and landscape architects work for a percentage of the total installation cost, on an hourly basis or for a set fee. The final contract may call for a combination of any two or all three. The fee arrangement is negotiable between you and the architect. There are several variations possible.

You can hire an architect or landscape architect to draw up a set of plans for a set fee or on an hourly basis. You then have the option of using the plans to get competitive bids from contractors or pool builders for the entire job. Or you can negotiate a contract for a builder to do a specific portion of the work and delay some parts of the project to either reduce the initial cost or to take on some of the work yourself.

Architects and designers can also be retained as consultants on an hourly-fee basis. If you wish to design your own pool, they can offer advice on specific aspects of the design. They can be used as a source of ideas or for solutions to landscaping or structural-design problems.

Architects or landscape architects charge the highest fees. Their academic training, ability to meet specific professional standards and assume broad responsibilities for a pool project may justify the cost.

CONTRACTORS AND DEALERS

Some building and landscape contractors offer pool-building services as part of an overall project. Some will subcontract pool work to a pool dealer or pool contractor; others will hire an experienced crew to install the pool.

Independent pool contractors usually provide design services and build custom-designed pools. Or they can help you choose a manufactured vinyl-lined or fiberglass pool, then install it.

Because they are not affiliated with a specific pool dealer or manufacturer, independent contractors are free to order a pool and support equipment from a variety of sources. This means you have more options in making your final choices.

Overall, most pools are sold and installed by pool dealers. Most dealers provide design and building services and function as their own contractors. Some employ their own crews to complete the basic work, but subcontract electrical, plumbing or landscaping work.

Some dealers only sell pools, support equipment, accessories and chemicals and help the buyer find a pool contractor to do the actual installation. Dealers who sell above-ground pools can either offer installation services or provide counsel to buyers who are installing their own pools.

Most pool dealers and pool contractors specialize in one type of pool, either sprayed-concrete, vinyl-lined or fiberglass. Pool dealers are most often the retail outlet for vinyl-lined, fiberglass or above-ground pools. A large pool dealer will usually stock a few basic pool models. Most often, pool orders are forwarded to the manufacturer and pool components shipped to the dealer.

Builders of sprayed-concrete pools are usually called *pool builders* or *pool companies*. All sprayed-concrete pools are custom designed in the sense that no two are built exactly alike. They are all built at the site from a custom design or by duplicating as closely as possible one of a selection of basic designs.

BEING YOUR OWN CONTRACTOR

In general, this book recommends that you do not act as your own contractor, unless you've had past experience contracting major building and remodeling projects. It's well worth the money a dealer or contractor charges to assume the responsibilities and headaches of coordinating the project.

Installing an in-ground pool requires experience, talent and special equipment not readily available to the average do-it-yourselfer. Taking on a major project like a pool can be risky. If you intend to be your own contractor just to save money, one serious mistake could wipe out any anticipated savings or leave you with a costly, poor-quality pool.

There are few advantages in being your own contractor if you can find a capable contractor and crew. To stay competitive, most pool builders employ experienced crews. They are usually in a better position than the homeowner to find qualified subcontractors at favorable rates.

For example, it is unlikely that you will save money by arranging for the basic pool excavation yourself rather than leaving the job to a pool builder.

It's also unlikely you'll save time. If you're working with subcontractors, it's difficult to schedule work so that when one subcontractor completes one phase of the work, the next subcontractor is ready to begin. A pool contractor or dealer is usually set up to schedule work so the job gets done quickly and efficiently.

If you have extensive technical or building experience, or past experience in contracting major building or remodeling projects, you may choose to be your own contractor. If you live in an area where there are no qualified pool dealers or experienced pool builders, you may have no other choice.

WHAT'S INVOLVED

Being your own contractor means you will be responsible for getting building permits, selecting the pool and arranging for individual subcontractors to take care of all phases of construction you cannot handle yourself.

Personal involvement in installing any pool will require a good deal of your time. For any pool, the steps that should logically be left to subcontractors are excavating, plumbing and electrical work. Steps that require certain expertise or specialized equipment, such as spraying concrete or lifting a one-piece fiberglass shell into the excavation, must also be subcontracted. Coordinating the efforts of these subcontractors may take more time than the actual work involved in building or installing the pool.

Excavation requires heavy equipment and experienced equipment operators. Even if you plan to install the pool yourself, this is one job that should be subcontracted. *Photo courtesy of Patio Pools, Tucson, AZ.*

Excavating companies are accustomed to working around power lines and underground utilities and will have the skill and equipment necessary to do the job right. But you should hire a company with experience in excavating for the type of pool you've chosen.

Most local building codes will require that all plumbing and electrical work be completed by licensed plumbers and electricians. Digging trenches for plumbing and electrical lines can be done by the homeowner, or by the company that does the pool excavation.

If you must act as your own contractor because you have no other choice, above-ground pools are the least complicated to install. Many are designed to be installed as do-it-yourself projects. All above-ground pools include detailed instructions to help the installer. The chapter, *Above-Ground Pools*, starting on page 97, covers buying and installing these pools.

Vinyl-Lined Pools—A vinyl-lined pool with prefabricated sidewalls is probably the easiest in-ground pool for the owner-contractor to install. Sidewall assembly and liner installation require only modest technical knowledge. Metal or plastic sidewalls are relatively easy to handle. The entire pool package can be delivered on a single pallet. The manufacturer will provide basic installation

Installing sidewalls and liner for vinyl-lined pools can be a do-it-yourself project. But a trained crew can do the work in less than a day, so you won't save much money by doing it yourself. Also, your involvement in actual installation may void a dealer's or manufacturer's warranty. *Photo courtesy of Heldor, Morristown, NJ.*

instructions and counsel when necessary. Basic installation procedures are outlined on pages 84-87.

You have the option of assembling a vinyl-lined pool yourself or subcontracting this phase of the work. Labor costs for actual pool assembly represent a relatively small part of the pool's total cost. An experienced crew can assemble a vinyl-lined pool in a day or less. So can a competent do-it-yourselfer. The major costs are the pool itself and hiring subcontractors for excavation, plumbing and electrical work.

Fiberglass Pools—One-piece fiberglass pools are delivered to the site as a single shell. Initial excavation is slightly more critical than excavating for a vinyl-lined pool. The hole shape must conform closely to the shell so there's a minimum of backfilling. You'll need to find an excavating company that has experience working with these pools.

Placing the pool requires a special crane and an experienced operator. Backfilling the excavation with sand must also be done correctly—any voids left under the shell may result in structural failure, causing leaks. It's best to let the company or dealer who sold you the pool assume responsibility for placing the pool and backfilling the excavation. Chances are, you'll find it just as economical to let the pool dealer assume responsibility for the entire project. Plumbing and electrical work should be done by licensed subcontractors.

Fiberglass-sidewall pools are installed similarly to vinyl-lined pools, but require experience in working with large amounts of concrete. It is best to hire a pool builder with experience in installing this type of pool. Mistakes in installation are critical and difficult to correct.

Sprayed-Concrete Pools—Spraying concrete is a technique that requires both a high level of skill and specialized equipment. It is extremely difficult for the owner-contractor to subcontract this and other specialized tasks to independent tradesmen, and coordinate the work. Most spray-gun operators work for pool builders. Other members of the pool builder's crew include excavators, workers experienced in placing rebar, plumbers, electricians and masons. The crew is used to working together and can do the entire job quickly and efficiently.

FINDING QUALIFIED HELP

Established pool manufacturers make quality products and materials that offer years of trouble-free service. Pool problems today are seldom due to poor materials or shoddy workmanship by the manufacturer. Quality controls are effective and most products carry adequate warranties.

Most pool owners who report problems can trace their difficulties to poor workmanship during installation or bad advice in selecting support equipment. Because a pool represents a sizeable investment, finding a good contractor or builder is essential. Here are a few tips on how to find qualified help.

SOLICIT RECOMMENDATIONS

Most builders of quality pools rely on personal recommendations from satisfied customers to generate new business. Ask for suggestions from friends or neighbors who have recently had pools installed. This is often the best way to find a good pool installer. Many pool owners are proud of their new pools. They are willing to show you the pool and discuss their experience in working with specific builders.

Ask pool designers and builders if you can see some of their recent work. Most reputable pool builders have a number of satisfied customers who are willing to show you their pools.

Stay alert for comments from pool owners who are *dissatisfied* with their installations. Pool builders obviously list their most satisfied customers as references. No pool company will voluntarily provide names of dissatisfied customers.

ASK POOL SUPPLIERS

Local pool-supply companies or pool maintenance companies are a good source for leads to pool builders, designers and landscape architects. They will be aware of local pool builders who have a reputation for quality work.

CHECK THE BUILDING DEPARTMENT

Your local building department may be willing to supply a list of recent pool installations. This may provide leads otherwise unobtainable. It will be up to you to contact the pool owner and ask permission to look at the pool.

You can also get information from examining recent building permits issued for pool construction. Permits are public record.

Building inspectors have first-hand knowledge of the quality of a builder's work. They know which builders are cooperative and strive to meet building codes. Try to to get recommendations from local inspectors.

CHECK WITH ARCHITECTS

If you have no other contacts, check the telephone directory for names of local architects and landscape architects. Call and ask them for names of pool designers and builders they may know personally or by reputation. Many architects subcontract pool work to local pool companies they can depend on.

At the same time, you may want to ask them if they're interested in designing your pool. If they are, make arrangements to see some of their installations. Pool design is a specialty, and not all architects and landscape architects design pools.

CHECK WITH POOL DEALERS

If you've found no other sources for recommendations, go directly to pool builders and dealers. Look in the Yellow Pages under the heading, *Swimming Pools*.

Visit several dealers to get a personal impression. Find out what specific pools they sell and what services they can provide. Is the dealer a member of the *National Spa and Pool Institute (NSPI)*? Does the dealer belong to any trade associations or local contractor's associations? Check with the local Better Business Bureau to see if any complaints have been filed against the dealer.

You may want to take advantage of your visits to exchange preliminary information. The dealer will want to know a few basic facts. Where will the pool be installed? Are there any obvious soil or terrain problems? What is the approximate size of the pool? Are there likely to be access problems? When visiting dealers, take along your site plan, described on page 9, and any other information you've accumulated.

Most dealers record specific details on worksheets as the first step toward preparing an estimate or firm quote. The process isn't too different from having remodeling work done on your home.

The dealer won't be able to give you a firm price in a preliminary visit. He or she should be able to describe similar installations or show you photos or blueprints of completed projects and tell you what each cost.

Get details from the dealer on warranties and follow-up services. Ask about zoning laws, building codes and other restrictions that might affect your plans and sources of financing.

COMPETITIVE BIDS

Designing, selling and installing swimming pools is a competitive business. So it's best to solicit bids or price quotes from two or three dealers or pool builders. No two builders are likely to arrive at exactly the same price for installing the same-size pool with the same support equipment.

Most pool dealers and builders are willing to provide quotes for pool projects. It's a time-consuming process, but competitive bidding is an accepted part of the business. There are several reasons some dealers may be reluctant to provide quotes. Most commonly, it's because they're too busy to take on the job or they're simply not equipped to handle it. In this case, find another dealer.

Sometimes a dealer won't commit to a firm quote because the prospective client has not provided enough information. There are many variables from job to job. Be as specific as possible when providing information to builders or dealers to obtain bids. The more details you can provide, the more accurate the bid will be.

You should have specific plans for the pool—a site plan and details on materials for surrounding deck, plants and pool structures. Architect's drawings are also helpful. If you've already chosen a pump, filter and heater, include the model number or requirements for each of these units, including sizes and capacities.

Request a quote on the information as provided. The bid should clearly specify the kinds and amounts of materials, the type of support equipment, including brands and model numbers, and the prices for individual components. The bid should also include the exact size and capacity of the pool and specific construction specifications. These are all items that will eventually be written into the final contract, discussed on page 38. Don't accept verbal prices or written quotes that aren't in sufficient detail. Items left out can lead to last-minute charges for extras when it comes time to sign the final contract.

ESTIMATES VS. BIDS

Understand the difference between an *estimate*, and a *bid* or *quote*. An estimate is usually a calculated guess based on the pool company's experience. It is intended to give you a general idea of what the project is likely to cost.

Most estimates are on the low side. An estimate is not a binding agreement to do the job for a certain price. Estimates are helpful during the planning stages of your pool to help you plan your budget and get an idea of what you can expect to buy for your money.

A bid or quote is a firm price based on careful study of the specifications

---

WHAT IS THE NSPI?

The National Spa and Pool Institute (NSPI) is the national trade association for the swimming pool, spa and hot tub industry. The NSPI sets quality standards for business ethics and construction practices in the pool industry.

Pool manufacturers, dealers, retail stores, pool builders and pool service companies are among those eligible for NSPI membership. Applicants to NSPI are referred back to one of NSPI's 56 chapters. The regional chapter checks the applicants' references and has final approval on acceptance for membership.

When choosing a pool dealer or builder, check to see if they're a member of the NSPI. Although this is no guarantee that the pool company will build you a top-quality pool at a fair price, it indicates that the company's business practices and reputation have been reviewed and approved by the organization. You can be assured that an NSPI member is a legitimate pool dealer or builder. Members are expected to conform to the high-quality standards set by the NSPI.

You can write or call the NSPI to get a list of participating members in your area. The NSPI will not recommend specific members. To request a list of local members, write NSPI, 2111 Eisenhower Ave., Alexandria, VA 22314.

Before You Build 37

you provide the dealer. Normally, the builder or dealer indicates that this is the price that will be included in a final contract if there have been no misunderstandings or additional work requested.

GETTING A FIRM BID

How firm a bid might be is often hazy. There are many variables in building or installing a pool. No matter how legally binding you may believe the bid to be, it is almost impossible to hold a reluctant pool dealer or builder to a quoted price. Should difficulties over price arise at any time before the final contract is written, the best solution is to seek out a new pool company. However, you should be somewhat flexible. The dealer or builder may have a legitimate reason for an additional charge because something essential to the installation was overlooked.

Ask that the bid be guaranteed for a specific number of days so you have time to collect other bids and make an evaluation. This also protects the pool company from price fluctuations of materials and labor if you don't make up your mind in a reasonable length of time.

Encourage the builder or dealer to make alternative suggestions that can improve the quality of the pool and equipment or reduce the cost. Discuss all specifications in detail. If you provide too little information, the pool builder or dealer will probably request the details that are missing.

The lowest price will not necessarily be the best value. Design talents, workmanship and post-installation service vary from company to company. Once you have several competitive bids, weigh the price against company reputation, services provided, and other signs of quality. If necessary, call the pool company to answer any questions you may have. Having confidence in a builder with a good reputation for quality, dependability and long-range service may justify a higher initial price.

A particularly low bid should be regarded with suspicion and examined carefully. Less-reputable dealers may submit an unrealistically low bid to shut out competitors. They then proceed to increase the final price through a series of extra charges that weren't clearly stated in the original bid. If this happens, you always have the option of rejecting the contract before signing it. The bid or quote is not a binding obligation on your part.

NEGOTIATING A CONTRACT

Most established pool builders are knowledgeable, provide quality materials and workmanship, meet all their obligations and deliver a finished pool at a fair price. Unfortunately, there are a few who don't meet these basic standards.

Negotiating a fair contract is a critical step for you and the pool builder. A clear, well-defined contract benefits both parties.

WHAT TO EXPECT

A properly executed contract will be written to provide you these benefits:
- Construction will start on time and be completed on time. Start and completion dates will be included in the contract.
- The work will be completed with as little disruption to property and utilities as possible. The contract will specify who is responsible for providing site access, relocating utility lines, and repairing any damage to property during construction.
- The finished pool will meet or exceed the minimum specifications of the contract. This includes pool size, quality of materials and workmanship and quality of support equipment.
- The final price will be the contracted price. Extra charges, if any, will be only those agreed upon in advance to cover changes you have requested.
- The site will be left free of debris.
- The pool will be filled and cleaned and all operating equipment left in perfect running order.

WRITING THE CONTRACT

Once you have selected the pool builder and all preliminary planning has been completed, all verbal agreements and cost estimates will be written into a binding contract. A properly prepared contract provides protection for you and the pool builder. It is essential to prevent misunderstandings and make sure all parties live up to the basic agreement.

Drawing up a contract should be a cooperative effort. The pool builder is anxious to get your business and will agree to most reasonable requests. The builder will also have an opportunity to explain reasons for including specific items in the contract.

The contract is usually prepared by the pool builder. It is often a standard form. Upon request, a reputable builder will give you a blank contract to examine prior to writing the final contract.

To complete the contract, the builder will go through the contract items to cover the details of your specific installation. You have a right to a completed, unsigned contract you can review with your lawyer before signing. You don't have to accept the contract as originally written. Until the contract is signed, you can agree with the builder to strike certain clauses or add details not included on the form.

You also have the option of having your attorney prepare the contract. This could be the wisest step if the pool is a part of a more complex building project. If you prepare the contract, the builder will specify points that must be included.

If you are employing an architect or landscape architect to handle pool details, he or she can prepare the pool contract. Completing the contract will involve all parties participating in the project. Examine the contract as carefully as you would if you were proceeding unaided.

Under current federal law, once the contract has been signed, you have three business days to change your mind.

SPECIFICATIONS

List in detail the specific dimensions of the pool. Specify the type of support equipment, and type and amounts of materials to be used. Include the manufacturer, model and type of each item to be installed. This would include such components as motor and pump, filter, heater, skimmer, diving board, solar equipment (if any), ladders, pool cover, pool-cover reel, automatic pool cleaning equipment, and so forth. Include specifications for pool deck, plumbing, wiring and lighting.

SITE PLAN

A site plan drawn to scale shows the pool's location on the property, the shape of the pool, the location of support equipment and all basic dimensions. Working from your original site plan, page 9, and other information, the builder will make blueprints or architectural-style drawings of the pool and its surroundings. Or the builder may agree to use plans provided by an architect or landscape architect. Compare the builder's plans or blueprints with specifications defined in the contract.

Check to see that the size of the pool is really as you imagined it to be. Are the drawings scaled correctly? Check to see that they are in proportion to the size of the lot and your home. Make sure the actual dimensions for the deck are similar to those shown in the drawings.

WORK SCHEDULE

Include the date work is to begin and the date it is to be completed—including site cleanup. Include specific provisions for weather delays. Specify when you will assume responsibility for maintenance and operation of pool equipment.

It is not unreasonable to include a penalty provision for failure to complete the work on a reasonable schedule. A penalty provision is negotiable. Usually it is a set dollar amount to be deducted from the final settlement for each working day the job remains unfinished.

VARIATIONS

It is not always physically possible to build a sprayed-concrete pool to the exact dimensions specified in the contract. The way the site is excavated, steel tied and concrete applied makes it difficult to form the exact shape specified in the plans.

In the contract, cover how much of a variation is acceptable without penalty. If the completed pool, including variation, is smaller than specified in the contract, you should be entitled to a reduction in the final price. The amount should be specified.

If the pool is oversized, you may agree to an extra charge to cover the costs of the pool up to a specific larger dimension. Or you may agree to share the added cost with the builder. You can insist that an oversize pool is the builder's error. Any such charges or added costs should be clearly stated in the contract.

OTHER UNKNOWNS

Anticipate unknown hazards. Excessive rock, uncharted utility lines,

Your pool contract should specify exactly what work the pool installer is responsible for and what follow-up services are provided. Pictured is a basic pool installation with minimal deck. Pool has been filled with water and support equipment tested. Construction debris has been removed from site and fence sections replaced at equipment-access location. This is often the work specified in a standard contract for vinyl-lined pool installation. Additional work, such as final grading or landscaping, can be written into the standard contract. *Photo courtesy of Heldor, Morristown, NJ.*

underground water and other unexpected natural or man-made obstacles can add to the cost of the pool. Make a provision for dealing with situations that are not wholly the responsibility or fault of the pool builder. There should be a limit on extra charges for such contingencies. The limit is negotiable.

It is often to your advantage to agree to share some of the cost of extra labor or materials necessary to deal with unusual problems. The builder will be more willing to do the work correctly. In all cases, the burden of proving the necessity of extra charges should be the responsibility of the builder. Extra work and resulting charges should be approved in advance by the homeowner.

Without this provision, it is good business practice for the pool builder to build in an allowance for unknown contingencies when producing the original quote. If there is no allowance for unknown problems in the contracted price, the builder is gambling. This could lead to financial complications that could jeopardize the successful completion of the job.

CLEANUP

Specify who is responsible for cleaning up the site when construction has been completed. The pool builder usually takes responsibility for removing excavated dirt and rock, and major debris. Light cleanup can be assigned to the builder, or you can do it yourself. The contract should specify who does what cleanup, and the amount of any price concessions offered you for doing part of the work. The contract should also specify who is responsible for damage to foliage, walks and other property.

ACCESS AND UTILITIES

The contract should state who is responsible for providing access to the site. Who is responsible for arranging to have utility lines removed or relocated? Who is responsible for paying to move and replace utility lines or other physical obstacles, such as walls or fences?

PAYMENT SCHEDULE

The pool builder will want to be paid as early as possible to cover day-to-day expenses of labor and materials during the construction period. Smaller companies often finance a project with short-term loans and must pay interest until the job is completed.

It is common practice to schedule a series of payments to be made as construction progresses. Progress payments are usually tied to specific stages of work. The amount of each

Before You Build 39

It's often hard to build a free-form pool like this to precise dimensions specified in plans. The contract should specify allowable variations in size. If pool exceeds maximum allowable size, contract should state who pays the difference. If pool is smaller than minimum size, contract should specify amount of rebate to customer, if any. *Design: Aquarius Pools, Sacramento, CA.*

payment should be in proportion to work completed.

If possible, arrange to make the final payment after the pool has been in operation long enough to be sure that everything is working properly. The final payment date should be a specified amount of time after completion of the pool. *Do not pay in advance for work that has not been completed.*

For manufactured pools that can be installed in a few working days, payment schedules are not as critical. Normally, you can be expected to make a down-payment to cover the pool itself and pay final costs when the installation has been completed and the pool is in operation.

Payment schedules should be negotiable. The exact payment schedule should be agreed upon and amounts and schedule included in the final contract.

LEGAL PROTECTION

There is always a possibility that the builder or dealer will not be able to finish the job. The reason why a contract is not fulfilled is not an issue. Resolve questions of ownership if there is a bankruptcy and include this information in the contract.

It is not unreasonable to ask the contractor to post a performance bond. If a bond is required, it should be specified in the contract. A performance bond is a form of insurance the builder must acquire to guarantee the project is completed as specified. If the builder defaults, the holder of the bond must provide the financing so another builder can complete the pool.

If no bond is provided, ask for mechanic's lien releases as the work progresses. These releases can be obtained by the contractor for work subcontracted and for materials acquired for the job.

Mechanic's lien releases protect you from claims against the contractor for unpaid materials or services. Under mechanic's lien laws, you are liable for money owed suppliers and subcontractors by your builder if you have not obtained releases.

INSURANCE

Before agreeing to have a builder begin work on your pool, make sure the builder has adequate liability and property insurance. This should be a condition of the contract. Insurance should cover injuries to employees on your property. It should cover damage to your property. Verify that the insurance is valid and that current premiums are paid.

Check with your own insurance agent. Describe the project involved and the amount and type of coverage carried by your pool builder. Make sure your personal coverage is adequate.

PERFORMANCE

Every contract should carry a *validity period*. This specifies how long the builder agrees to honor prices included in the contract if building is delayed.

Warranties—The contract should include specifics on what is guaranteed, by whom and for how long. The builder will usually guarantee workmanship and construction materials. Warranties for support equipment are usually carried by the manufacturer of the individual components. Warranties for manufactured pools, including vinyl liners, are honored by the pool manufacturer. Get equipment literature and warranty cards from the builder. Federal law requires that you be told what items are covered by warranties.

The contract should specify who is responsible for obtaining building permits and building approval from local agencies. As a condition of the contract, the builder should agree to meet all requirements of zoning laws, building codes and local covenants.

HOW TO AVOID TROUBLE

There are thousands of pool builders and dealers who are capable of producing a quality, trouble-free pool at a fair price. Unfortunately, there are a few builders and pool salesmen who try to take advantage of the potential client's enthusiasm or lack of knowledge to sell inferior products or shoddy construction.

In negotiating with a pool builder or pool salesman, there are several signs that should warn you to proceed cautiously or, better still, find a more reputable dealer.

QUICK CLOSES

Beware of salesmen who seem too anxious to close a sale and get a signed contract. A reputable pool dealer expects to spend time with each customer. It may take four or five conferences to prepare cost estimates, arrange installation details, choose support equipment and negotiate contract details.

"BAIT-AND-SWITCH" TACTIC

This tactic is most often used by disreputable dealers of above-ground pools. A dealership will advertise their economy models or run a special sale on several lower-cost models. When you go to buy the pool, the salesman will try to convince you that the pool you've chosen is too small, incomplete, poorly designed, and so forth. He or she will then try to sell you a larger, more expensive pool that "better suits your needs." Or the salesman will try to sell you accessories that are "essential" to the use of the pool.

The best way to avoid this tactic is to know what is included in the pool package you've selected. Make sure the basic price includes all equipment and accessories necessary to install and operate the pool. For tips on selecting above-ground pools, see pages 98-100.

QUICK SIGN BONUS

Be suspicious of a salesman who offers a price break, special bonus or something "free" for signing "today" or "this week" as a pressure tactic for a quick close. Nothing is offered free. Whether it's a diving board or a year's supply of chemicals, the cost will be included in the total cost of the project. Haste in signing a contract could be costly.

SPECIAL DEALS

Beware of salesmen who claim they are offering you a low price so they can use your pool as a model installation to show potential buyers in your neighborhood. A similar approach is to offer to build a pool "at cost" so it can be used for promotional or advertising photography.

It is unlikely the special price is really special and the pool may be of suspect quality. An appeal to your vanity or interest in a "deal" is an approach used to sell pools or other home improvements by disreputable companies.

Reputable dealers will often ask an owner's permission to show a new pool to prospective clients, or take photographs for their sales portfolio—but only after the pool is built, and only if the owner is satisfied with it.

FREELANCERS

Beware of salesmen who have no formal affiliation with a pool builder or dealer. The salesman will get a signed contract for a pool, then sell the project to the lowest bidder. This is not illegal unless the salesman misrepresents his affiliation.

Make sure you are talking to a formal representative of the specific pools the salesman is discussing. There is no legal way to prevent an independent salesman from forming a company to obtain pool contracts. The protection against this tactic is to ask for and check references from homeowners who have bought pools from the salesman. You can avoid this trap if you follow the recommendations beginning on page 36 for finding qualified help.

LOW BIDS

Be suspicious of bids that seem unrealistically low or significantly lower than bids from other pool builders. A low bid may be submitted to eliminate competition. Once the low bidder has isolated the buyer, a series of added costs are tacked on to cover items not clearly accounted for in the original proposal.

This problem can be avoided if you provide a complete set of specifications when you obtain the bid, and make sure the bid reflects those specifications. See page 38 for details on what information to provide dealers when seeking bids.

BLANK CONTRACTS

Beware of a salesman who tries to get you to sign any contract with blanks that have not been completely filled in. Be suspicious of a salesman who hesitates to provide a copy of a blank, standard contract for you to examine in advance.

CASH PAYMENTS

Beware of a salesman who offers substantial discounts for payment in cash. The company could be insolvent or trying to hide the transaction. The same holds true for dealers who offer price breaks for making advance payments. Once all or a substantial portion of the project is paid for, there is little pressure on the company to install a satisfactory pool. A payment schedule should be in proportion to the work completed.

Never make out checks in the salesman's name or pay cash. Checks should be made out to the company by name. You never know what the status of an individual salesman might be with the company he or she represents.

NO REFERENCES

References from satisfied customers are the most common means for a reputable pool company to solicit new business. Beware of salesmen who refuse or are unable to provide the names of recent pool buyers.

Established pool builders will not be offended if you ask for recommendations or question their experience or qualifications. Quality pool builders know that their success depends on good products and service. Much of their business comes from leads provided by satisfied customers.

Before You Build 41

Spas and waterfalls can share the pool's support equipment. Basic components must be sized to handle the additional load. Design: Aquarius Pools, Sacramento, CA.

42   Selecting Pool Equipment

CHAPTER 4

Selecting Pool Equipment

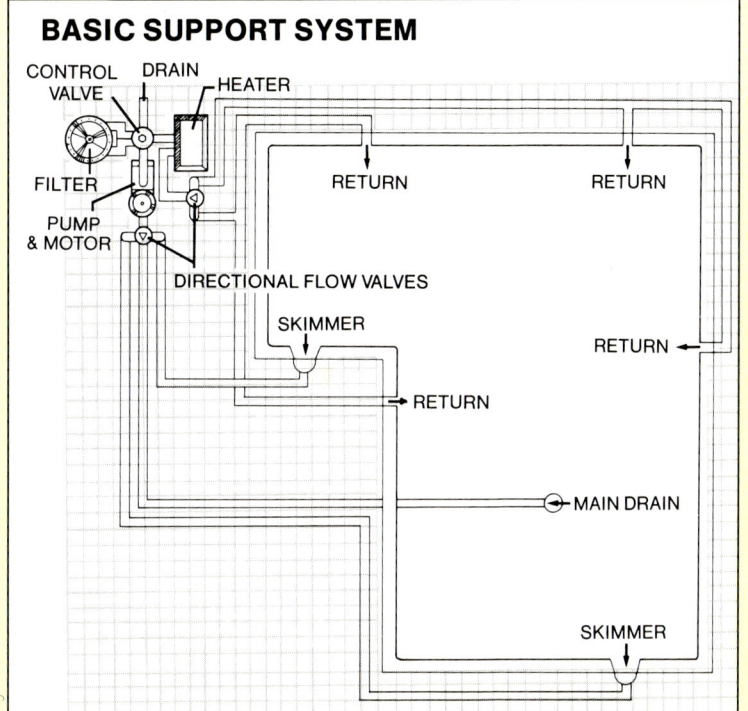

BASIC SUPPORT SYSTEM

(Diagram showing: CONTROL VALVE, DRAIN, HEATER, FILTER, PUMP & MOTOR, DIRECTIONAL FLOW VALVES, SKIMMER, RETURN, MAIN DRAIN)

Installing or building the pool shell is the most dramatic step in creating a new pool. A structurally sound shell will provide many years of satisfactory use with a modest amount of care. But equally important is the installation of quality support equipment (pump, filter, heater) and related plumbing and equipment.

Most annoying, day-to-day pool problems can be traced to undersized, mismatched or poor-quality support equipment. All components must be sized to handle the filtration and heating requirements of the pool. They should not only function effectively as individual components, but work well together as a system. For years of trouble-free service, choose the best-quality components you can afford.

One way a pool builder can make a bid competitive is to specify undersized components in the quote. Skimping on size and quality is false economy. Too small a pump will not deliver the required flow through the filter for effective filtration. A small filter is inefficient and requires frequent cleaning. An undersized heater will use more energy and may not have the capacity to raise the water temperature to a comfortable level.

When soliciting bids for your pool installation, check the size and quality of the support components specified in each bid. The bid should specify each component by brand and model number. If a pool dealer or builder recommends specific components, ask to see product literature provided by the equipment manufacturer.

An effectively working support system and proper chemical treatment make it possible to recycle pool water almost indefinitely. Except in cases of extreme chemical imbalance, only water splashed out of the pool or water lost to evaporation need be replaced.

This chapter will help you choose the right-size pump, filter and heater. It also covers surface skimmers, automatic cleaning equipment and major accessories installed when the pool is built—automatic chlorinators, diving boards and pool slides. Information on installing support equipment is on page 95. Details on servicing support equipment start on page 127.

HOW THE SYSTEM WORKS

The pump pulls water into the system through the main drain at the pool bottom and through the skimmer at the water surface. Water is pumped through a filter to trap fine particles of dirt and other debris. From the filter, water is directed through the heater and piped back into the pool. The drawing at left shows how basic support equipment is plumbed to a pool.

The support system also purifies water by circulating sanitizing chemicals that destroy harmful bacteria and other microorganisms. The filter, combined with chemical treatment, keeps the pool clean and safe for swimming. Complete details on pool maintenance start on page 117.

Each member of the support system must be sized to filter and heat the pool's total water volume in a predetermined amount of time. Support equipment can be designed to handle the pool only, or serve both a pool and attached spa.

CODE REQUIREMENTS

Local building codes may limit the options you have in selecting components. Codes may specify how you must dispose of waste water.

For example, if local codes prohibit water backwashed through the filter from being discharged into the sewer system, you have several alternatives. Waste water can be directed to a dry well on your property. You can include a *separation tank* on a diatomaceous earth filter to remove sediment from backwashed water or buy a cartridge filter so no backwashing is

Selecting Pool Equipment 43

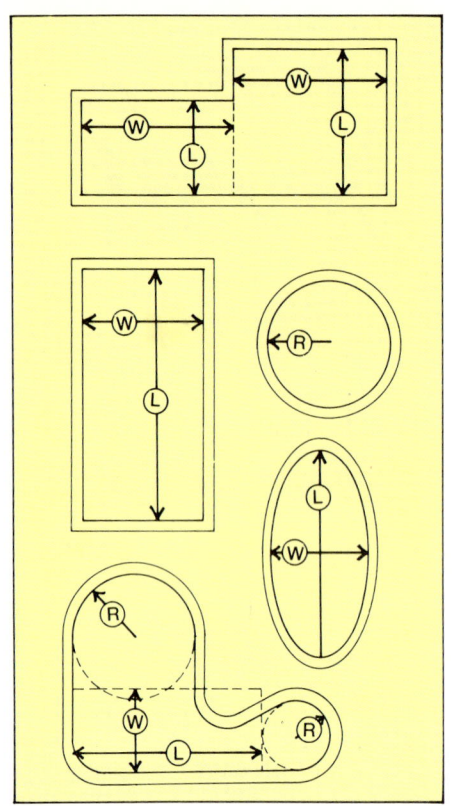

This drawing shows where to take measurements to determine the surface areas of the pool shapes shown. Refer to text at right to determine surface area in square feet and figure pool capacity in gallons.

required. Specific types of filters are discussed on pages 48-50.

Codes limiting water use may specify what kind of filter you can install. High-rate sand filters, which can require several hundred gallons for backwashing, may be impractical in areas where water is in short supply.

Codes may determine where support equipment can be located on your property. Codes usually include specifications on plumbing and wiring. They may even specify the type of filter you can install.

State or local energy-use restrictions may dictate the type of heater you install. Such restrictions are usually tied into energy-conservation programs or current availability of fossil fuels or electricity in your area. See page 50.

OTHER EQUIPMENT

In addition to the basic pump, filter and heater, there are other pieces of automated equipment that can be plumbed into the support system. They include automatic pool vacuums, pool sweeps, and chlorinators. A heater can be replaced or supplemented with a series of solar panels to provide solar heating.

Surface skimmers, discussed on page 53, are often called accessories, but are installed as a standard part of the support system on all modern in-ground pools.

HOW TO SIZE EQUIPMENT

The best way to size equipment for your pool is to gather all the basic data on your pool's requirements and consult a pool dealer or builder. They are experienced in matching equipment to a number of different pool situations. Also read literature and specifications provided by pump, filter and heater manufacturers. The literature will often contain helpful charts and formulas to help you with your calculations. The following information will help you determine your pool's requirements so you can select the correct-size equipment.

POOL CAPACITY

There are several factors that together determine the size and type of components for a support system. To correctly size all components, you must first know the number of gallons of water in the pool. This is referred to as the pool's *capacity*. Total capacity determines how many gallons of water have to be pumped through the filter and heater per minute (flow rate) to recirculate all the water in a given number of hours.

Manufacturers of standard vinyl-lined or fiberglass pools can tell you exactly how many gallons of water each model will hold. The builder of a sprayed-concrete pool should be able to give you an estimate of capacity before building begins. The dimensions of a completed sprayed-concrete pool may differ slightly from those called for in the original specifications.

For purposes of selecting support equipment, a reasonably accurate estimate of pool capacity will be satisfactory. You can estimate capacity using measurements indicated in your pool plans.

How Many Gallons?—The basic formula for figuring pool capacity in gallons is to multiply the pool's surface area by its average depth from waterline to pool bottom. The resulting figure gives you the number of cubic feet of water in the pool. One cubic foot of water equals 7.5 gallons. Multiply number of cubic feet by 7.5 to get total gallons.

To determine the average pool depth, add the depths of the shallowest and deepest parts of the pool and divide by 2. This is how the formula applies to different pool shapes:

Round Pools—Take the radius of the pool (the distance from the center to the edge), multiply it by itself, then times 3.14, times the average depth of the pool: $r^2 \times 3.14 \times $ *average pool depth*.

A pool 24 feet across has a radius of 12 feet. If the pool has an average depth of 5 feet, the capacity is determined as follows: *12 x 12 x 3.14 = 452 square feet*. Multiply 452 by the average depth of the pool, 5 feet, to determine the number of cubic feet: *452 x 5 = 2,260*. Multiply 2,260 by 7.5 and you will have the number of gallons in the pool: *2,260 x 7.5 = 16,950*.

Rectangular Pools—Multiply length by width by average depth. Multiply that total by 7.5 to determine the number of gallons.

Oval Pools—Find the centerpoint of the pool. Measure the pool width through the centerpoint (shortest dimension), as shown in the drawing at left. Then measure the pool length (longest dimension). Multiply these two numbers, then multiply the total by 3.14. Multiply that total by the average depth: *length x width x 3.14 x average depth*. Multiply the result by 7.5 to determine the number of gallons.

Irregular Pools—Most pools are a combination of standard geometric forms. If possible, divide the pool into basic geometric shapes, figure the gallons in each section, then add them together.

For example, an L-shaped pool is made up of two rectangles. Figure the number of gallons in each rectangle separately, then add the totals. Free-form pools can often be divided into a series of ovals and circles.

CHOOSING A PUMP

The first pumps used in swimming pools were originally designed to provide running water to homes in rural areas. They were adapted for pool use with few, if any, design changes.

In recent years, pumps and pump motors have been designed specifically for swimming pools. They are long-

44 Selecting Pool Equipment

lasting, safe and superior to early models. National electrical codes now include specifications for pool motors and pumps. These codes cover corrosion, grounding and details on water exposure from flooding, rain or broken pipes.

SIZING FACTORS

The pump is the heart of the support system and should be the first unit chosen when planning a system. The pump must have adequate power to cycle the pool's total water volume through the filter in a given number of hours. It must also be sized to overcome resistance in the plumbing system. Once pump size has been determined, the filter is matched to it. See page 48.

If the pool is to include a spa that uses the same support equipment, sizing a pump becomes more complex. In addition to handling the additional filtration requirements of the spa, the pump must have enough power to operate the spa's hydrotherapy jets. In some systems, an additional pump is installed to operate the jets. If your pool will include a spa, the pool designer or installer will be able to select the correct-size pump or pumps to operate it.

For effective filtration of dirt and debris, the pool's total water volume must be cycled through the support system in a given number of hours. This is called the system's *turnover rate*. Turnover rates vary slightly for different pools, depending on pool use and how much dirt and debris accumulates in the pool.

Once you've established the desired turnover rate, you can then calculate the required *flow rate* through the system. This is the number of gallons the pump cycles through the system per minute.

When the flow-rate requirements have been established, water resistance in the plumbing system, called *head loss*, or *total dynamic head*, is computed. Pump manufacturers supply performance charts with their pumps for sizing purposes. The charts list the various flow rates each pump will deliver under different head losses. You use the chart to select the pump that delivers the required flow rate against the head loss in the system.

The following information tells how to compute turnover rate, flow rate and head loss. To compute head loss, you'll need to work with your pool designer or dealer to decide where to locate the support equipment so plumbing requirements can be determined. See *Designing an Efficient System,* page 46.

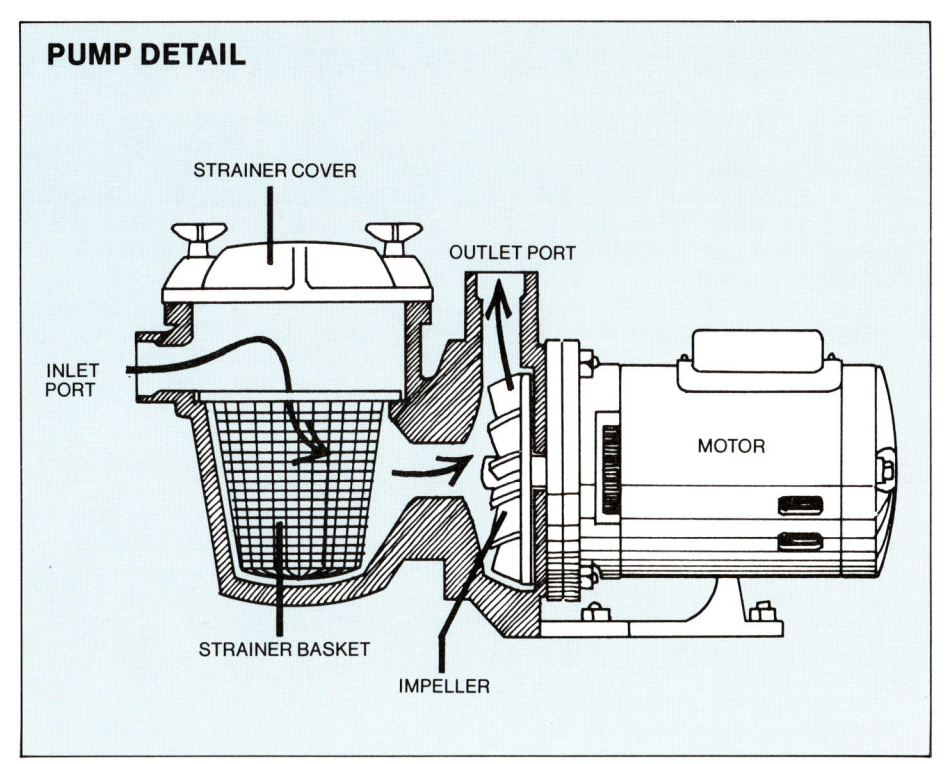

DETERMINING FLOW RATE

The first step in sizing a pump is to determine the desirable number of hours for one complete water turnover or recycling period—the *turnover rate.*

The desired turnover rate will vary from pool to pool. The best turnover rate will be just enough to maintain good water quality at the minimum expenditure of energy.

The best way to determine the turnover rate is to seek the advice of a pool builder or dealer in your area. The standard turnover rate for residential pools is 8 to 10 hours.

When the turnover rate has been established, divide pool capacity in gallons by the turnover rate in hours to determine gallons per hour. Divide by 60 minutes to determine the required flow rate in gallons per minute (gpm).

As an example, an average 15x30' pool with a shallow end 3 feet deep, and a deep end 7-1/2 feet deep, has a capacity of about 21,000 gallons of water. Use the formulas on page 44 to determine the gallon capacity of your pool.

Using an average turnover rate of 8 hours, 21,000 gallons divided by 8 equals 2,620 gallons-per-hour flow rate. Divide 2,620 by 60 to arrive at a flow rate of 35 gallons per minute.

The right pump will be of the size necessary to produce the required flow rate to operate the filter efficiently.

DETERMINING HEAD LOSS

The pump causes water to flow. The filter, heater, water lines and all other components resist flow. To size the pump, you'll need to determine the amount of *flow resistance* or friction in the system.

In plumbing terms, flow resistance is called *head loss* and is expressed in feet. Head loss is determined by pipe diameter, length of pipe run and number of elbows in the system. Added together, these factors determine the total head loss, referred to as *total dynamic head (tdh)*. Head loss is used to determine *back-pressure*, which is the flow restriction expressed in pounds per square inch (psi).

Head-loss or back-pressure figures are required to size the pump, using manufacturer's performance specifications. The pump must be sized to deliver the required flow rate against

Selecting Pool Equipment 45

DESIGNING AN EFFICIENT SYSTEM

An efficient support system is designed with a minimum of water resistance, or *total dynamic head*, in the plumbing system. There are a number of ways to reduce total dynamic head, or head loss, in a system.

In planning the pool, locate support equipment as close to the pool as possible. This will reduce power needed to pump the water through the system. It will also reduce heat loss in water flowing through the return line from the heater to the pool.

Support equipment is typically plumbed with 1-1/2-inch pipe. For installations where water is pumped long distances, pipe diameter should be increased to 2 inches or more. Larger-diameter pipes create less resistance.

Most pools are designed with the return lines below the pool's water level to create a *closed system*.

Once a closed system is filled with water, water in the return lines causes a siphoning effect that lifts water up and through the system. In a closed system, the height of the pump or filter above the pool has little effect on resistance created in the system. The same principle applies to roof-mounted solar panels. A larger pump may be needed to circulate water through the panels to overcome added head loss caused by additional pipe and fittings—not because the panels are well above pool level.

Each 90° elbow in the plumbing system creates the same resistance as about 10 feet of straight pipe. Two 45° elbows cause less resistance than one 90° elbow. Where codes permit, flexible PVC pipe may be used instead of elbows to reduce total dynamic head. Gradual bends create less resistance than sharp ones.

A simple plumbing system with large-diameter pipe, a minimum of elbows and *full-flow fittings* is the most economical system to operate. Full-flow fittings and valves create less flow resistance than standard fittings and valves.

DETERMINING RESISTANCE

A basic hydraulic law states that friction increases as water flow or gpm increases. In chart form, it's possible to plot a friction-loss curve on a graph that demonstrates how friction increases as the gpm or flow rate increases.

In designing a pool support system, components will vary as to how much each contributes to friction loss. Each part of the hydraulic system can be examined to determine pump requirements. Friction loss in the entire system—pipes, filters and heater—produces the total dynamic head. Total dynamic head is expressed in feet. Pool builders usually have access to technical data that tells them how many feet of head loss each foot of various diameter pipes contribute to the system. Fittings and elbows also have head-loss ratings. Added together, the amount of pipe and number of fittings and elbows determine the total dynamic head.

Water resistance in the system is also measured in terms of back-pressure, measured in gallons per minute (gpm). When total dynamic head is reduced, so is back-pressure in the system. High pressure through the filter does not increase its efficiency. Too much pressure can be inefficient. Only the amount of water flowing through the filter (flow rate) determines the filter's cleaning efficiency. Unnecessarily high pressure requires unnecessary energy. Too rapid a flow can create turbulence in sand filters.

In designing the system, the goal is to keep total dynamic head and back-pressure as low as possible in proportion to flow. Friction is reduced by using large diameter pipe, full-flow fittings and as few elbows as possible. Use long bends of pipe instead of elbows whenever possible.

---

back-pressure, or total dynamic head in the system.

The amount of head loss in a system depends on the distance water must be pumped from the pool to the filter and heater, the interior diameter of the pipe used and the number of *elbows*, (45° or 90° fittings) in the system.

Support-system design is usually worked out before installation begins. Start by letting the pool designer or builder know where you want to locate the support equipment. The closer the equipment is to the pool, the more efficiently it will operate. The less plumbing involved—pipe runs, elbows and other fittings—the lower the head loss. The less head loss, the smaller the pump required to produce the desired flow rate. Tips for designing an efficient support system are discussed above.

When the plumbing system is designed, head loss and back-pressure can be computed and the correct-size pump chosen.

In most cases, the pool dealer or builder will design the support system. He or she will know head loss figures for various diameter pipes, elbows, valves and other fittings in the system. Pipe and fitting manufacturers and suppliers can also provide head-loss figures for the components they sell.

The total dynamic head of plumbing systems for average-size residential pools ranges from 35 to 60 feet. Many pool builders will install a pump that exceeds the total dynamic head of the system, especially if the owner is considering adding a solar-heating system in the future. The additional plumbing required for solar will increase total dynamic head in the system.

If a pump supplier is given the pool specifics—capacity, required flow rate and plumbing details, he or she can recommend a specific-size pump, based on manufacturer's performance charts.

If you elect to design or install the system yourself, seek counsel from an experienced pool designer or installer.

WHAT TYPE OF PUMP?

Pumps used to circulate water through the support system are called *centrifugal pumps*. These pumps use a shaft-mounted impeller powered by an electric motor. The centrifugal force of the spinning impeller creates the flow through the pump.

Individual manufacturers produce pumps made of bronze, cast iron and high-impact plastic, in a variety of sizes. Basic pumps for swimming pools have strainer baskets on the intake side to trap debris that might clog the pump's impeller.

All pumps used for pools today are *self-priming*. That is, they do not have to be primed with water each time they're operated. Pumps used for older pools had to be primed before every use or positioned below the pool's water level. Occasionally found in use in older pools, they are impractical for new installations.

In theory, self-priming pumps never have to be primed once they are in service. However, air in the system can cause suction starvation of the pump.

Repriming the pump is done by filling the strainer pot on the pump with water and allowing water to run back into the incoming line. Air can be bled out of the system through a relief valve in the top of the filter.

Most pumps are water-cooled. A pump can overheat and get damaged if operated when dry. Complete details on servicing and maintaining pumps are on page 128.

PUMP SIZES

Pool pumps come in standard sizes, usually identified by horsepower (HP). Standard pool pumps range from 1/3HP to 2HP. Larger pumps, up to 3HP are used to power hydrojets for systems that incorporate spas.

In a spa system, it takes about 1/4 to 1/2HP to run each jet. In small pool-spa combinations, a pump sized to power jets may produce too much pressure, or head, to operate the filter efficiently. In such cases, either separate pumps, or the two-speed pump discussed below, are installed. If a two-speed pump is used, the low speed is used for filtration, the high speed to operate the jets. A valve is installed so water bypasses the filter when the pump is in high-speed mode.

ONE-SPEED OR TWO-SPEED?

One-speed pump motors have been the standard for many years. Recently developed two-speed motors now give the pool owner an option.

One-speed motors turn the pump shaft and impeller at a single, constant rate. The advantages in using one-speed pumps are that they are dependable, long-lasting and the most economical to buy.

Two-speed pumps were adapted for swimming pool use to reduce the cost of operating the filtration system.

Energy-efficient two-speed pump operates at high speed to overcome initial pressure in the plumbing system, then kicks back into lower speed to operate equipment. High-speed mode is also used to operate hydrojets in an attached spa, or swim-current jets in a pool.

They are more expensive than one-speed pumps, but operate more efficiently. At lower speeds, a two-speed pump operates with less noise. It also consumes less energy to cycle the same amount of water. The higher initial cost can usually be recovered in one or two years in energy savings, which can reduce the long-range cost of operating a pool. So it makes economic sense to install a two-speed pump.

The motor that powers the two-speed pump is actually two motors in one. When the pump is switched on, it begins operation at its highest speed. When the initial head loss or back-pressure has been overcome and water is flowing through the system, the pump automatically drops to a lower speed.

In one example, the high-speed phase turns the pump at 3,450 revolutions per minute (rpm) and the low-speed is 1,750 rpm. When the pump switches to low-speed operation, the flow is lowered by a factor of 2, which reduces flow by 50%. The head or water pressure is dropped by a factor of 4, which reduces pressure to 1/4. The power required (kilowatts) is reduced by a factor of 6, (which reduces power consumption to 1/6). Reducing power consumption to 1/6 also cuts energy costs to 1/6 while the pump is operating at low speed.

The result is this: If flow is reduced by 50% during low-speed operation, it will take twice as long to filter the same amount of water, but will require only 1/3 the power consumption to do it. Running the system 10 hours at half-speed is more efficient than running the system at full-speed for 5 hours. Not all two-speed pumps are as efficient as the example cited here.

Constant half-speed operation distributes the chemicals evenly, operates the pump at the minimum noise level and produces the desirable number of gallons per minute through the system at approximately 1/3 the energy cost. The lower electric bill will repay the higher investment early in the life of the pump.

In determining size for a two-speed pump, horsepower and rpms for the high-speed phase are used to calculate the size needed to overcome head loss in a specific system.

DETERMINING ENERGY EFFICIENCY

The energy efficiency of a pump can be determined by dividing the gallons of water pumped in one hour by the pump rating in kilowatts. Gallons per hour is the pump's flow rate (gpm) multiplied by 60. Refer to manufacturer's literature for ratings. For pumps rated in horsepower, determine kilowatts by multiplying horsepower by 746. The higher the number, the more efficient the pump.

Selecting Pool Equipment **47**

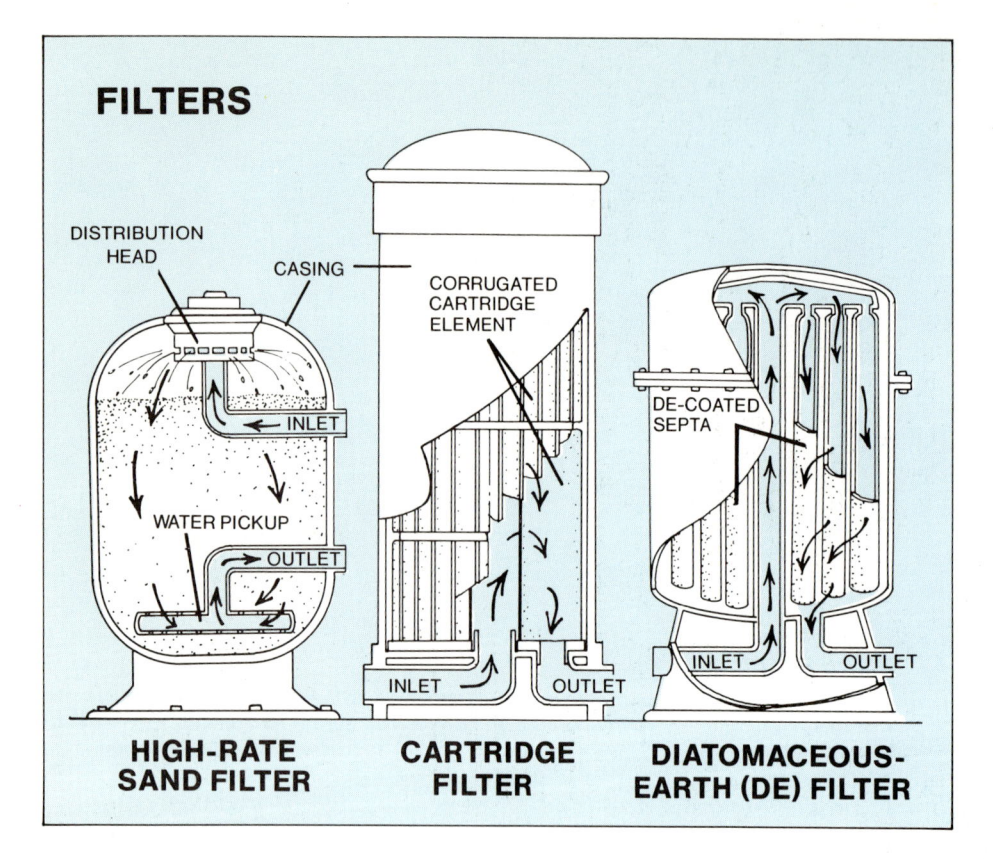

FILTERS

HIGH-RATE SAND FILTER
- DISTRIBUTION HEAD
- CASING
- INLET
- WATER PICKUP
- OUTLET

CARTRIDGE FILTER
- CORRUGATED CARTRIDGE ELEMENT
- INLET
- OUTLET

DIATOMACEOUS-EARTH (DE) FILTER
- DE-COATED SEPTA
- INLET
- OUTLET

CHOOSING A FILTER

The purpose of the filter is to remove fine particles of dirt and debris from the water. Water pumped through the filter and treated with the right pool chemicals can be recycled almost indefinitely.

There are currently three types of filters being used in residential pools. *High-rate sand filters* and *diatomaceous earth (DE) filters* are the traditional pool filters. *Cartridge filters* are comparatively new for pool use. All three types are effective and provide good service. They are made of stainless steel, fiberglass or plastic.

In most cases, the type of filter recommended by your pool builder or dealer will be one commonly used in your geographical area. One type isn't necessarily superior to the others. Any quality filter should last 10 years or more, if correctly maintained. Pool builders may recommend filters they have used successfully in the past and have experience servicing. Complete information on cleaning and maintaining filters starts on page 130.

The final selection should be a matter of personal preference. In some areas, the homeowner isn't offered a choice. A limited water supply or restrictions on waste-water disposal may have forced local communities to specify the type of filter you can install.

WHAT SIZE FILTER?

All pool filters have a *filter area*, measured in square feet. In high-rate sand filters, it is the surface area of the top layer of sand. In DE filters it is the surface area of the grids, or *septa*, that hold the DE material. In cartridge filters, it is the surface area of the cartridges.

DE filters have a capacity of about 2 gallons of water per minute per square foot of filter area. Cartridge filters have a capacity of 3/4 to 1 gallon per minute per square foot. High-rate sand filters are rated at 20-22 gallons per minute per square foot. Although sand filters have the highest capacity per square foot of filter area, the area is relatively small compared to DE or cartridge filters.

The pool's capacity and turnover rate will determine the size of the filter. These elements are also used to size the pump. After you've chosen a pump, filter capacity, in gallons per minute, is then matched to the flow rate of the pump.

The initial cost of a filter is usually in proportion to its capacity and filter area. The most economical filter is the minimum size capable of effectively filtering the water of a specific pool. The minimum size also must be cleaned most frequently.

An investment in an oversize filter will increase installation costs, but will reduce maintenance time. The larger the filter, the less often it needs cleaning or backwashing.

Regardless of the filter size, it is important that water flows through the filter at the rate for which it was designed. Larger capacity filters have higher minimum-flow requirements. If the filter is too large, it won't be operating at maximum efficiency.

HIGH-RATE SAND FILTERS

Sand is the oldest and most common medium for filtering water. High-rate sand filters are still popular because they're effective and easy to maintain. Depending on use, the sand can be used continuously for several years before it needs replacement.

The principle of a high-rate sand filter is simple. Sand traps dirt particles when a non-turbulent flow of water is forced through sand in the filter.

In operation, water flow in a high-rate sand filter stirs up the top few inches of sand to keep dirt particles from clogging the top surface too rapidly. Early sand filters had little surface turbulence. The sand surface became quickly saturated, so the filter required more frequent backwashing.

Sand for the filters is available at pool dealers and suppliers. Most filter manufacturers recommend sand of *.45-.55 millimeters*—the size of the sand grains—with *1.6 uniformity coefficient*—the variation in size of sand grains. This is also called *#20 silica sand*. Clean sand of this size will trap 15-micron particles.

As the sand collects contaminants, the micron size of particles lodged in the sand continues to be reduced until the pores are clogged and the filter needs backwashing. A micron is one 1,000th of a millimeter. The filter operates most effectively during midcycle. Backwashing before it is necessary actually reduces the efficiency of the filter.

Most sand filters have a pressure gage to register pressure in the tank. Some manufacturers recommend checking the pressure when the system is being operated with a clean filter, and backwashing it when the

48 Selecting Pool Equipment

pressure increases by approximately 10 psi.

Another method for systems with relatively high operating pressures is to backwash when the pressure increases by 50% over the pressure when the system is clean. Some filters operate with as little as 2 to 5 psi of pressure; others may begin at 10 to 15 psi.

An alternative to a pressure gage is a water-flow gage that measures the flow between the filter and the pool. As the filter collects dirt, the flow is restricted. The filter needs cleaning when the flow drops below a certain level.

Your pool dealer or builder can probably make an accurate estimate on how often a certain size sand filter will require backwashing when installed in your pool. No two pool systems are exactly the same, so there is no chart or graph to tell you the specific pressures for operating or cleaning the system.

One disadvantage to high-rate sand filters is they can require up to several hundred gallons of water for backwashing. A diatomaceous earth filter uses less water for backwashing. Cartridge filters are not backwashed.

If you live in an area where water is in short supply, or where there are local restrictions against disposing of waste water in the sewer system, a cartridge filter, or DE filter with a separation tank to catch waste, may be more practical than a high-rate sand filter.

DIATOMACEOUS EARTH (DE) FILTERS

The filtering medium in a diatomaceous earth filter is sedimentary rock composed of microscopic fossil skeletons of the *diatom,* a tiny freshwater marine plankton. This fossil material has a highly porous silica structure with many channels and passages to trap suspended particles in water flowing through the filter.

DE is capable of trapping 5-micron particles. This makes it the most efficient of all the filters in cleaning or *polishing* pool water. A relatively thin coat of DE on the filter *septa,* the elements or grids inside the filter, is more effective than a 1-foot-thick layer of sand. The septa are made of a synthetic fabric that isn't affected by pool chemicals.

The most common type of DE filter is the vertical tank filter. The actual configuration of the filter septa inside depends on the model and manufacturer. They are typically in parallel panels, tubes, fan-shaped panels or stacked diaphragms. All models function basically the same.

The grid material used for the septa is intended only to support the DE filtering material. It has no ability to filter without a coating of DE. If a filter is allowed to run with no DE coating, the pores in the septa may become clogged with material that can't be washed free. This can cause permanent damage and make it necessary to replace the septa.

To coat the filter septa, a DE solution must be introduced into the filter after backwashing. The manufacturer of each filter will provide specific instructions on adding DE.

The most common method is to mix DE with water to form a slurry or thin, creamy mixture. The slurry is poured directly into the skimmer while the pump is running.

The amount of DE added is determined by the number of square feet of filter area. The ratio is usually 1 pound of DE for approximately every 10 square feet of filter area. The pool industry commonly measures DE by volume, not weight. A 1-pound coffee can holds about 1/2 pound of DE.

DE filters are cleaned by backwashing. Most DE filters include a backwash valve to reverse the flow in the tank and to expel waste from the system. A gage on top of the filter tank registers the pressure inside the tank. When the DE has become clogged with waste material, the pressure builds and registers on the gage.

There is no way to predict exactly how much pressure will register on the gage when the system is operating with a newly cleaned filter. Each system is different. Cleaning is normally required when the pressure climbs 8 to 10 pounds. Too frequent cleaning is a waste of time and materials.

A filter not cleaned often enough puts a strain on the pump motor by forcing it to operate against greater back-pressure. It also reduces the volume of water that can be cleaned each hour.

Some DE filters are designed to include separation tanks to collect discharged water heavy with DE sediment. The system functions in a

Pressure gage on filter indicates when filter needs cleaning or backwashing. In most systems, cleaning is required when gage shows an increase of 5-10 psi over normal operating pressure.

similar way to a household vacuum cleaner. Solid wastes are trapped in a bag in the separation tank. After backwashing has been completed, the bag is removed, emptied into the garbage, hosed off and replaced in the separation tank.

A dry well can be used only if the filter has a separation tank. If no separation tank is used, sediment in the water will eventually fill the well, clogging it. Check local codes for specific requirements for disposing of waste water. A DE filter uses 1/4 to 1/3 less water than a high-rate sand filter.

CARTRIDGE FILTERS

Cartridge filters are easier to clean, more convenient and less complicated than a sand or DE filter. The reusable cartridges look somewhat like an automobile oil filter and work on the same principle.

One or more corrugated polyester cartridges are suspended in the filter tank. Water is pumped through the filter and passes through the cartridges. Particles in the water are trapped in the cartridge fabric.

The initial cost of most cartridge filters is less than a sand or DE filter of comparable capacity. This advantage can be offset by the cost of replacement cartridges. But the cartridge filter is not swimming's contribution to the disposable world. Filters can be reused a number of times before they need replacement.

Cartridges are manually removed from the filter to be cleaned or replaced. Instructions are on page

Replaceable cartridges come in different sizes to match filter shape and capacity. Cartridge filters for pools may use one or more cartridges. Some filters use a dozen or more of the smallest size shown here.

131. Cartridge filters are not backwashed. A set of cartridges can be used until worn or damaged. How long they last depends on the pool's use and maintenance. Usually, the initial set of filters used to clean the water in a new plastered pool will get severely impacted and have to be replaced.

A cartridge filter will not remove minute particles as effectively as sand or DE filters. It requires more square feet of filter area than a DE filter. A cartridge with 72 square feet of surface is comparable to 36 square feet in a DE filter. This is important only in sizing a filter for the system. Cartridge, sand and DE filters with similar filtering capacities are about the same physical size.

Cartridge filters usually have a pressure gage on top of the tank. When the pressure rises from 8 to 10 psi over the starting pressure, the cartridges need cleaning or replacement.

The most common type of cartridge filter is located between the pump and heater in the filtration system. Cartridge filters are available that are incorporated with the skimmer. They are located just below the skimmer basket and plumbed to the main drain, with the drain inlet just above the skimmer basket.

These filter-skimmer combinations are recommended for small to medium-size pools and are often used in vinyl-lined and above-ground pools. The pool owner has the option of installing two skimmer-filters to reduce cleaning frequency. The filters are removed for cleaning through a flush cover in the pool deck.

CHOOSING A HEATER

Including a heater in the support system depends on whether or not you want to extend the swimming season. In most parts of the country, a heater is not needed during summer months but can extend the swimming season through spring and fall months. In warmer climates, a heater will allow swimming most months of the year. There are a few areas in the country where climate makes a heater marginal; that is, where supplementary heat is needed too few days to justify the cost of the heater.

The initial cost of the heater and anticipated price increases in gas or electricity are the main reasons a pool owner may decide not to include a heater in the original pool plans.

The arguments for including a heater are persuasive. The initial cost of a heater represents a minor percentage of increase in the total cost of a pool. A heater will extend the swimming season and enable you to make greater use of your pool.

If high energy costs are a concern, there are a number of options that will help keep costs down regardless of geography. The number of energy-saving features incorporated into the pool and support system have more effect on energy costs than the size or type of heater.

You can use the heater sparingly, settle for a shorter swimming season and accept cooler water temperatures. Regular use of a solar blanket or pool cover can cut heating costs as much as 50%. Should you ever decide to sell your home, a heated pool will have more appeal to a potential buyer than an unheated one.

The type of heater you select will be influenced by local fuel costs and the availability of natural gas. Where natural gas is available, a gas-fired heater is usually the most economical. Where natural gas isn't available, or its use is restricted, you have a choice between oil-fired or propane heaters, or electric-resistance heaters. The cost of oil or propane is usually higher than the cost of natural gas.

Electric-resistance heaters are used in some areas where the cost of electricity is reasonable or where natural gas isn't available. Electricity is also used to power heat pumps, which operate on a different principle than resistance heaters.

A solar-heating system is an alternative to a conventional heater. A solar system can be designed to circulate water through solar panels as the exclusive source of heating, or it can be utilized in a system with a conventional heater as a backup. See pages 58-73 for details on solar heating.

SIZING THE HEATER

Heater-size requirements are determined by three basic factors. You will need to know the surface area of the pool, the desired water temperature for swimming and the average air temperature during the coldest month you anticipate using the pool. Once these figures are known, minor adjustments can be made for altitude, pool location and wind patterns. This information will make it possible for the pool supplier to help you pick a specific type and model heater for your pool.

Finding Surface Area—By the time you are ready to choose a heater, you should already know the surface area of your pool. Obtaining this information was necessary for selecting a pump and filter. To find the surface area of various-shaped pools, see page 44.

Check Average Temperatures—The local weather bureau will be able to provide information on average air temperatures for each month of the year. Based on your own experience with local weather conditions, you will have to determine how many months a year you intend to use your pool. Extending pool use into cooler spring and fall months adds significantly to fuel costs and requires a larger heater.

Select Water Temperature—Ideal water temperature is a matter of personal preference. The National Spa and Pool Institute recommends 78F (26C) as an acceptably comfortable temperature that requires minimum energy use. Many pool owners prefer a temperature a degree or two above that. The American Red Cross suggests 78F to 82F (26C to 28C) as a safe, healthy temperature range for

50   Selecting Pool Equipment

swimming. Temperature is a trade-off between comfort and cost. For every degree temperature is raised above 78F, fuel costs will rise approximately 10%.

With the preceding information, it is possible to size a heater in one of two different ways. Subtract the average air temperature in the coldest month you will be using the pool from the desired pool temperature. The difference averages 20F to 25F in most parts of the country.

This will give you a figure called *desired temperature rise* or *desired degree rise*. Most heater manufacturers provide a simple chart that enables you to combine the pool surface area with the desired degree rise to pick a specific heater for your pool.

Working with Btu's—A more technical approach is to calculate the number of British thermal units (Btu's) required to heat the volume of water in your pool. A Btu is the amount of energy required to raise the temperature of 1 pound of water 1 degree Fahrenheit. Fossil-fueled heaters are rated in Btu's. Electric heaters are rated by kilowatt input, which is convertible to Btu's. One kilowatt equals 3412 Btu's.

The Btu ratings given for fossil-fueled heaters are usually their *input ratings*. Input rating, expressed in Btu's per hour, is the *total amount of heat* generated by the heater. All heat generated by fossil-fueled heaters is not transferred directly to the water flowing through them. Some heat dissipates or is lost through the heater's ventilating system. To correctly size a heater, you must know its *output rating*. The output rating, also in Btu's, is the amount of heat actually transferred to the water.

Some heater manufacturers also provide output ratings for their heaters. If not, you'll need to know the efficiency rating of a heater to determine the correct output rating. The American Gas Association claims gas-fired pool heaters average about 70% efficiency.

The heater's *input rating* multiplied by heater efficiency will equal the *output rating*. Electric heaters are virtually 100% efficient in terms of heat transfer, so the input and output ratings are essentially the same. However, electricity is usually a higher energy cost, so electric heaters aren't necessarily cheaper to operate.

HEATER SIZING CHART

BTU INPUT	100,000	125,000	175,000	250,000	400,000
BTU OUTPUT @ 70% EFFICIENCY	70,000	87,500	122,500	175,000	280,000
DESIRED TEMP. RISE	\multicolumn{5}{c}{**MAXIMUM SURFACE AREA IN SQUARE FEET**}
10°	800	1,000	1,400	2,000	3,200
15°	530	660	925	1,325	2,100
20°	400	500	700	1,000	1,600
25°	320	400	550	800	1,300
30°	250	330	450	650	1,050
35°	225	280	400	550	900

To use chart, first determine desired temperature rise, at left. Then determine surface area of pool in square feet, page 44. Opposite desired temperature rise, select closest pool-surface area figure that exceeds that of your pool. Then choose a heater with Btu input that most closely matches, but exceeds, input figure at top of column. It's always better to slightly oversize the heater.

[1] Figures are based on 3-1/2 mph average wind and average pool depth of 5.5 feet. Reduce input ratings by 4% for each 1,000 feet above sea level. Figures assume output ratings based on 70% heater efficiency.

[2] Pool-surface areas in chart are rounded off to nearest 25 square feet. Surface area of your pool should not exceed selected figure.

When the surface area of the pool and the desired degree rise are known, use the chart above to determine the heater Btu output required to heat your pool.

Adding the Variables—The information just given is for choosing a heater that will operate under ideal conditions at sea level. Altitude reduces heater efficiency. For each 1,000 feet above 2,000 feet altitude, add 4% to the calculated surface area of the pool before determining heater size.

If your pool is located in an open windy area, determine the heater size by pool surface area and desired degree rise, then select the next larger size heater. Windy conditions greatly accelerate heat loss. A cover is essential to protect an exposed pool. If the pool is indoors, heat loss is reduced and a heater with a smaller Btu output may be adequate.

Spas and Hot Tubs—An attached spa or hot tub can be designed to operate with the same support system used to heat and filter water in the swimming pool. A spa contains much less water than the smallest swimming pool. A heater capable of heating a pool will usually have the capacity to heat a spa.

Because spas and tubs have higher water temperatures than pools, they're usually not heated on a continuous basis. Most spa users find it convenient to size the heater large enough to heat the water quickly before each use.

Raising the temperature in an average 500-gallon spa from 75F to 105F (24C to 35C) requires a 30F temperature rise. If you want a 10F temperature increase each 30 minutes, it would require a heater with a Btu output of approximately 125,000 Btu's. As heater capacity is increased, the time needed to raise water temperatures is decreased. As a rule, a gas heater will raise water temperatures faster than an electric heater of equivalent size. Also, coil heaters, or *flash* heaters, will heat water more quickly than tank heaters.

BIGGER IS BETTER

Buying a larger heater is one of the few instances where long-range savings make it economical to spend more money on the initial purchase. Money saved by installing an inexpensive, marginal heater can be quickly lost in higher fuel bills. An undersized heater must operate more hours and consume more fuel to raise water the same number of degrees as one that is correctly sized.

The larger the heater, the more quickly the water can be heated to swimming temperature. If the pool is not being used regularly, you can

Selecting Pool Equipment 51

POOL HEATERS

COIL HEATER
- OUTLET
- INLET
- COIL
- INSULATION
- BURNER

TANK HEATER
- OUTLET
- VENT
- INLET
- BURNER

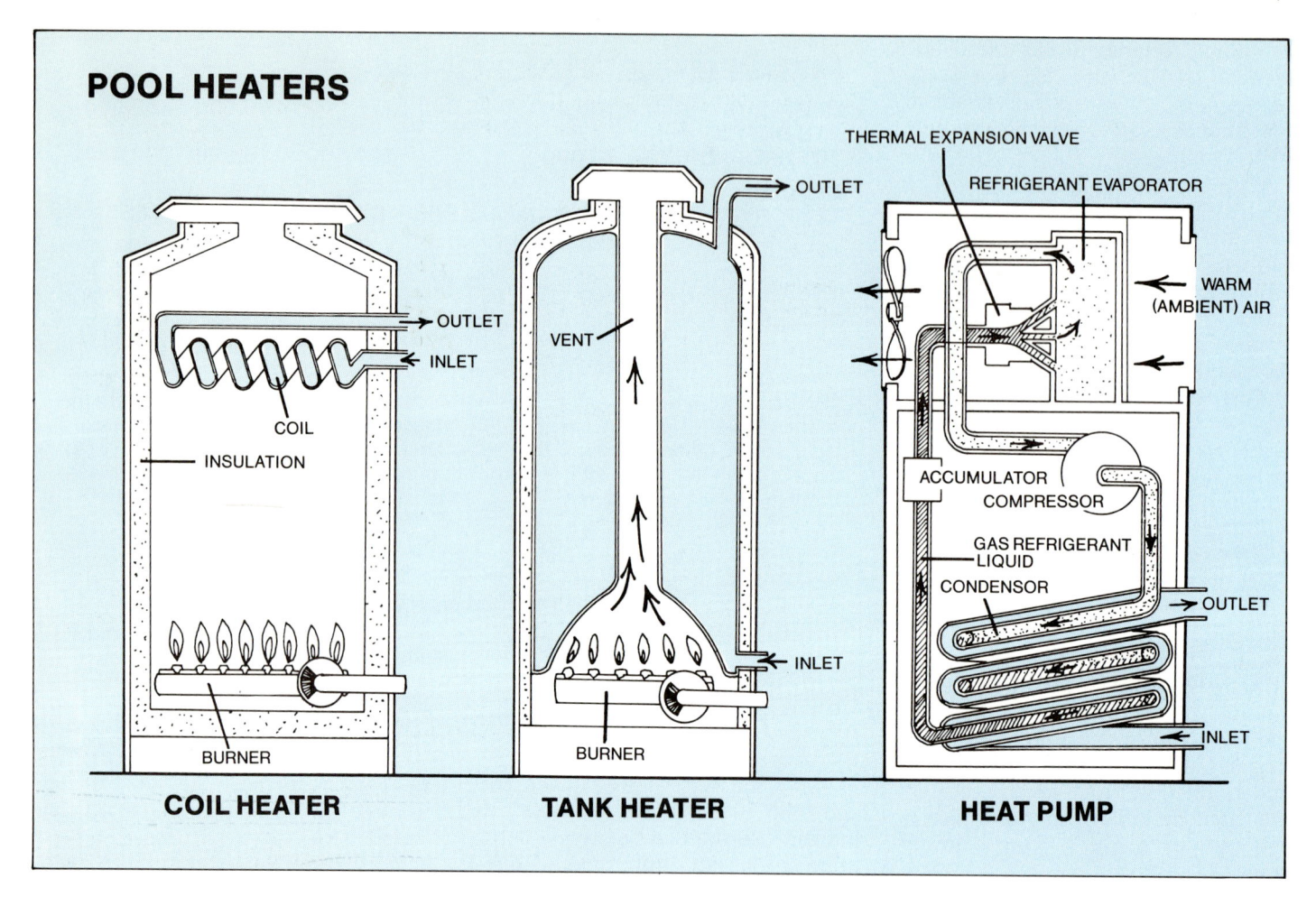

HEAT PUMP
- THERMAL EXPANSION VALVE
- REFRIGERANT EVAPORATOR
- WARM (AMBIENT) AIR
- ACCUMULATOR
- COMPRESSOR
- GAS REFRIGERANT LIQUID
- CONDENSOR
- OUTLET
- INLET

lower the thermostat setting to save energy, then boost the temperature in a few hours for weekend swimming.

In windy or cold weather, an undersized heater may labor and still not be able to heat water quickly enough to maintain swimming temperatures. In choosing a heater, it is better to oversize than undersize—to a point. A heater one or two sizes larger than the minimum required will not be a waste of money.

TYPES OF HEATERS

The selection of a specific heater is a matter of personal preference combined with the type and supply of energy available. The initial purchase price, the cost of installation and the average annual cost of fuel are the three important factors to consider. Of these three, the annual fuel cost is most important. Energy costs over a period of years will actually determine how economical a heater you have chosen.

Where natural gas or fuel oil is available, these heaters are usually the most economical to operate. Many of the newer gas heaters have electric-spark ignitions rather than pilot lights.

Such intermittent ignition devices are more energy efficient than a continuously burning pilot light. Also, at least one state, California, requires intermittent ignition devices on all new gas-heater installations for pools. It is likely that other states will soon pass similar energy-conservation laws.

At altitudes below 2,000 feet, a main-line gas pressure of 5 inches *water column pressure* (wcp) is usually required for a gas heater. Your local gas company will be able to tell you if there is sufficient pressure in lines to your home.

Electric-resistance heaters are usually the most expensive to operate. New materials, insulation and design improvements have helped produce electric heaters that are more economical to operate than earlier models.

Electrically operated heat pumps designed for pool use have also been improved. Although heat pumps are much more economical to operate than conventional gas or electric heaters, they do have some limitations, as described on page 53.

Solar-heating systems are worth considering for their long-range economical operating costs. Initial installation costs are high and payback periods vary depending on climate and system efficiency. Solar systems are discussed in detail in the following chapter.

Because energy costs vary from place to place, local pool dealers will be the best sources for estimating operating costs of the various heaters available. Current energy rates are available from your local utility company.

These are the most common types of heaters used for residential pools:

Coil Heaters—These consist of finned copper coils or copper tubes enclosed in a combustion chamber. The coils are heated and the heat is transferred to water being pumped through them. As a type, they are called *flash heaters*. Coils or tubes can be heated with an open flame or electricity.

Open-flame, gas-fired coil heaters are the most common and usually the most economical to operate.

Where natural gas is not available,

52 Selecting Pool Equipment

coil heaters can also be adapted to use heating oil or propane as fuel. A tank is required to store bulk heating oil. Liquid propane requires special pressure tanks that must be purchased or leased from the propane supplier. Propane tanks should never be stored indoors.

Electric coil heaters operate on the same principle as gas or oil-fired open-flame heaters. They are effective only for small pools or spas, as they aren't capable of handling a large volume of water.

Tank Heaters—These are most commonly used for residential hot-water heaters. Gas-fired models use an open flame to heat a large tank of water from below. Electrical models have heating elements immersed in the water tank. Tank heaters are less expensive than coil heaters. They have a slow recovery period and are practical only for small pools. They take much longer to heat water than coil heaters.

Heat Pumps—Increasing fuel costs have created new interest in heat pumps for pool heating. They are the most expensive heaters on the market, but offer substantially lower operating costs than most other heaters. Heat-pump manufacturers claim operating costs are less than half the cost of natural gas heaters and up to 75% less than electric-resistance heaters.

A heat pump operates on the same principle as a refrigerator or air conditioner, but in reverse. A refrigerator extracts heat from inside the refrigerator box and expels it into the air. A heat pump has a compressor in a non-reversing refrigeration circuit that extracts heat from the air and transfers it through a condenser to the pool water.

Because a heat pump pulls heat from the air, it is not practical in cold, dry climates. Most heat pumps are designed to function with air temperatures between 47F and 105F (8C and 45C). A properly maintained heat pump should last approximately 10 years.

Heat pumps are not produced in as many sizes as other types of pool heaters, but the models available are sufficient to heat most residential pools. The most popular models are rated at 52,000 Btu's and 98,000 Btu's.

Because heat pumps are relatively new for pool heating, they are not as widely distributed as other types of pool heaters. As the manufacturers become more active in the pool market, the number of outlets should increase.

SURFACE SKIMMERS

A skimmer serves a double purpose in a pool. It's an important part of the water-circulation system. It prevents oil, suntan lotion, floating algae, leaves and other debris from collecting on the water surface. Most skimmers include a filter basket that traps leaves, twigs and larger materials before they are sucked into the filtration system. On most pool skimmers, the filter basket is removed for cleaning by opening a lid that sits flush on the pool deck. These are called *top-loading skimmers*. *Front-loading skimmers* are designed for above-ground pools and spas. On these, the basket is removed from the front, through the skimmer opening to the pool.

Skimmers in modern pools are installed when the pool is built. Technically, a skimmer is an optional piece of equipment, but no modern pool is built without one. Add-on units are available to hang on the side of above-ground pools or on the side of older pools without built-in skimmers.

Almost all skimmers today are made of durable plastic and installed as prefabricated units. By buying the skimmer separately, you have a choice of many different models designed for many different purposes.

In the basic skimmer, water is sucked in from the pool surface. The amount of flow is controlled by a *weir*. This is a gate that rises and falls with the water level so only a thin sheet of surface water is taken in. This water passes through the filter basket and on into the filtration system.

More sophisticated skimmers are designed with many optional features. Some come with attachments for pool vacuums. You can buy a skimmer with a built-in low-water protection device that automatically turns off the pump if the water level falls below the skimmer opening. Skimmers also are designed to add water automatically when the water level is too low. A skimmer is available that integrates a cartridge filter. See page 50.

Skimmers are produced with au-

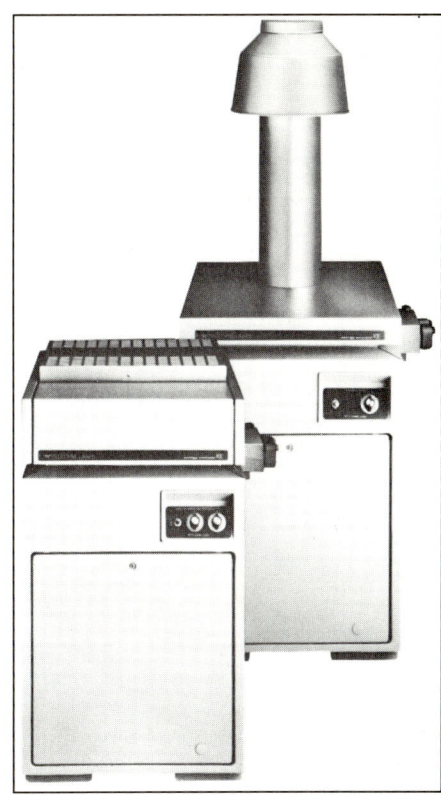

Shown are two basic models of gas heaters for pools. Left is outdoor low-profile model. Right is indoor stacktop model. All heaters enclosed in a building or shed require a vent stack. Manufacturer also offers outdoor stacktop model for installation in equipment sheds. *Photo courtesy of Teledyne Larrs, North Hollywood, CA.*

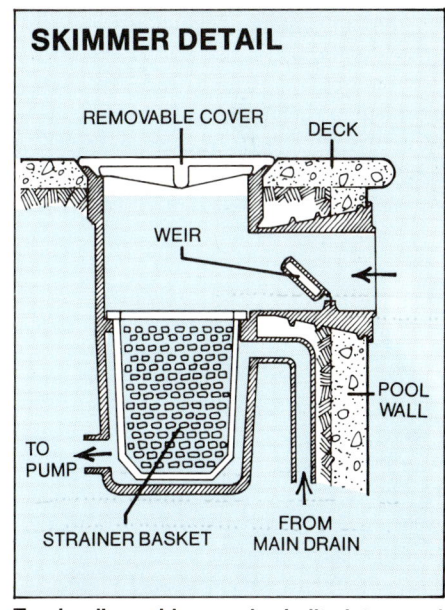

Top-loading skimmer is built into pool deck. Weir controls water flow.

Selecting Pool Equipment 53

Front-loading skimmers are most often used for above-ground pools and fiberglass spas. Skimmer basket is removed through water inlet. On this model, the basket is attached to the weir.

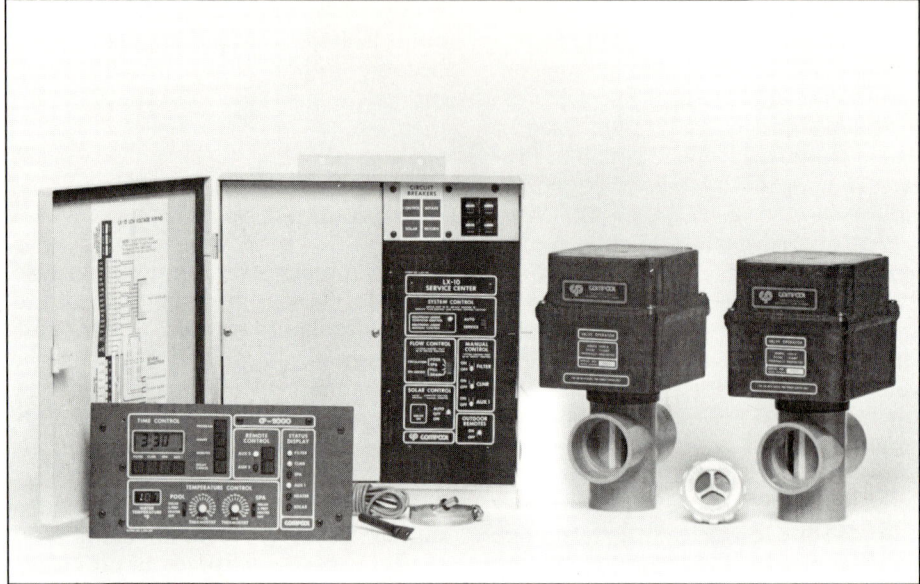

Programmable timer features six program settings per day to control operation of filter, pump, pool cleaner, spa and auxillary equipment. Includes separate thermostats for pool and spa, solar-heating controls, LCD time readout, LED temperature readout and status-display lights. Optional relay units can be installed to operate two additional pieces of equipment. Display panel, lower left, can be installed in any convenient location. System also includes subpanel with switches, and automatic valves installed in plumbing lines. *Photo courtesy of Compool, Mountain View, CA.*

Top-loading skimmers are used for practically all in-ground pools. Access to skimmer basket is through cover plate in pool deck.

Most support systems use a basic time clock to control filtration time. Turning yellow dial sets time of day. Indicators around the dial set start and stop times for equipment.

tomatic chlorinators that leach chlorine into the pool. Skimmers can be plumbed with adjustable flow controls that balance water flow into the system from the main drain and skimmer. Water is pulled into the system equally from the drain and skimmer.

An effective skimmer draws water off the surface at a high velocity. This is more important than the volume of water sucked into the system. When possible, build the skimmer into the downwind side of the pool so wind across the pool surface will push debris toward the skimmer.

EQUIPMENT CONTROLS

Support equipment for all modern pools is automatically controlled by some type of timing device. The least sophisticated and most widely used device is the time clock shown at left. It automatically runs the pump for filtration, and can be set for any length of time during a 24-hour period.

More sophisticated versions of the basic time clock have two or more functions, or *stations*, for operating the filtration system several times each day, or to operate pump, heater and other accessories, such as the pool-cleaning system, at predetermined times. Time clocks are used in conjunction with a *fireman* switch so the heater turns on and off only while the pump is running.

When additional equipment or accessories are added, such as a solar-heating system, a spa, automatic pool cleaners, or underwater lights, additional time clocks can be wired into the system, if necessary.

The time clocks are most often located in a switchbox mounted next to the electrical subpanel for the equipment. The subpanel houses circuit breakers for connections between the equipment and circuits to the main service entrance of the house. Subpanel and switchbox are located as close to the equipment as legally possible to simplify wiring.

The disadvantage of time clocks is that they must be manually reset when you want to change heating or filtration times. If there is a power outage, the entire timing system must be reprogrammed.

54 Selecting Pool Equipment

PROGRAMMABLE TIMERS

Modern electronic and computer technology have recently been applied to pool and spa control systems. Several manufacturers offer electronic programmable timers that automatically operate the on and off times of pump, heater, pool-cleaning system and other accessories. These timers are much more sophisticated than standard time clocks.

Programmable timers vary in the number of functions they perform. The most sophisticated—and expensive—ones offer fully automated control of a solar-heated pool with a backup heater, pool-cleaning system and attached spa. They can be operated by remote control stations located in different parts of the house or yard, or by hand-held remote-sending devices.

Some timers include thermostat controls for spa and pool. Others can be programmed to run equipment for different lengths of time on different days. Most have LED or LCD readouts for time of day and pool or spa temperatures. Indicator lights show which pieces of equipment are operating at any given time.

Most programmable timers offer one or more auxiliary functions to operate accessories, such as automatic chlorinators, spa hydrojets, pool lights, and so forth. Capabilities and optional features of these timers vary.

When choosing a programmable timer, make sure it has some sort of safeguard device so it cannot be misprogrammed to run equipment out of sequence. Another safeguard is a built-in battery that operates the timing device during a power outage. This way, the timer won't have to be reprogrammed after a power failure.

Ask pool dealers and suppliers for literature on the various units available and choose the one that best suits your pool system and your budget.

Some innovative pool designers and builders have adapted remote sending units and telephone responders to equipment controls. These devices enable any piece of equipment or accessory to be operated from almost any location, either using a hand-held or console sending unit, or by activating equipment over the telephone. Such gadgetry is better applied to spas for turning on heater, air bubbler or hydrojets before use.

With the sophisticated control devices now available, it is possible to operate pool and spa as part of an overall automated system for the home. The available devices and their capabilities are too numerous to describe here.

AUTOMATIC POOL VACUUMS

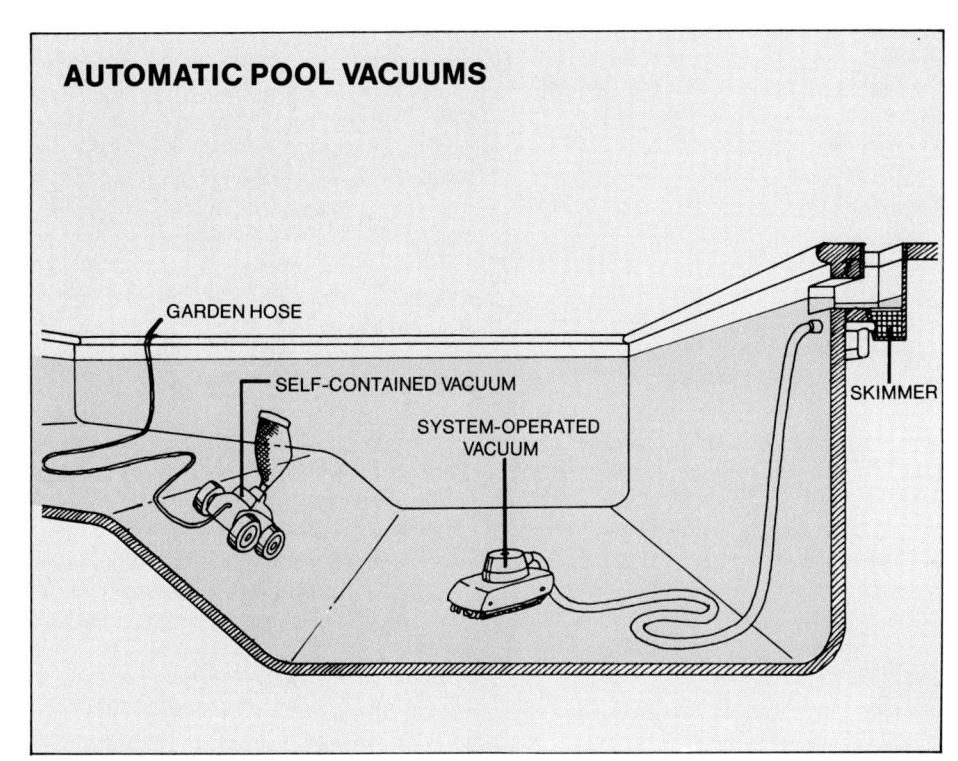

Self-contained vacuum operates using pressure from garden hose. System-operated vacuum is attached to suction line below skimmer.

POOL ACCESSORIES

There are many optional accessories designed to reduce pool maintenance or to make using your pool more enjoyable. The built-in maintenance accessories discussed here are integrated into the basic support system. They are planned for when the support equipment is installed. Other pool-maintenance accessories are discussed on page 139.

Slides and diving boards should also be planned as part of the original pool design. For safety, they require minimum pool depths and deck clearance.

You can use a pool without most accessories. Some, like ladders, hand rails, safety lines, floats and steps, should be included if they add to the safety of the pool design.

AUTOMATIC CHLORINATORS

Regular testing of pool water will indicate which chemicals are needed and how often they must be added to maintain good water quality. Most automatic chlorinators that dispense chlorine won't eliminate testing. They will help cut maintenance time and reduce the chance of damage if routine maintenance is neglected for a short time.

The simplest chlorinators consist of chlorine sticks or tablets placed in a floating dispenser. Sticks and tablets are also available that can be placed in the skimmer basket. They dissolve slowly, releasing a metered amount of chlorine into the water. This system is often described as *semi-automatic*.

More sophisticated chlorinators are plumbed into the return line of the circulation system and dispense measured amounts of chlorine into the water. Some use chlorine sticks or chlorine cartridges specifically designed for the dispensers. Chlorine flow can be adjusted for the need of a specific pool.

Chlorine Generators—These devices convert ordinary salt into chlorine gas

Selecting Pool Equipment 55

POOL SWEEPS (AGITATORS)

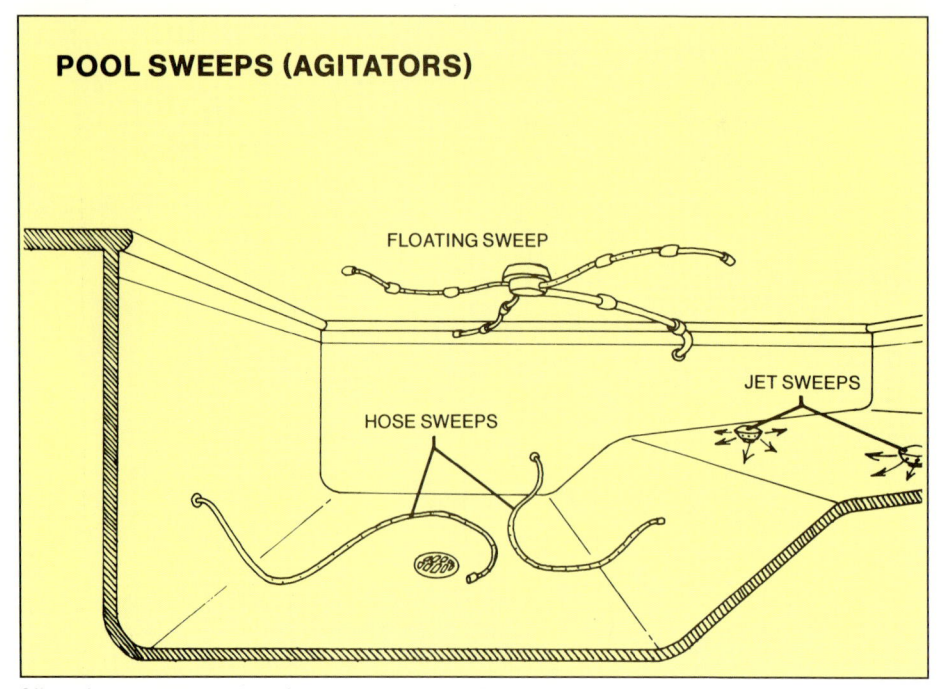

All pool sweeps operate using water pressure from support system.

Floating sweeps are attached to the pool's return inlet and float on the pool surface. Two or more hoses are attached to the floating head and swirl around the top of the pool propelled by the force of the water entering the pool. Water pressure forces surface debris into the skimmer and dislodges dirt from the sides of the pool to be sucked up by the main drain. Some models have heads with a rotating water jet that helps remove dirt on tile above the waterline.

A second type of agitator is built in when the pool is installed. Returning pool water is directed through a series of flexible tubes that extend from the sides and bottom of the pool. Water pressure causes the tubes to move gently across the pool floor and walls to push dirt into the pool's main drain. When the cleaning cycle has been completed, the tubes automatically retract out of sight into the pool walls.

The cost of the system is in initial installation. Once the system is in place, it operates almost energy-free by the force of water returning to the pool from the filtration system. There are no moving parts. The agitator is operated by the same pump used to run the support system. A slightly larger pump may be required to overcome additional head loss in the plumbing system. Head loss is discussed on pages 15-16.

A third type of agitator system utilizes jets built into the pool bottom. Returning pool water is directed across the bottom of the pool to move dirt toward the main drain so it can be sucked into the filtration system. The jets are installed and plumbed when the pool is built. Some types of jet systems may require a separate pump.

DIVING BOARDS

A diving board is the single accessory that has the most influence on pool design. Without a board, the pool need only be deep enough for swimming—about 3-1/2 to 4 feet. The minimum recommended pool depth for a diving board is 7-1/2 feet.

If you intend to include a diving board, you have the option of designing the pool first, then sizing a board to meet depth and width dimensions of the pool. If you're an enthusiastic diver who has always dreamed of having a 3-meter board, the pool must be deep enough and wide

---

through electrolysis. The system passes an electric current through a brine solution (salt dissolved in water) contained in a holding tank in the unit. The chlorine produced is then injected into the pool's plumbing system downstream of the pump, filter and heater. The brine solution and electric current are housed in the unit and do not directly interact with the pool water.

Fully automated chlorinators and chlorine generators are available that test the water and maintain the correct pH balance and chlorine level. When pH and chlorine sensors on the units detect a change in levels, the correct amounts of chlorine and pH-balancing chemicals are automatically fed into the pool water. The units shut off when levels have been corrected.

Even the most automated chlorinating systems are still only part of a complete pool-maintenance program. For details on water treatment and using pool chemicals, see the chapter, *Pool Care & Repair,* starting on page 117.

AUTOMATIC POOL CLEANERS

If you want to do as little maintenance as possible and can't justify hiring a pool-maintenance company, there are an increasing number of automatic devices designed to do most of the work for you. They fall into two basic categories—*automatic vacuums* and *automatic pool sweeps,* or *agitators.*

Automatic Vacuums—These roam the bottom of the pool inhaling dirt and debris. Some will climb sidewalls and steps. Others float on the water surface and collect debris through vacuum hoses that hang from the float head.

There are two basic types of automatic vacuums. One type ties directly into the filtration system. Dirt and debris are sucked off the pool bottom and sides and into the support system where the filter removes it from the water. The other type is self-contained. The cleaning unit is lowered into the pool and operates independently of the filtration system. The unit is plugged into a 120-volt outlet and is self-propelled. It has its own filter and bag to catch debris.

Automatic vacuums can be switched on and off manually or controlled with a timer. They will keep an average-size pool clean by operating several hours a day.

Agitators and Pool Sweeps—Pool vacuums operate by sucking water and suspended particles of debris into a filter bag or the support system. Agitators and pool sweeps use water pressure in the return line from the system to sweep pool walls and bottom. The principle of agitators and pool sweeps is to agitate the water to dislodge dirt and debris from pool walls and bottom. The suspended dirt is then directed into the main drain where the regular pool filter can remove it.

56 Selecting Pool Equipment

POOL SLIDES

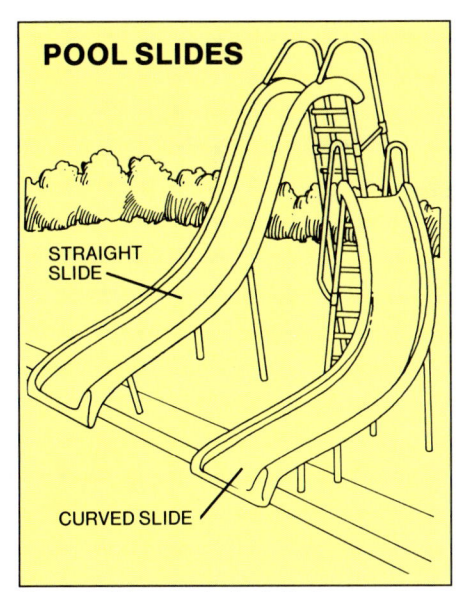

Curved slides can be installed on a narrower pool deck than straight slides. Other than that, the type you choose is mainly personal preference.

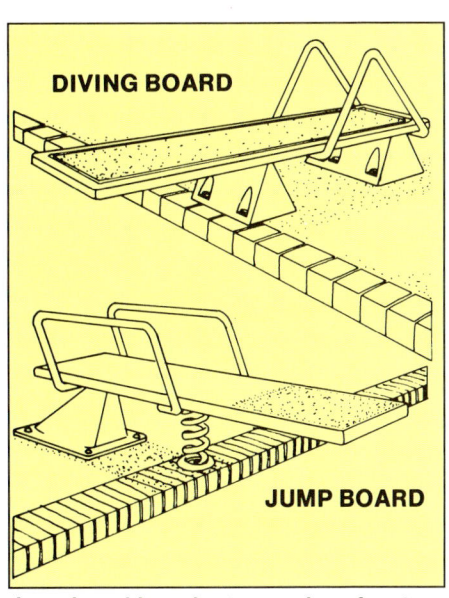

Jump board is a shorter version of a standard diving board. Most jump boards use coil springs to provide bounce.

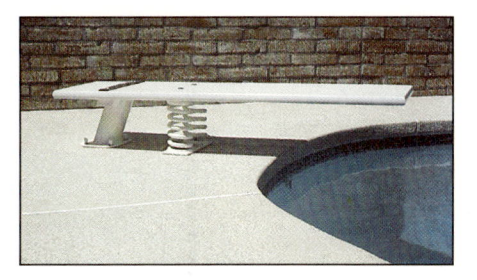

Most pool slides are fiberglass with metal supports. They come in several basic colors to match other pool accessories.

DIVING BOARD SPECIFICATIONS

Maximum board height above water	20"	26"	30"	40"
Maximum jump board length	6'	8'	8'	8'
Maximum diving board length	8'	10'	12'	12'
Minimum pool length	28'	30'	33'	36'
Minimum width at deepest point	15'	15'	18'	18'
Minimum depth at deepest point	7.5'	8'	8.5'	9'

enough to make it safe to use the diving board you have chosen.

The National Spa and Pool Institute has published minimum standards for pool dimensions for diving safety. You will have a greater margin of safety if pool dimensions exceed minimum requirements. The above chart gives NSPI recommendations for diving board and pool specifications.

Note from the chart that the minimum safe dimensions for a pool with a 10-foot diving board 26 inches above the water, is 30 feet long, 15 feet wide at the deepest point and 8 feet deep at the deepest point. If you already own a pool or are designing a pool that meet or exceed those dimensions, you can safely install any board no longer than 10 feet at a maximum above-water height of 26 inches. Specific recommendations for minimum standards and more detailed pool dimensions are available from the National Spa and Pool Institute (NSPI), 2111 Eisenhower Ave., Alexandria, VA 22314

The name, *diving board*, evolved when boards were made of wood. Most diving boards today are made of fiberglass. Some fiberglass boards do have laminated wood cores. Most boards for residential pools are 8 to 12 feet long and 18 inches wide. Larger boards 20 inches wide are available in lengths up to 16 feet.

There are many styles of diving boards. All operate on the same principle. The end of the board is secured and a fulcrum is located under the board—usually a third to half the distance from the back end of the board to the diving end.

Where space is a problem, *jump boards* that require less space than a diving board are a reasonable substitute. Most jump boards are anchored at the back end and the board rests on a heavy coil spring to provide the bounce. There is no fulcrum. Other types are short versions of traditional diving boards. See drawing above.

Diving-board bases are usually bolted to the pool deck. This means boards are more easily installed when anchor bolts can be positioned before the deck is poured. Fiberglass and metal are the most common materials for bases. Many diving boards have hand rails available as an option. The manufacturers of individual diving boards will have specific instructions for their installation and clearance requirements.

SLIDES

Pool slides are popular accessories, especially with children. They come in many sizes, shapes and colors. Almost all slides are made of fiberglass and are supported by metal frames.

Slide manufacturers recommend a minimum water depth of 4 feet for even the smallest slide. Larger slides that stand as much as 12 feet above the pool deck need a pool depth of at least 5-1/2 feet.

A standard straight slide may require up to 14 feet of deck space from the edge of the water. Curved slides that begin parallel to the edge of the pool use from 6 feet to as little as 3 feet of deck area.

Some slides have water jets to keep the slide surface wet and slippery. Make sure the slide is installed with the lip extending over the edge of the pool. Water that runs down the slide should drip into the pool. The slide should be far enough away from the diving board or pool ladders so there is no danger of slide users striking other swimmers or pool equipment.

Selecting Pool Equipment

Pools with black or other dark-colored shell will absorb more of sun's heat than a light-colored pool. Dark color can raise pool temperature 5° to 10° on a sunny day. *Design: Eric Armstrong, Landscape Architect, Morro Bay, CA.*

Solar Heating & Energy-Saving Ideas

CHAPTER 5

Solar Heating & Energy-Saving Ideas

Most homeowners considering a new swimming pool look at solar heating from one of two extreme points of view. The pessimist looks first at the high initial cost of a solar-heating system. The need for all the extra gadgetry and a roof covered with solar collectors is discouraging. The simple solution is to install a conventional pool heater and hope future energy price increases are moderate.

The solar enthusiast looks at a solar system as a moral statement. A solar-heating system saves energy and natural resources. Once the initial investment has been recovered, heating is almost cost free. It's a form of revenge against high utility bills.

The truth lies somewhere in between. A solar-heating system is less dependable and more complex than a standard gas, oil or electric pool heater. The system has little protection against a series of days when clouds block the sun. Additional plumbing, extra thermostats and control valves mean there is more to take care of than in a standard heating system.

It is true that energy from the sun is free. Collecting it is not. Operating the system requires only slightly more energy to run the pool pump, but the initial investment in a complete system can cost several thousand dollars. A solar system requires more maintenance than a standard heating system and must be combined with other conservation measures to be truly cost-effective.

Pool owners in most areas of the country still need a conventional backup heater to guarantee comfortable temperatures. Supplementary heat may be necessary if overnight temperatures fall well below average or if there is a period of several consecutive cloudy days. How much backup heating is required to lengthen the swimming season often depends less on geography than on the size of the system, the number of sunny days and how often a solar cover is used.

In northern areas of the country, solar heat can extend the season up to 2 months. In milder climates, solar can increase the season by as much as 4 months. In hot climates, the system may allow swimming most of the year.

WHY BUY SOLAR?

The arguments in favor of solar heating are persuasive. Fuel costs will continue to rise. Some states offer tax incentives for installing a solar-heating system in a new pool. Credits are also offered for replacing traditional heaters with solar as the primary heating source. The conventional heater becomes a backup heater.

Solar heating reduces dependency on outside energy. This could be useful if service is disrupted or during future energy shortages. When energy is in short supply, one of the first conservation measures a community may take is to restrict energy use for nonessential purposes, such as heating swimming pools.

At some point, money saved in heating bills will equal the initial cost of the system. When that day has been reached, pool-heating costs will be near zero.

The payback time for an active solar installation depends on a number of factors. These include climate, pool-site conditions, fuel costs, conservation measures, year-to-year weather conditions, frequency of pool use and available state or federal tax credits. In combination, these factors determine when the money you've saved on heating bills equals the cost of the system.

The most optimistic proponents estimate a payback period of 2 to 5 years. More conservative estimates run as long as 8 to 10 years. There is no accurate way to predict a payback period. There are too many variables. Once a system is in use, it is difficult to know what daily, monthly or seasonal heating costs might have been had solar not been installed.

Solar Heating & Energy-Saving Ideas 59

Solar panels can be cost effective in northern parts of the country during summer months. This pool is located in Connecticut. Panels are mounted on roof of pool house. *Design: Chapman Pools, Old Lyme, CT.*

Solar is most popular in conservation-minded regions of the country that have a high number of sunny days each year. Most solar installations are in Florida, California and the Southwest. However, there is no geographical limitation on solar energy for pool heating. Solar systems will work in all parts of the country.

Some areas with gloomy winter weather still have enough sunny days during the summer months to justify a solar system. Many of these areas are also high energy-cost areas. Where energy is expensive, a system doesn't have to be as efficient to have a reasonable payback period.

A solar system is a long-range option for reducing pool-heating costs. There are many other simple ways to hold down heating and maintenance costs. This chapter examines available solar systems and explores the many ways you can save energy and reduce pool-heating bills.

SOLAR POOL SYSTEMS

In recent years, escalating fuel costs and interest in energy conservation have stimulated research in solar technology. The emphasis has been on home-heating systems and domestic hot-water systems. Pool heating is a perfect application for solar.

Solar systems used to heat pools have two major advantages over residential heating systems.

First, a pool system requires lower operating temperatures than a system designed to heat a home or domestic hot water. It can also be less efficient. The swimming season is the time of year when solar heat is plentiful. The sun is hot, high in the sky and the days are long.

Second, pool water provides the mass to store heat. Bulky heat-storage systems required for home heating are unnecessary. Water mass in a covered pool will lose minimal heat during a series of cloudy days. Poor weather also discourages swimming. This is when the pool is more likely to be kept covered.

Unlike pocket computers or video recorders, where new technology and mass production brought on significant price decreases, wider use of solar heating has not greatly reduced the price of the system or its components. The reason is that solar-heating systems are built from stock or modified components already widely used in industry. Motors, pumps, copper or plastic pipe, valves, heat sensors and the materials used to build solar panels are not new.

Prices for solar equipment have not plummeted. But better quality materials, more efficient components and a better understanding of the technology have helped produce more efficient systems. Many solar collectors for pools are made of corrosion-resistant plastics capable of withstanding constant exposure to sun, weather and pool chemicals.

By definition, a solar-heating system that depends on pumps and other mechanical components is *active*. A *passive* heating system utilizes all possible natural methods of capturing heat from the sun without mechanical devices. In practice, an efficient active system also incorporates passive energy-saving ideas.

Passive solar heating depends primarily on locating the pool in a wind-protected area where it will have maximum exposure to the sun. Everything

OPEN-LOOP SYSTEM

CLOSED-LOOP SYSTEM

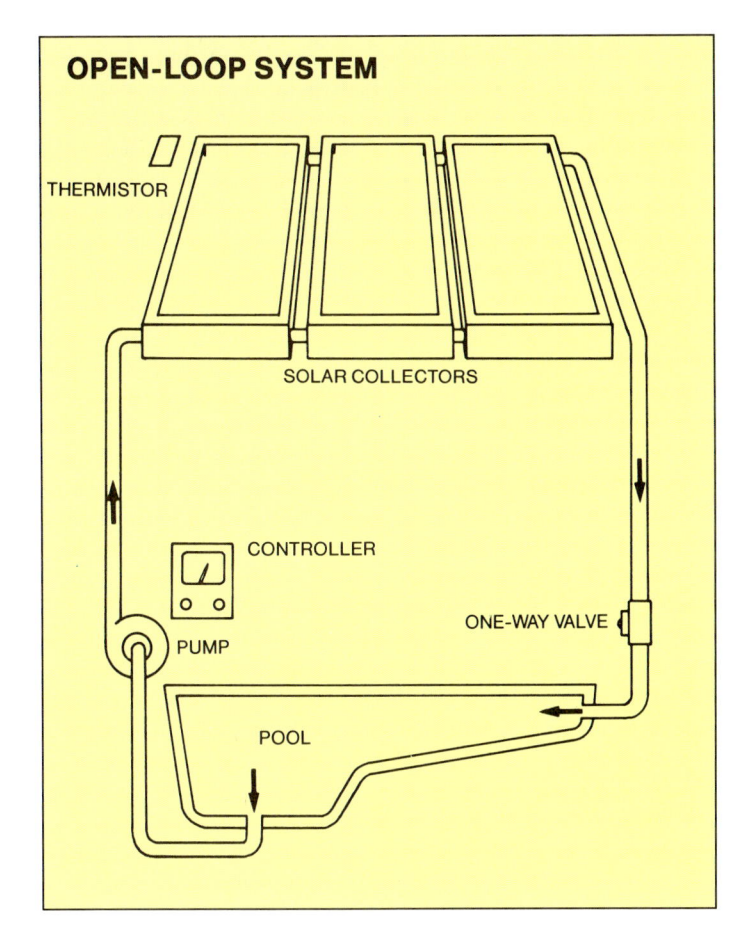

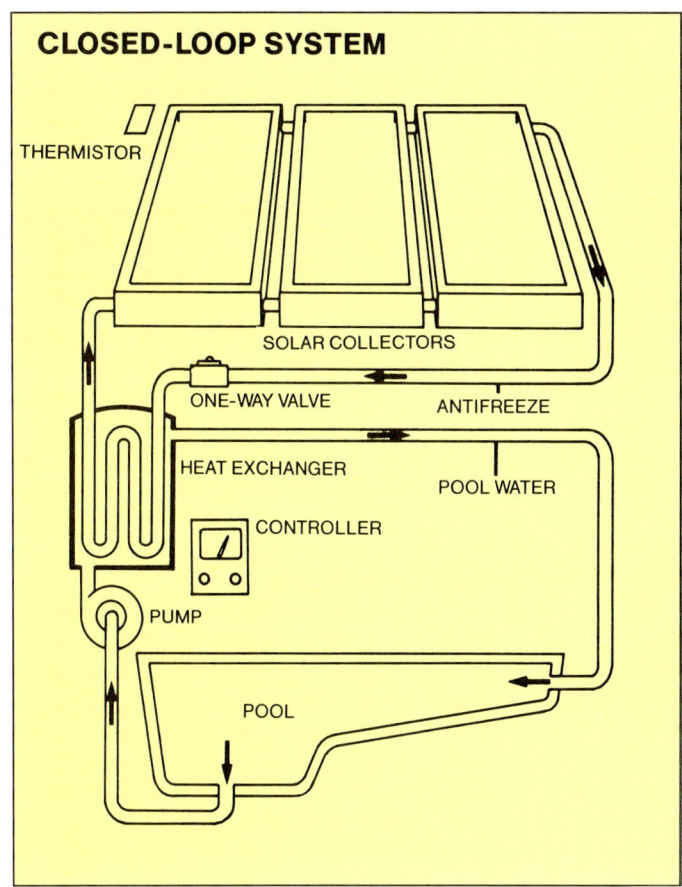

possible is done to encourage natural heat gain and to prevent heat loss. Using a pool blanket or solar cover is the single most effective way of preventing heat loss. See pages 69-71.

ACTIVE SOLAR SYSTEMS

Active systems can be air or liquid. Air systems are normally limited to space heating for homes. Fans force air through a series of ducts into solar collectors. Air heated in the collectors is pumped into a heat-storage area, usually a rock bin. Heat is drawn from storage to heat the house when heat is needed. Systems that use liquid as a heat-transfer medium can also be adapted to space heating.

Swimming pools are almost always heated with active liquid systems. If the liquid pumped through the solar collectors is pool water, it is an *open-loop system*. A *closed-loop system* circulates antifreeze through the collectors. Heat collected by the liquid passes through a heat exchanger where it is transferred to pool water. The heated pool water is then pumped back into the pool. The drawings above show open- and closed-loop systems.

Closed-loop systems using antifreeze and a heat exchanger are more expensive than open-loop systems and are not commonly used for swimming pools. One advantage of a closed-loop system is that you don't have to drain the collectors when temperatures fall below freezing. This is an advantage in areas where temperature differences between day and night are extreme. An open-loop system can be designed to drain automatically when temperatures fall below freezing.

Another reason for considering a closed-loop system for pool heating is that hard or improperly treated pool water can cause scale buildup or corrosion in metal solar collectors. A closed-loop system eliminates the danger of damaging the panels by alkaline or poorly conditioned pool water. In areas where hard water is a problem., a closed-loop system will usually last longer than a metal open-loop system. Open loop systems with plastic collectors better withstand hard or chemically treated water.

HOW COLLECTORS WORK

Solar collectors or solar panels are the most visible components of an active solar-heating system. They are usually located on a south-facing roof, pool building or hillside. Collectors installed on flat roofs or ground are mounted in frames angled toward the sun.

The water or antifreeze solution is pumped through a series of metal tubes (copper, aluminum or steel) or plastic channels in the collector. The collector absorbs heat from the sun. Liquid passing through the collector absorbs the heat.

If the liquid is pool water, it is pumped back into the pool. Systems with backup heaters are designed so solar-heated water automatically bypasses the heater. When the water drops below a certain temperature, it is automatically routed through the heater to raise it to the desired temperature. The drawing on page 62 shows how a typical system works.

TYPES OF COLLECTORS

Solar collectors are made in many different styles. The traditional and oldest system involves running cop-

Solar Heating & Energy-Saving Ideas

TYPICAL SOLAR SYSTEM

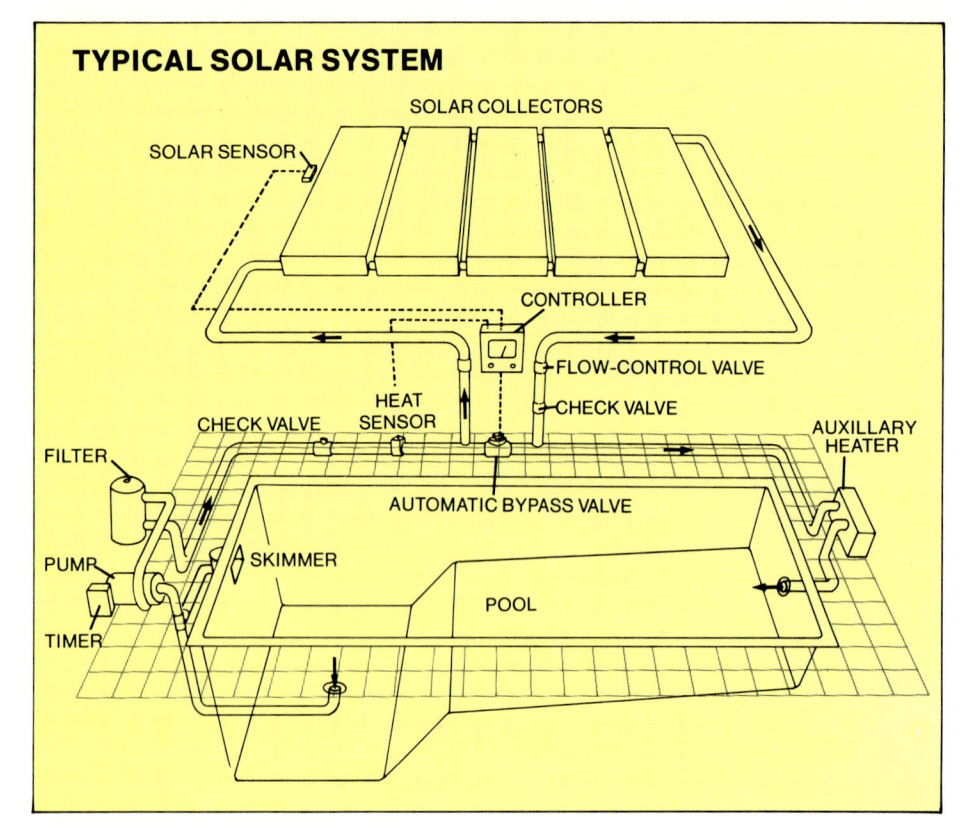

per, aluminum or steel tubing through an enclosed flat box to pick up heat collected from the sun. These are called *flat-plate collectors*. Flat-plate collectors come in the form of rigid panels. Some modern flat-plate collectors use plastic tubing or channels instead of metal ones.

Another type of collector uses black-plastic tubing or a flexible plastic sheet with integral channels. The black tubing or sheets are not enclosed in a panel, but exposed directly to the sun.

If you want a solar collector completely hidden from sight, you can install a *deck-collector*. These are collectors embedded in a concrete pool deck or nearby concrete patio. See page 65.

Flat-Plate Collectors—A flat-plate solar collector is like a sandwich. A metal sheet protects the bottom of the collector. A sheet of insulation is placed on top of the metal. Another sheet of metal, called an *absorber plate*, has metal tubes welded or bonded to the top surface. This is the part of the collector that absorbs heat from the sun and transfers it to the liquid running through the collector. A similar style has two sheets of metal bonded together with integral passages for liquid to pass through rather than through metal tubes. The absorber plate is painted flat black or coated with a heat-absorbing material called a *selective surface*.

Most metal-tube collectors are boxed in an insulated metal or wooden housing. The entire unit is often referred to as a *solar panel*. The most common panel size is 4x8'.

Metal tubes in the panel are spaced and sized to create a flow pattern that produces the most efficient heat transfer from the absorber plate to the liquid passing through the tubes. The collectors are designed with tubes far enough apart to draw maximum heat from the absorber plate, yet close enough to eliminate *hot spots* between tubes. The surface of an effective absorber plate is cool to the touch because most of the heat is being transferred to the liquid.

Collector Materials—Copper is an excellent heat conductor. Aluminum is also a good conductor. Aluminum is less expensive than copper, but is subject to electrolysis, or deterioration, if another metal is used in the same system.

Steel is the least expensive, but it is difficult to protect from rusting and is rarely used for collectors. Stainless steel, which best resists corrosion, is the most expensive material to use in collectors. It is less conductive than copper or aluminum and is not commonly used in solar collectors. Stainless steel is used in heat exchangers.

Recently, panels using plastic channels instead of metal have become popular for use in solar pool-heating systems. They are practical for pool heating because efficiency is less critical than for collectors used to heat domestic water or a home. Plastic will not conduct heat as effectively as metal.

Plastic collector panels are made of heat-absorbing black polypropylene and similar extruded inert plastics. Special additives protect the plastic from damage by pool chemicals and ultraviolet rays. Plastic has grown in popularity because it is the least expensive and the most corrosion resistant. These panels are available glazed or unglazed. Unglazed, flat panels are most often used for swimming pools. The drawings at right show typical metal and plastic collector panels.

Some plastic panels are designed so that after several years of use, they can be disassembled and flipped over to expose the side that has been protected from weather. As improvements have been made in materials, solar-collector warranties offered by suppliers have been extended to as much as 10 or 15 years.

Glazed and Unglazed Panels—Solar panels that have a cover of clear or translucent glass or a clear acrylic plastic are called glazed panels. The glass or plastic cover traps the heat in the collector, so more heat is absorbed by the absorber plates.

Unglazed panels do not have a glass or plastic cover. They do not produce as high a water temperature as glazed panels. Unglazed panels are most often used to heat pools. They are less expensive than glazed panels. Pool water doesn't require the high temperatures generated by glazed panels.

In areas where there is a constant cool wind, glazed panels are more efficient and reduce heat loss. They are often used for pools with spas, because they can produce the high temperatures required to heat spas to a comfortable temperature.

Flexible-Plastic Collectors—Several types of solar collectors are not housed in rigid panels. One type uses lengths of black-plastic tubing arranged in a flat-coil configuration. These are mounted directly on the roof. Another type consists of 4-

62 Solar Heating & Energy-Saving Ideas

FLAT-PLATE COLLECTOR PANEL

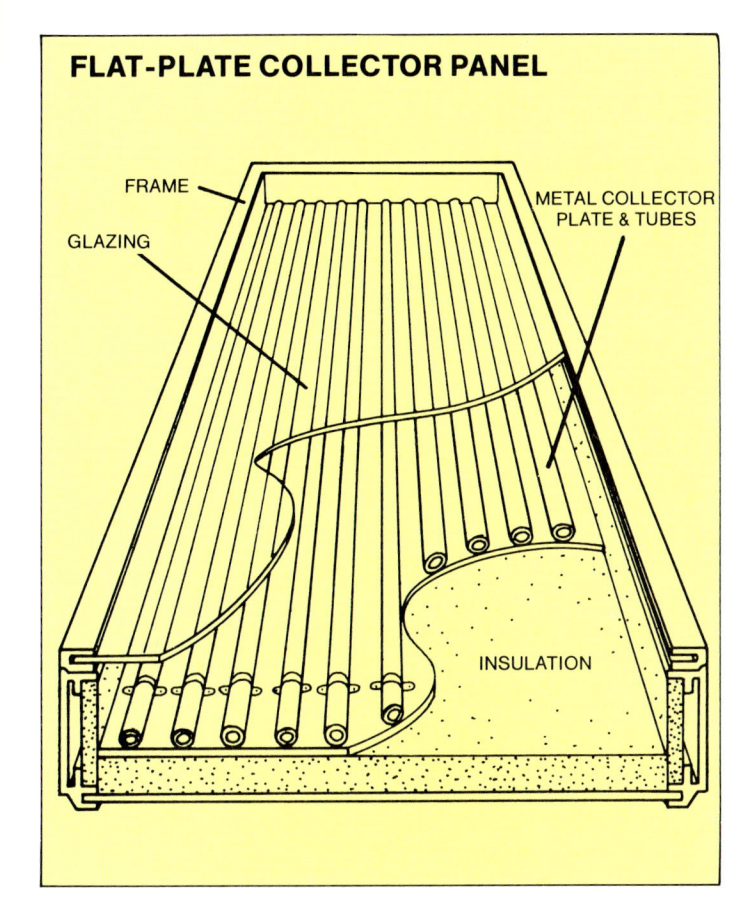

- FRAME
- GLAZING
- METAL COLLECTOR PLATE & TUBES
- INSULATION

PLASTIC COLLECTOR PANEL

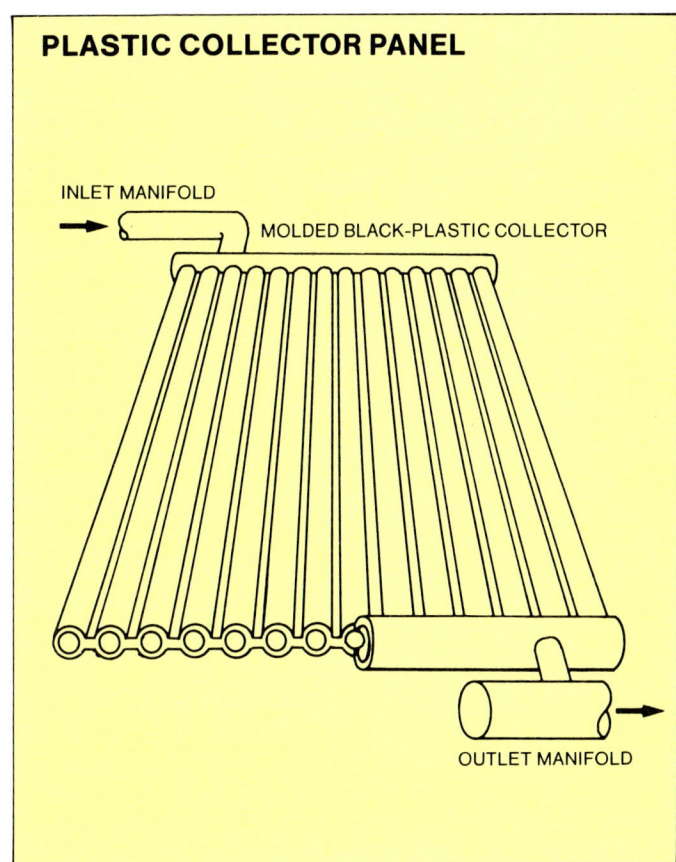

- INLET MANIFOLD
- MOLDED BLACK-PLASTIC COLLECTOR
- OUTLET MANIFOLD

inch-wide roll-out tube mats which are connected together and bonded to the roof.

These collectors are not as efficient per square foot of collector space as flat-plate collectors. They are less expensive per square foot, so the overall cost is about the same.

One advantage of these collectors is that their angle in relation to the sun is not as critical as a flat-plate collector. Also, they are less noticeable on the roof and easier to install. In sufficient quantity, flexible-plastic collectors will produce the temperatures required for heating pool water.

SIZING A SYSTEM

The effectiveness of a system will vary depending on climate, wind conditions, orientation to the sun and the type of collectors and other components used to build the system. The key to effectiveness is the number of square feet of collector compared to the square footage of the pool surface.

There is no all-purpose formula to determine how many square feet of collector are needed to heat a specific pool. Conditions vary from site to site and pool to pool. Collectors vary in efficiency. A typical ratio for unglazed collectors is about 3 square feet of collector for every 4 square feet of pool surface. A pool with a surface area of 400 square feet will need approximately 300 square feet of collector area. A 4x8' collector is 32 square feet. Nine or 10 collectors would be needed to heat a typical pool of 400 square feet.

When shopping for collectors, gather the same information required for sizing a heater, page 50. You'll need to know the surface area of the pool in square feet, desired pool temperature and the average temperature of the coldest month you'll be using the pool. With this information, the pool dealer or solar dealer can determine the Btu requirements of the pool and recommend the correct number and type of panels.

Selecting Pump and Filter—The addition of a solar collectors to the basic support system will require slightly more power to pump water through the system. The extra plumbing required and the collectors themselves will add water resistance, called *head loss*, to the system.

Determining head loss, or *total dynamic head*, in the support system is one of the factors required to size the pool pump for effective filtration. Information on how to figure head loss is described on page 45.

Most solar systems will add 6 to 10 feet of head loss to the support system. If you're adding a solar-heating system, determine the pump requirements for the pool and basic support system—filter, heater and plumbing. See pages 44-47. Then add the additional head loss created by the solar system.

Many solar manufacturers provide head-loss data on their collectors. In many cases, adding solar requires buying a pump one size larger than required for the same system without solar. Additional energy required to operate a solar system is an insignificant part of the support system's overall operating costs.

Because a solar-heating system is a closed system, no extra energy is required to pump water up to the collectors. The pump merely keeps water moving through the system. Gravity and the siphoning effect in the return lines balances pressure in the incoming lines to the collectors. In other words, the height of the collectors above the pool have no effect

Solar Heating & Energy-Saving Ideas 63

HILLSIDE MOUNT **ROOF MOUNT** **GROUND-LEVEL MOUNT**

on the amount of power required to pump water to them.

Selecting a Backup Heater—The capacity of the backup heater will depend largely on how much backup heating you wish for the solar system. If you have an indoor pool, or anticipate swimming on cloudy or overcast days, the backup heater should be sized to heat the pool without the help of the solar system. Check with local pool builders with experience installing solar systems. They will be familiar with local weather conditions and the performance of systems they have installed. Complete details on selecting pumps, filters and heaters are included in the chapter, *Selecting Pool Equipment*, starting on page 43.

For example, a system designed to provide 85% of the desired heat may be the most economical. You have the option of supplementing the system with a backup heater or simply not swimming when clouds or weather allow water temperatures to drop. You may settle for a season shorter by two or three weeks a year.

In some areas of the country, heating is rarely required during the summer. A solar-heating system to extend the swimming season by one or two months may not make economic sense.

LOCATING COLLECTORS

There is no easy way to hide solar collectors. Collectors need the greatest possible exposure to the sun. Most collectors are placed near the pool on the roof of the house, garage or a pool building.

In the Northern Hemisphere, solar panels face south to take maximum advantage of the sun throughout the day. The angle of the panels depends on the latitude of your area and which times of the year you want maximum efficiency from the panels.

A south-facing sloped roof is ideal. Collectors can also be placed at ground level on flat ground or on a south-facing slope. Collectors on flat ground are supported by frames that provide the correct angle for maximum heat gain. Typical locations for collectors are shown in the drawing above.

If the pool is situated on a south-facing slope, the collectors may be located at ground level. By placing the collectors on the downhill side of the pool, *natural convection* will help move water from the pool through the collectors and back, slightly reducing the load on the pool pump. Natural convection causes warm water to rise and cold water to sink.

Roof-Mounted Collectors—Frames of roof-mounted collectors must be firmly secured to the roof. Collectors will expand and contract from the heat of the sun and must be designed to tolerate some movement. The system selected to attach collectors should allow clearance between the backs of the panels and the roof. This will allow air to circulate. Some local and state building codes specify a minimum clearance. Manufacturers will recommend how their specific collectors are to be mounted.

Collectors mounted on flat roofs are held in frames so the surface of each collector will face the sun. Elevated panels must be secured against the wind. Where cool winds are the norm, glazed panels are the most efficient to reduce heat loss.

Solar panels require little maintenance. Access is necessary only to permit occasional cleaning. Dirt or dust accumulating on the panel will filter out the sun and reduce the efficiency of the system.

Solar-panel suppliers in your area

64 Solar Heating & Energy-Saving Ideas

South-facing slope is ideal location for mounting solar panels. Here, panels are mounted above pool. System would be slightly more efficient if it were possible to mount panels below pool's water level. *Design: 20th Century Pools, Buena Vista, CA.*

will be able to recommend the specific angle the panels should be tilted toward the sun. The angle will vary depending on latitude. Panels should face true south or up to 10 degrees to the west.

You may prefer maximum heating early and late in the season and place the panels to catch full sun when it is low in the southern sky. At extreme southern latitudes, panels perpendicular to the path of the sun in July will be facing almost straight up. Most panels are placed somewhere in between.

Sophisticated systems have collectors that automatically track the sun. Collectors with parabolic reflectors concentrate the sun's rays on a single metal tube running the length of the collector. A polished-metal reflector focuses all collected energy on the tube to produce much higher temperatures than are required for pool heating.

The high initial cost make parabolic collectors impractical for pool heating and too expensive for most home heating installations.

Flat-plate collectors can be installed with adjustable supports and flexible hoses so the angle can be changed manually during the year. The system is practical for ground-level installations where panels are already frame-mounted. For most rooftop installations, the minor amount of heat gained is usually not worth the extra effort.

DECK COLLECTORS

It is possible to build an active solar-heating system with collectors hidden in the pool deck, a masonry patio or even a driveway. One type consists of copper coils embedded in the concrete deck surrounding the pool. When the sun heats the deck, heat is drawn from the deck by water circulated through the copper pipe. The deck is the collector. There is no access to embedded coils, so diligent water maintenance is essential to prevent coils from corroding or building up mineral deposits.

Another type of deck collector has prefabricated-plastic solar grids that are embedded in concrete. A vapor barrier is placed on the ground underneath the collectors. A sheet of urethane foam provides insulation between the vapor barrier and the grid. Concrete is poured directly on top of the grid to form the pool deck. Plastic panels are less expensive than copper and are corrosion resistant.

Concrete is not an effective heat conductor. It does store heat well. An effective system using heat collected from a pool deck will require a larger collector area than other types of solar systems.

Collectors embedded in concrete must be drained during freezing weather to prevent expansion that can

Solar Heating & Energy-Saving Ideas **65**

COIL-TYPE DECK COLLECTOR

PLASTIC DECK COLLECTOR

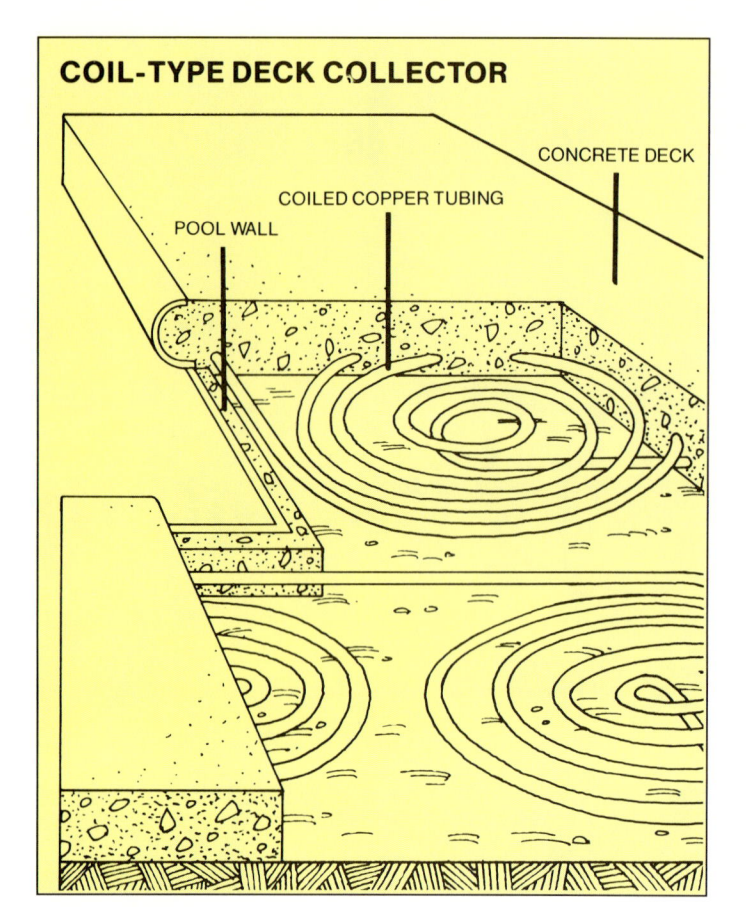

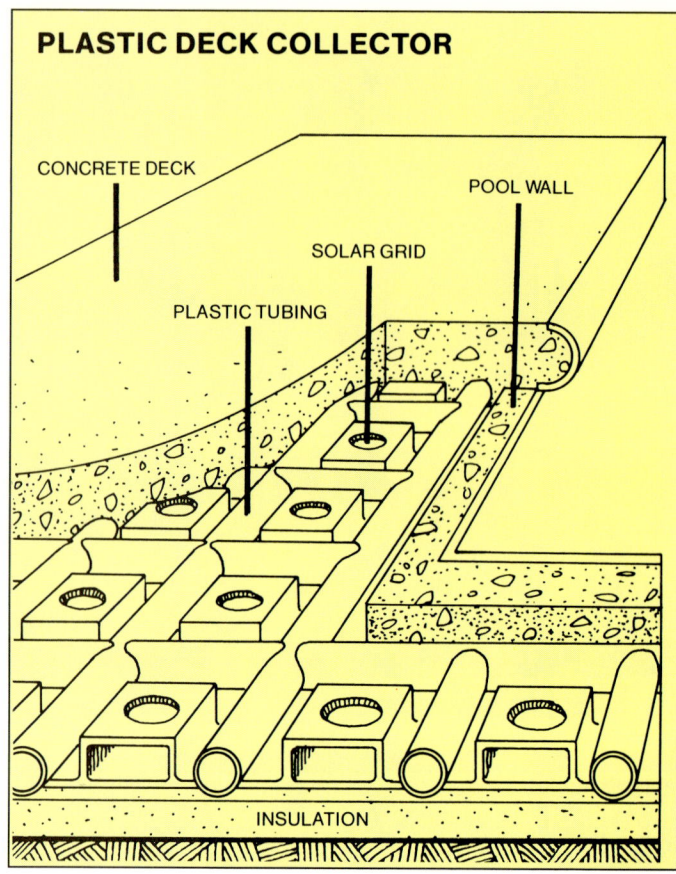

damage the collectors and crack the concrete. Typical deck collectors are shown in the drawings above.

Heat-Exchangers—Most solar systems pump water directly from the pool, through a filter, then through the solar collectors. Utilizing a heat-exchanger offers an alternative that reduces collector damage from corrosion or water freezing in the system.

An antifreeze liquid is circulated continuously through the solar panels to pick up heat from the sun. This heated liquid is brought into indirect contact with pool water in a heat-exchanger. The heated pool water is pumped back into the pool. This is referred to as a *closed loop system*—see page 61.

For pool heating, the primary advantage of a heat-exchanger is that it protects the collectors from chemicals and alkaline or acidic pool water. Designers of pool solar-heating systems agree that balanced water from a properly maintained pool will not cause scaling or damage metal tubes in solar collectors. Most damage to collectors—caused by imbalanced pool water—is irreversible. A heat exchanger protects the system's components.

PLANNING EFFICIENTLY

It is technically possible to design a solar-heating system that will maintain an ideal pool temperature almost 100% of the time during a normal or extended swimming season. However, in most cases this would be costly and inefficient.

The most efficient system produces the highest practical amount of heat for the lowest possible cost. Once that point has been reached, any increase in the amount of heat provided is at an accelerating cost. It becomes less expensive to boost temperatures with a backup heater than to add more collectors for additional solar-heating capacity.

If eight collectors can provide a specific pool with the desired heat 80% of the time with no backup heater, 10 collectors won't provide adequate heat 100% of the time. It could take a 50% increase in collectors to improve output another 5%.

ADDING SOLAR

If you are building a new pool without solar heating, you have the option of adding a solar system at a future date. Size the pump, filter and heater with solar use in mind. Rough in the basic plumbing for the system so future conversion costs will be minimal.

Adding a solar system to an existing pool is called *retrofitting*. If you want to add solar to your present pool, you'll first have to determine if your present pump is capable of handling the additional water resistance created by the system. Have a solar installer or pool installer check your present support system to see if it can be retrofitted for solar at a reasonable cost. If you have to replace the pump, filter and heater to accommodate solar, the additional cost may not justify the anticipated savings.

USING PASSIVE SOLAR ENERGY

There are two effective ways to hold down pool-heating costs. The first is to take advantage of natural ways to utilize passive solar heat from the sun. The second is to do everything possible to reduce heat loss. You don't have to install an active solar-heating system to take advantage of these energy-saving ideas.

When you are planning a pool,

select a site that has maximum exposure to the sun. Review the priorities involved in choosing a suitable site, discussed on pages 9-13.

Equally important, protect the pool from the wind. A pool loses heat in three ways. Under most circumstances, about 10% is lost through the pool shell into the ground. Another 30% is lost from heat radiating into the air. The greatest loss, 60%, is through evaporation to wind blowing over the pool surface. The stronger the wind current, the greater the loss.

NATURAL HEAT GAIN

In addition to choosing a pool site with maximum exposure to the sun, there are three ways to enhance natural heat gain.

Shallow Pools—An increasing number of pool designers are recommending shallow pools for several obvious reasons.

A pool depth of 3-1/2 to 4 feet is adequate for swimming and all pool activities except diving and using larger pool slides. See page 57.

A shallow pool heats more quickly from the sun. It uses fewer gallons of water than a deeper pool with the same surface area. There is less water to pump, filter and heat.

Dark-Bottom Pools—Light colors reflect heat and dark colors absorb heat. A pool with a black or other dark-colored bottom will absorb more heat than a traditional light-colored pool.

Water temperatures in dark-bottom pools are estimated to be from 2° to 5° warmer than the same size pool with a light bottom. There are too many variables in pools, climates and locations to have produced sophisticated test data.

For maximum natural heat gain, you can design a shallow pool with a dark bottom.

In the Southwest and other sunbelt areas, a dark-bottom pool may work too efficiently. High July and August temperatures can create uncomfortably warm water for swimming.

A pool with a dark bottom can be esthetically appealing. Some homeowners like the effect and choose a dark-bottom pool as much for appearance as for its energy-saving potential. Dark pools reflect the images of surrounding trees and shrubbery. They can be designed in free-form shapes, using rocks and other natural materials, to simulate a forest pool.

Bubble-type solar pool cover traps sun's heat. Solar covers are an inexpensive way to heat a pool. *Photo courtesy of Cantar Corp., Carlstadt, NJ.*

Floating collectors trap heat in air space between water and underside of collector, creating a greenhouse effect. Hexagonal units are designed to fit any shape pool. Each unit covers about 7-1/2 square feet of pool surface. They're sold under the trademark, *Solar Petals*. *Photo courtesy of Engineering & Research Associates, Tucson, AZ.*

Solar Heating & Energy-Saving Ideas

Dark-bottom pools fit some landscapes better than others. This pool was designed to give the impression of a forest pond. The same pool might look out of place in a formal landscape. *Design: Barnett-Hendricks Pools, Inc., Cherry Hill, NJ.*

Shallow pools are more efficient than deep pools in collecting heat from the sun. *Design: 20th Century Pools, Buena Vista, CA.*

Most landscape designers will agree that black-bottom pools look more at home in naturalistic landscapes, but would look out of place in a formal, structured landscape with sparse foliage. In certain types of landscapes, an aqua or other light-colored pool will give a more refreshing feel and better complement surrounding plants, pool structures and the home.

The water in dark-bottom pools requires frequent monitoring. Algae, scale and cloudy water are less noticeable than in a light-colored pool.

Underwater Collectors—A unique passive solar-heating system consists of plastic mats that cover the pool bottom. Each mat, about 2 feet square is covered with rows of perforated blisterlike domes. There are holes around the base of each dome and a single hole in the top of the dome. See drawing at right.

When the sun strikes the dark blue or black plastic mats, they absorb heat. Heat is transferred to water trapped in each dome. The warmed water rises by convection through the opening in the dome top. Colder water rushes in through holes in the bottom to take its place.

This continuing cycle gradually raises the temperature in the whole pool. The mats are made of injection-molded PVC plastic. Anti-algae compounds are incorporated into the plastic.

PREVENTING HEAT LOSS

As a law of physics, cold is the absence of heat. Heat flows from warm objects into cooler air or objects. Heat that can be retained is heat that doesn't have to be replaced. Conserving existing heat is cheaper than replacing lost heat.

The most effective way to reduce heat loss is by covering the pool. Uncovered pools that might drop 10° to 15° overnight can be protected with pool blankets that reduce heat loss to 2° or 3°. Pool enclosures will also reduce surface heat loss.

As mentioned, only about 10% of a pool's heat is lost through the bottom and sides of the pool. The rest is lost through the water surface. Insulating the water surface makes sense.

Windbreaks—Wind robs a pool of heat. In naturally windy areas, choose a site where the pool has as much existing wind protection as possible. Take advantage of existing buildings, fences, shrubbery or trees. Where a fully sheltered site is not possible, protection against excessive heat loss from wind can be controlled by adding natural or artificial wind barriers.

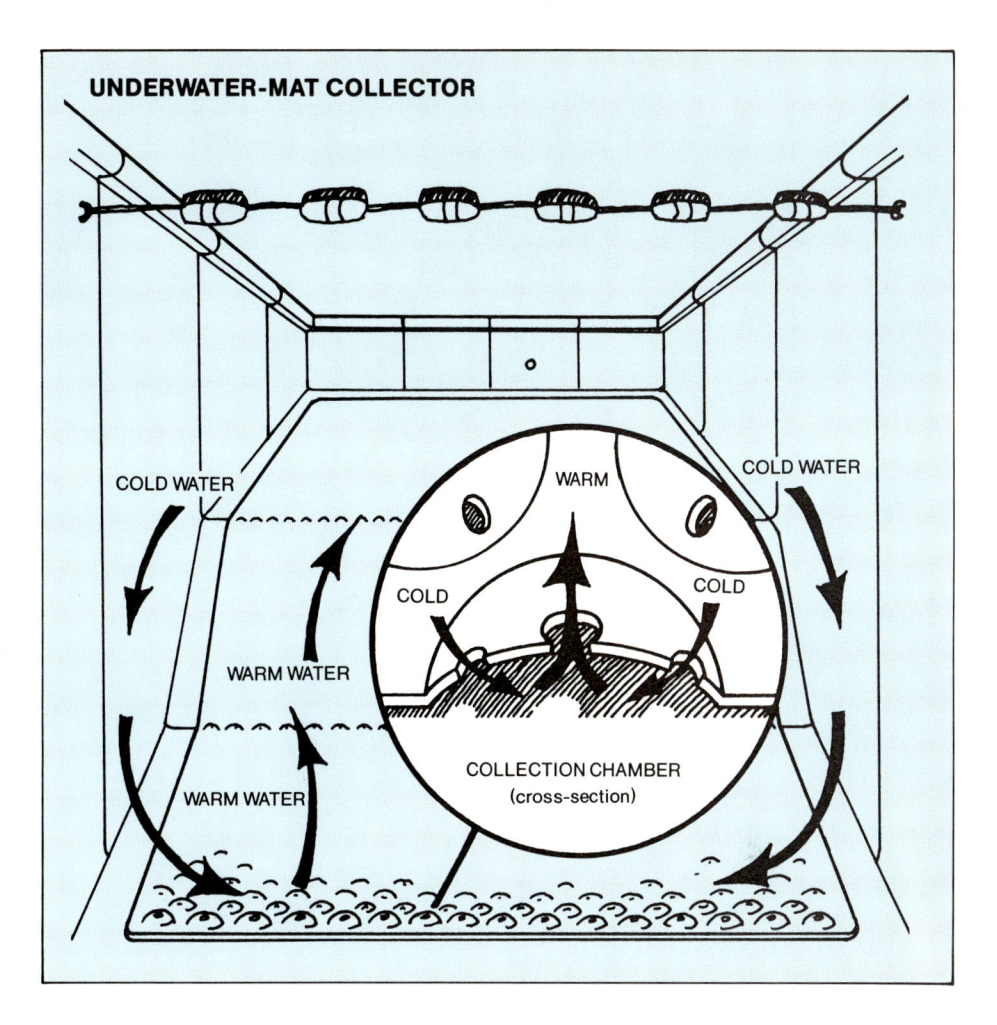

Trees, bushes and shrubbery are ideal windbreaks. Natural foliage permits some circulation of air on hot days, yet is capable of reducing the effect of strong winds. Wind control is an important factor in planning a pool. For information on selecting a pool site, see pages 9-13.

It's impossible to generalize about wind conditions. Every pool site has its own climate. Determine any prevailing wind patterns that may exist. Look for problem areas where wind may be funneled between buildings. When you have a good idea of wind patterns, have your local nursery suggest specific plants that will thrive in your area and offer good wind protection. Trees and other poolside plantings are discussed on pages 107-108.

Fences and walls provide an immediate solution to wind problems. You won't have to wait for foliage to mature. Solid fences and walls are usually not the most effective wind barriers. Wind washes over them and continues unhindered several feet behind the barrier. The most effective fences have openings that break up the wind and diffuse its force.

In planning pool landscaping, the goal may be a pleasing combination of natural and artificial barriers—walls, fences or pool buildings, enhanced with trees and shrubs. Proper placement will save energy and help reduce heat loss. Details on specific pool fences and tips on general landscaping for controlling wind are discussed on pages 108-109.

Pool Covers and Enclosures—You can use several different types of covers for swimming pools. A floating *pool blanket* is used for insulating the pool to prevent heat loss when the pool is not in use.

A solid *pool cover* is more sturdy than a pool blanket. It can be woven or solid plastic and is used to cover the pool during the off-season or overnight. A cover will help hold heat

Solar Heating & Energy-Saving Ideas   69

Winter pool cover is used to keep debris out of pool during off-season and prevent water and chemical evaporation. Water filled bags keep cover in place. *Photo courtesy of Cantar Corp., Carlstadt, NJ.*

Air-supported bubble enclosure allows year-round swimming, can be removed in summer months. *Photo courtesy of Air Structures Inc., Sacramento, CA.*

in the pool, but its main purposes are safety and to keep the pool clean.

A *solar cover* both insulates the pool and allows sunlight to penetrate, heating the water.

A *pool enclosure* can be a permanent or temporary structure that partially or fully encloses the pool to permit swimming inside or under cover.

Although the terms *pool blanket* and *pool cover* are sometimes used interchangeably, these items are usually defined as follows:

Solar Cover—These are clear or lightly tinted translucent plastic designed to increase heat gain while the sun is shining. They are called *solar covers* because they allow the sun's rays to filter into the water and heat it. The most common solar cover has air bubbles built into the plastic sheeting. The cover prevents evaporation and retains heat. Dead-air space in the bubbles acts as an insulator.

Foam Blanket—A thin layer of insulating foam sandwiched between sheets of plastic is designed to float on the pool surface. Foam blankets have better insulating qualities and hold more heat in the pool than thinner solar blankets. One disadvantage is that foam blankets block the sun and prevent direct solar gain. They are also heavier to handle than thinner plastic solar blankets.

Foam Slabs—These 1- to 2-inch-thick slabs of rigid-foam insulation have the best insulating properties of all blanket materials. Slabs are cut in sections that piece together to cover the pool surface. They must be removed individually and stacked before the pool can be used for swimming. Like foam blankets, they prevent direct solar gain.

Pool Covers—During the off-season, pools are covered to help maintain the water's chemical balance and keep debris out of the pool. Some covers are designed to prevent children from falling in the pool. Many of these are sturdy enough to support an adult's full weight.

Most covers are made of woven plastic, or plain or reinforced plastic sheeting. They are held in place with water-filled plastic tubes or have grommets for securing them with rope. The use of covers for winterizing is discussed on pages 137-138.

In addition to their value during the off-season, the covers conserve heat and help keep the pool clean during

Greenhouse-type pool enclosure allows maximum solar gain, prevents heat loss. Pool can be used year round. Photos show outside and inside views of same enclosure. *Design: Aqua-Rama of Atlanta, Marietta, GA.*

Solar Heating & Energy-Saving Ideas 71

Hand-operated reel makes cover removal easy. Automatic cover reels are also available. Photo courtesy of Cantar Corp., Carlstadt, NJ.

the swimming season. This reduces the energy needed to operate the pump and filter system.

Some covers provide protection for small children or animals falling into the pool. Most covers and blankets that float on the water surface to prevent heat loss are not designed to support the weight of a child. If this is a specific feature you want in a pool cover, check the manufacturer's specifications. Floating covers and blankets usually carry the warning that they are not designed to support weight.

Pool Enclosures—There are four types of pool enclosures that either make year-round swimming possible or add several months to a normal season. Each one can keep out insects and most of the debris that finds its way into unenclosed pools. The pool is also protected from heat-draining winds.

The air-supported dome, or plastic bubble, is the least expensive and most widely used pool enclosure. A small air pump maintains sufficient air pressure to keep the dome inflated. You have the option of leaving the dome in place all year or just during marginal spring and fall swimming months.

The metal-frame canopy-type enclosure supports a plasticized fabric cover and is similar in design to a tent. These come as prefabricated kits. The advantage of this system over an air-supported bubble is that the light metal framework provides rigid support so no air pump is required. The frame also makes it possible to open the sides during warm weather or to install windows. The structure can be permanent or disassembled in the off-season.

A greenhouse or rigid metal-frame building with a solid roof and walls is usually a permanent installation. These structures come prefabricated or can be custom designed. Some prefabricated greenhouses, either free-standing or house additions, can be adapted to house a pool.

Prefabricated pool structures are available with clear or colored acrylic-plastic sheets or fiberglass sections. These structures can be built with permanent doors, windows and ventilating fans. See photos on page 71.

Custom free-standing pool buildings can be built like any conventional building. The main difference is that they usually have large areas of glass or clear-plastic panels to maximize solar gain. They must also be designed to vent excess moisture. All metal fixtures should be corrosion-resistant. Building materials should be water-resistant.

A custom-designed room addition to the house is the most expensive type of pool enclosure. It does have the advantage of becoming a permanent part of the home. As with other permanent structures, a good portion of the building cost can be added to the home's appraised value.

HANDLING COVERS

Uncovering and covering a pool each time you swim can be troublesome. Unfortunately, if you want the benefits of a cover, you have no alternative.

There are pool blankets and covers that work automatically. They wind up on power-driven or hand-cranked reels. These make handling blankets less cumbersome.

When you do use a cover, completely remove it before using the pool. A pool is unsafe if a swimmer can be trapped under the cover or hidden from view.

SMALL STEPS MEAN BIG SAVINGS

Using a pool cover may be the single most effective way of reducing pool heating costs. But an effective energy-saving program incorporates a series of smaller steps that conserve water and pool chemicals and reduce maintenance expenses.

Pool-equipment manufacturers recognize that high energy costs can discourage homeowners from installing a new pool. Their interest in developing energy-efficient components have resulted in heaters, pumps and filters that use less energy.

Here are a few additional steps to reduce the costs of enjoying a pool.

HEATING THE POOL

An efficient heater maintains the pool temperature at a comfortable level. How and when the heater is used will affect your total pool heating bill.

Pool Temperature—A pool heated to 78F (26C) is suitable for most pool activities. Temperatures required for children playing in the shallow end may be warmer than for someone swimming laps. Experiment to find the lowest comfortable temperature.

Check the temperature with a pool thermometer. Once you have settled on the minimum comfortable temperature, set and mark the thermostat at that level. If necessary, put a lock on the thermostat so swimmers can't change the setting.

Many swimmers unfamiliar with heating pools don't understand that it can take several hours to raise the water temperature a few degrees. Water may feel cool when you first enter the pool. Resist the temptation to turn up thermostat. Chances are,

72 Solar Heating & Energy-Saving Ideas

you'll have finished the swim long before the temperature rises one degree.

The NSPI estimates that lowering the water temperature from 82F (28C) to 78F (26C)—just 4°—will reduce energy consumption by 40%. Each degree the temperature is raised over 78F (26C) increases energy use on an accelerating basis.

When the heater will not be used for a week or more, shut it off and turn off the pilot light. Some gas heaters come equipped with electric-spark ignitions, eliminating the need for a continuously burning pilot light. These heaters are more energy-efficient. Also, a well-maintained heater will save energy. See page 132.

If you use your pool only on weekends, lower the temperature a few degrees when you are finished swimming. Reset the thermostat in time to reheat the pool for the following weekend.

Pool Seasons—Heating a pool to get an early start on the season or to extend the season into the late fall can accelerate heating costs. Short days and cool nights make it expensive to keep a pool at swimming temperature.

It is up to you whether you want to extend the pool season into the cooler months. If you do, you'll have to install a heater capable of heating the pool water to a comfortable temperature during cool weather.

If the heater is undersized, temperatures on marginal spring or fall days may make it literally impossible to heat the pool to a desired temperature. For information on choosing the right-size heater, see page 50.

Locating Support Equipment—The closer the support equipment is to the pool, the more efficiently it will operate. The pump won't have to work as hard to overcome pressure in the plumbing system. Also, less heat will be lost through pipe walls if pipe runs are shorter. Initial plumbing costs will also be less.

Local codes may dictate minimum and maximum distances from pool to support equipment. For maximum efficiency, locate the equipment as close as legally possible to the pool.

Pump and Filter—The cost of filtering water can be reduced by cutting the number of hours the system is in operation. Most pool owners operate filter systems an arbitrary number of hours each day. The system needs to be run only long enough to maintain good water quality. Running the system more hours than necessary wastes energy.

Reduce filtration time until you reach a point where water quality deteriorates. Then increase times by a small amount each day until the filter is keeping the water clean.

If you are planning a pool, an energy-efficient two-speed pump motor will cut your energy bill. Two-speed motors are designed to overcome the inertia of starting the pump and initial water resistance in the system.

When the pump overcomes resistance, the motor kicks into a lower speed that uses much less energy. Two-speed pumps are more expensive than one-speed pumps, but the additional cost is made up quickly in energy savings. Additional details on selecting a motor and pump are on pages 44-47.

Set the filtration system so that it operates from early morning through mid-morning hours. An ideal 8-hour cycle will be from 4 a.m. until noon. This avoids the heavy, midday peak electrical usage period. The water will also be at its best during the hours the pool is most likely to be used.

During periods when the pool is used lightly, reduce filtration hours. Increase filtration time for periods when the pool is in heavy use. Selecting the correct-size pump and filter will help hold down equipment operating costs.

WATER CONSERVATION

Water is scarcer and more expensive in some areas of the country than in others. In areas were water is in short supply, conserving it can be as important as saving energy.

In selecting a filter, choose a system that requires a minimum amount of water to clean. Backwashing a sand filter requires the most water—as much as several hundred gallons. A diatomaceous earth (DE) filter uses much less water for backwashing than a sand filter.

A cartridge filter, which requires no backwashing, uses only the water necessary to hand-clean the cartridge. For complete details on pool filters, see pages 48-50.

A pool cover designed to reduce heat loss will also help reduce water evaporation by as much as 95%. The best way to conserve water is to install a smaller, shallow pool.

USING CHEMICALS

The best way cut pool-chemical use is to keep the water chemistry in balance. Frequent testing and chemical applications will make it unnecessary to make large adjustments to bring the water back into balance.

INSULATED POOLS AND EQUIPMENT

Though a pool blanket or cover is the most effective way to prevent heat loss, there are other steps you can take. The basic steps are to insulate the pool shell and to insulate the plumbing system.

Insulating the Pool Shell—Most above-ground pools lose more heat through sidewalls than in-ground pools. Now many above-ground pools are available with insulated sidewalls. Consider insulated sidewalls if you plan on heating your above-ground pool.

There is some controversy among pool designers as to whether heat loss through in-ground pool shells justifies the cost of insulating them. Some argue that because heat loss through sidewalls of in-ground pools is minimal—about 10% of total heat loss—it is usually not cost effective to insulate them.

There are pool builders today who are using rigid polyurethane foam to insulate sprayed-concrete and fiberglass pools. They contend that the cost of the insulation will soon be recovered in energy savings. For vinyl-lined pools, a thin layer of insulation is placed between the vinyl liner and the pool walls.

Talk to several pool dealers and builders in your area about the cost and benefits of insulating the pool shell. Such insulation is more practical in some areas than in others.

Pipes and Equipment—Insulating pipes and fittings in the pool's plumbing system will help prevent heat loss and help keep water in the pipes from freezing during winter months. This procedure is standard in cold climates where the pool and its equipment must be winterized. See page 137.

In cold climates, support equipment can be housed in an insulated enclosure. Tank-type heaters can be covered with an insulating jacket to prevent heat loss.

Solar Heating & Energy-Saving Ideas

Spraying concrete is the most dramatic—and critical—step in building a gunite or shotcrete pool. *Photo courtesy of Patio Pools, Tucson, AZ.*

CHAPTER 6

How Pools Are Built

Completing all the preliminary steps before work actually begins on your pool can seem like an endless process. From the moment work starts, all the time spent planning will have proven well worthwhile.

The information in this chapter isn't intended to provide instructions for installing your own in-ground pool. It will provide the information you need to understand basic installation processes for the major types of in-ground pools. It will help you work knowledgeably with the contractor and crew, so you'll know what to expect as building progresses.

There are a few steps you can take to reduce final pool costs if you want to become directly involved. Most are in planning, site preparation, landscaping and other property improvements that take place once the basic pool is in the ground. The information on page 17 explains some of your choices.

Weigh the cost of your own time and skills against potential savings. Rarely does a homeowner correctly estimate how much time even the simplest project can take. If cost is a primary concern, consider an above-ground pool designed as a practical do-it-yourself installation.

Vinyl-lined Pools—Improvements in materials and manufacturing techniques have produced vinyl-lined pools that builders can quickly assemble. Wall panels for vinyl-lined pools are prefabricated and can be easily assembled in a variety of custom shapes. Nuts, bolts and other hardware are furnished with the pool package. Bolt holes line up and shell assembly requires little shaping or modification.

Vinyl liners can be custom designed to fit almost any shape. Steps and other custom touches that at one time required building special forms, are now available in a variety of prefabricated plastic components.

These improvements have reduced the time required to install the pool. They have also reduced the opportunities for a homeowner to save money by making a pool a do-it-yourself project. Labor costs are a decreasing percentage of the total cost of a completed pool. This reduces practical opportunities for saving money by becoming involved in the installation of the basic pool shell.

After the pool site has been excavated, you can assemble the vinyl-lined pool package, if you're handy with tools and follow instructions carefully. The pool manufacturer will supply basic assembly instructions with each pool ordered. The job will require at least one helper to assemble the pool walls and to install the vinyl liner. It usually makes more sense to hire an experienced crew to do this work.

Depending on the pool manufacturer and pool builder, your involvement in construction could negate a warranty that applies to a vinyl-lined pool installed by an authorized dealer. Installing the shell is the most critical step in building. Mistakes could be costly.

Most pool builders will discourage direct involvement by an inexperienced homeowner. Interest and enthusiasm may be appreciated, but the contribution may be minimal. After excavation is complete, an experienced crew trained to work together can install a vinyl-lined pool in 3 to 5 working days. The easiest work for the homeowner is also the easiest work for an experienced crew. Much of the heavier work, particularly excavating, is impractical for the homeowner.

Sprayed-Concrete Pools—Gunite and shotcrete pools require special preparations and equipment. They are wholly impractical as do-it-yourself projects. Shaping and tying steel to form the skeleton of the pool is a key step in construction that must be completed correctly. Spraying concrete to create the shell requires special equipment and is a skill acquired only with experience.

Plastering, electrical work and plumbing are jobs best left to tradesmen experienced in pool installations.

How Pools Are Built 75

Clearing the site is the first step in pool installation. You can do the work yourself or let the pool builder do it. Tree removal often requires heavy equipment. *Photo courtesy of Patio Pools, Tucson, AZ.*

Most building codes will require use of a state-licensed electrician and plumber.

Fiberglass Pools—The excavation for installation of a one-piece fiberglass pool shell is similar to that of a gunite pool. The ground is contoured as closely as possible to the final shape of the pool. Work to prepare a fiberglass shell for installation is largely completed at the factory. The shell is delivered to the site in one piece. It is relatively light in weight, but it still must be lifted by a crane into the excavation.

If access is a problem, the pool can be lifted over most houses by a large crane and placed in the excavation. If access is not a problem, a small crane, either a component of the delivery truck or a separate vehicle, will lift the shell off the truck and place it in the excavation. A small crane requires no more access room than the truck delivering the shell.

Fiberglass-sidewall pools are similar to vinyl-liner pools in installation. The difference is that these pools have concrete bottoms, which are poured after the walls have been assembled and set in a concrete footing. The excavation is then backfilled with gravel or concrete. Like vinyl-lined pools, installing the sidewalls is relatively quick and easy. However, the concrete work involved requires specialized skills and exacting work. The job is best left to a pool contractor with experience installing these pools.

In recent years, sprayed-concrete pools, vinyl-lined pools and fiberglass pools have dominated the pool market. The success of these systems has all but eliminated most other types of pool construction for both design and cost reasons.

The installation steps described in this section are for typical vinyl-lined, sprayed-concrete or fiberglass in-ground pools. Instructions for homeowner installation of above-ground pools are included in the chapter, *Above-ground Pools,* page 101.

THE BASIC STEPS

Regardless of the type of pool you are installing, certain phases of work are roughly the same. These include site preparation, excavation, plumbing, wiring and setting up support equipment. The only phase that really differs between the basic types is the actual installation of the pool shell.

No two contractors may approach a job in exactly the same way. There will be variables caused by site access, terrain, soil conditions, equipment available to the contractor, the skills of individual crew members and even the weather.

The installation methods and sequences described in this chapter are those most often followed for installing the various types of pools. As with most construction, there is more than one *right way* to install a pool. For the reasons above, the builder you use may not precisely follow the methods described here.

Basic Installation Sequence—In brief, simplified form, the pool builder will follow this sequence of steps to install your pool:

Step 1—Prepare the site for construction. Remove foliage to clear the site or to provide access. Level or contour terrain where required. Specifications for grading and other site work should be included on the original site plan.

Step 2—Stake out the dimensions of the pool and deck, working from the site plan included in the contract.

Step 3—Locate underground utility lines—gas, electric and water—that will be affected during construction. Sewer lines, septic tanks and leach fields must be protected from damage by excavation or from being driven over by heavy equipment.

Step 4—Excavate to prepare for building or installing the pool shell. Run trenches for plumbing and electrical wiring from pool excavation to support-equipment site, and any required trenches to sources for gas and electrical hookups.

Step 5—Remove excavated material and clean site of construction debris.

Step 6—Rough in plumbing for main drain, skimmers, suction lines and return lines. Position rebar if sprayed-concrete pool.

Step 7—Rough in conduits for wiring for underwater lights and support equipment. Position niches for underwater lights if gunite pool.

Step 8—Install or build pool shell. Finish and trim. This includes adding coping, plastering and tiling gunite pools, installing underwater lights, drain covers, handrails and other trim pieces.

Step 9—Install and connect pump, filter, heater and other support equipment.

Step 10—Install pool deck around pool.

Step 11—Fill pool, clean, and test support equipment.

Step 12—Clean up site and landscape area. Add other pool structures, such as patio, gazebo or pool house.

PREPARING THE SITE

The contractor will work from the site plan included in your pool contract to locate the pool on the property and to establish digging lines for excavation.

Access must be provided for excavating equipment. A backhoe usually needs a path 8 to 10 feet wide for entry to the site. Access is also needed for the truck delivering pool components and building materials, and for the truck that hauls away excavated dirt and rock.

Heavy planks must be laid across fragile walks or patio areas to protect them from the weight of trucks and other heavy equipment.

Prior to signing a contract, discuss the specific details of site preparation. There are many tasks you can do to cut installation costs—transplanting plants, removing fence sections for access, trimming trees, or arranging to have utility lines relocated. Determine who is responsible for each step necessary to prepare the site for the builder. Include this information in the contract. See page 38.

EXCAVATING

Digging the hole for each basic type of pool requires a different technique.

Excavation is critical for sprayed-

Wall is removed to allow access for heavy equipment. *Photo courtesy of Patio Pools, Tucson, AZ.*

concrete pools. The excavation must be sculptured as closely as possible to the final pool shape. The major cut is completed by backhoe. Final shaping is completed with handtools.

For vinyl-lined pools, the excavation is completed to conform to the final cut and shape of the pool bottom. The depth and slope for the liner chosen follow specifications provided by the pool manufacturer.

For vinyl-lined and fiberglass-sidewall pools, excavation walls are cut oversize so there is working room for assembling the sidewall panels. Because the space behind the sidewall panels must be backfilled later, the cut should be only large enough to permit work to be completed behind the wall and to position support struts. Poured-concrete pools are excavated in the same way to permit the erection of forms.

For one-piece fiberglass pools, the excavation is shaped as nearly as possible to the final shape of the pool shell. Only enough space need be allowed for connecting the support equipment. Gaps between the fiberglass and earth walls are backfilled when the pool is in place, usually with sand. Unstable or wet soil may make other pool types more practical.

How Pools Are Built 77

Know what soil conditions are before excavating begins. Rocky soil like this may require heavier equipment than that used for sandy soil or loam. Solid rock may require drilling and blasting. *Photo courtesy of Patio Pools, Tucson, AZ.*

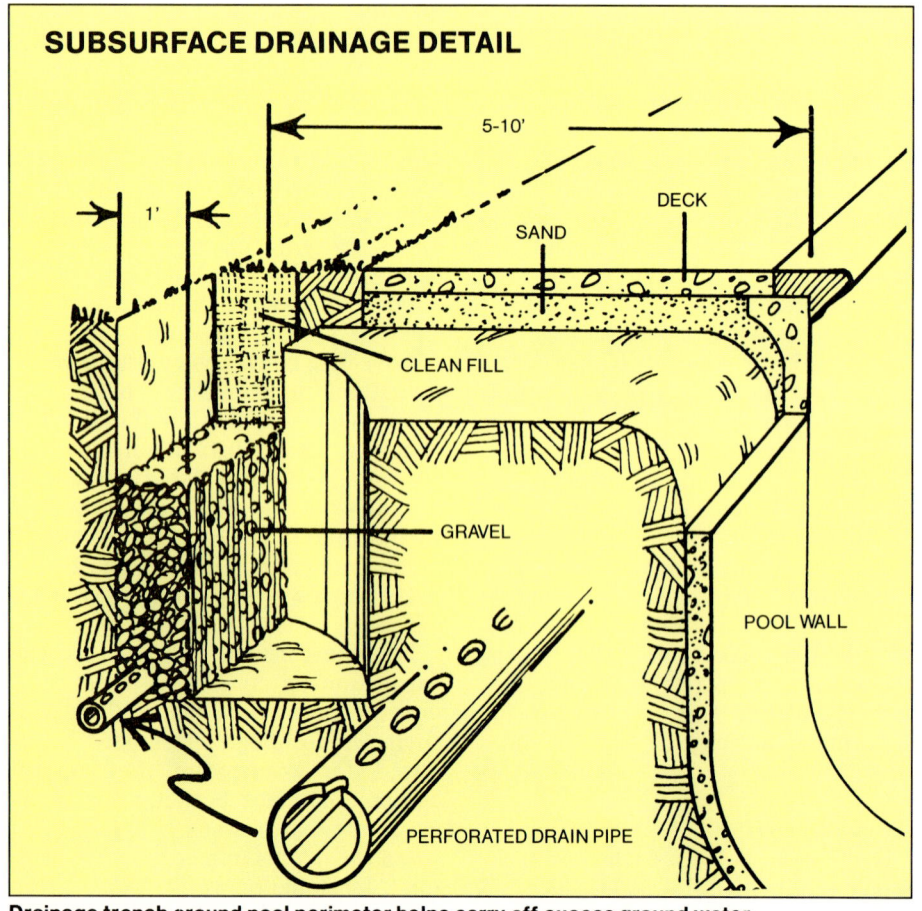

SUBSURFACE DRAINAGE DETAIL

Drainage trench around pool perimeter helps carry off excess ground water.

SAND, SOIL AND ROCK

The pool builder must work with existing site conditions. Excessively sandy, wet or expansive soil, underground water and rock are conditions that cause most excavating problems.

If you suspect a soil problem, have a soils engineer conduct tests prior to picking a site for the pool and certainly before starting excavation.

Sandy Soil—Sand makes it difficult to cut an excavation that has stable walls. Walls that may collapse are not too serious if you are installing a vinyl-lined or fiberglass pool.

Sprayed-concrete pools require a stable excavation shape until concrete is applied. A common solution for unstable walls is to shape the walls, then cover them with a light coat of concrete. This light shell stabilizes the walls until the rebar can be positioned and the final concrete coat added.

Wet Soil—There are two types of wet soil. One type is water-soaked soil created by heavy rain or runoff. This problem will be solved with time. Water that fills the bottom of an excavation can be pumped out. Remaining water will eventually evaporate or soak into the ground. Building need only be delayed until the soil dries at the bottom of the excavation.

Ground water is a more serious problem. If ground water is the result of a high water table or an underground spring, the best solution is to relocate the pool to a dry area away from the spring or to a higher site above the water table.

If relocating the pool is not possible or practical, a subgrade drainage system can be installed to carry away excess ground water. A typical system requires digging a trench about a foot wide around the perimeter of the pool 5 to 10 feet from the pool walls.

Gravel is placed in the bottom of the trench, then perforated drainage pipe is placed on the gravel bed and covered with a final layer of gravel. The trench is then filled with dirt to ground level. See drawing at left.

Water in the soil seeps into the gravel and into the pipe. Water in the pipe drains into a dry well or is directed to an area well below pool level. The difficulty with installing a drainage system is that there is no guarantee the system will be effective enough to solve the problem.

An experienced soils engineer should be retained to conduct soil tests and provide specifications for the drainage system. Specifications should include where to trench, how deep to dig the trench, the materials to use and a system for disposing of water collected by the system.

In addition to excavating problems, excessively wet soil can create upward pressure on the bottom of an empty pool. This is called *hydrostatic pressure*. When the pool is full, the weight of the pool water counteracts hydrostatic pressure from below. Hydrostatic pressure may cause an empty pool to shift and damage its plumbing and deck. In extreme cases, excessive ground water has caused fiberglass-pool shells and sprayed-concrete pools to *float* out of the excavation.

If underground water is suspected in any pool installation, install a *hydrostatic valve* at the main drain. The cost is insignificant when compared to cost of repairing a pool damaged by ground water. See drawing at right.

Hydrostatic valves are designed to open automatically or manually. They are seated in a gravel bed that collects water under the pool. When the pool is drained and there is upward pressure exerted on the bottom of the pool shell, the valve will permit ground water to run into the pool. This relieves hydrostatic pressure.

Automatic valves contain a float that is raised when water pressure underneath the shell is greater than pressure from above. Water will drain into the pool and relieve pressure. The float forms a seal to prevent pool water from draining out during normal operation.

Manual valves have a faucet-type handle that is opened with a long, forked pole when the pool is being drained or is empty. When the pool is refilled, the valve is closed.

Expansive Soil—This is a heavy clay soil that absorbs moisture and swells. Expansive soil can exert enough pressure to crack concrete pools or collapse the walls of vinyl-lined or fiberglass pools. If a soil analysis indicates potential problems with expansive soil, there are several steps you can take.

Sprayed-concrete pools can be built with thicker walls and extra steel reinforcing. Additional reinforcing will be needed for the walls of vinyl-lined pools. Fiberglass pools can be reinforced by backfilling the excavation with concrete. These structural-strength problems should be solved by a structural engineer who can determine stresses and pressures. The engineer can write specifications for the job.

Discuss the problem with your pool builder. Most builders retain outside technical help to solve unusual building problems. This should be the builder's responsibility.

Another solution is to remove expansive soil from around the pool walls and replace it with clean fill—normal, dry compacted soil—to act as a buffer between the expansive soil and pool walls to absorb pressure.

The problem can be avoided or minimized by taking steps to keep expansive soil dry. The first step is to make sure there is good natural drainage away from the pool. Joints between the coping and the deck, or between separately poured sections of the deck, can be sealed with a compressible expansion joint to keep water from seeping down between coping and deck sections.

A drainage system similar to one designed to remove underground water may also help keep excess moisture out of the soil.

Loose Fill—A pool installed in loose fill is a double risk. This problem will occur most often in newer housing developments where the terrain was recontoured.

A full pool can settle into loose fill and damage support equipment and the pool deck. An empty pool may be forced up out of the ground. When wet, loose fill will act almost as a liquid. The empty pool shell may float like a boat.

Sprayed-concrete pools are the most practical to install in loose fill. The common solution is to sink concrete piers through the loose fill and anchor them to rock or to footings poured in solid, stable soil. Rebar in the piers is tied into the rebar in the pool shell. When concrete is applied, the completed shell will be anchored to solid ground under the fill.

A soil test will show you the nature and depth of the fill. The pier system should be designed by a structural engineer. He can determine the dimensions necessary to support the weight of the filled pool.

Rock—Before deciding to excavate a site in excessively rocky soil or areas where you suspect solid rock, have a soils engineer make test borings every few feet at the pool site. This will determine what type rock exists below the surface and how extensive the rock really is. Some types of rock are easier to remove than others. For example sandstone is easier to remove than granite.

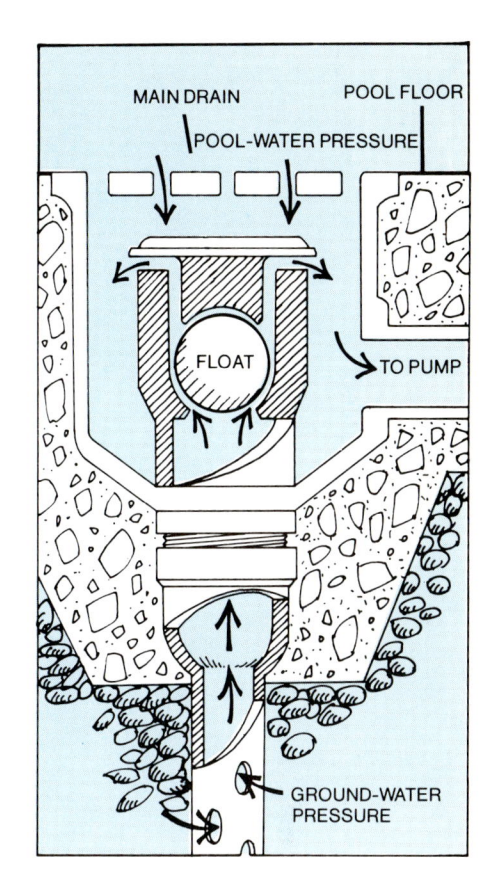

Get estimates on extra labor and equipment costs involved. Loose rock or heavier boulders may only require heavier excavating equipment. Solid or extensive rock could require expensive drilling an blasting. Hauling removed rock from the site will also be expensive.

If rock removal will add substantially to the excavating cost, look for an alternative site. If no rock-free or suitable site exists, consider an above-ground pool or a shallow pool. You will have the consolation of knowing rock provides the best possible pool foundation.

INSTALLING THE POOL

Every contractor will install a pool in a slightly different way. No two installations are exactly alike and no two pool builders approach a job exactly

HILLSIDE POOL DETAIL

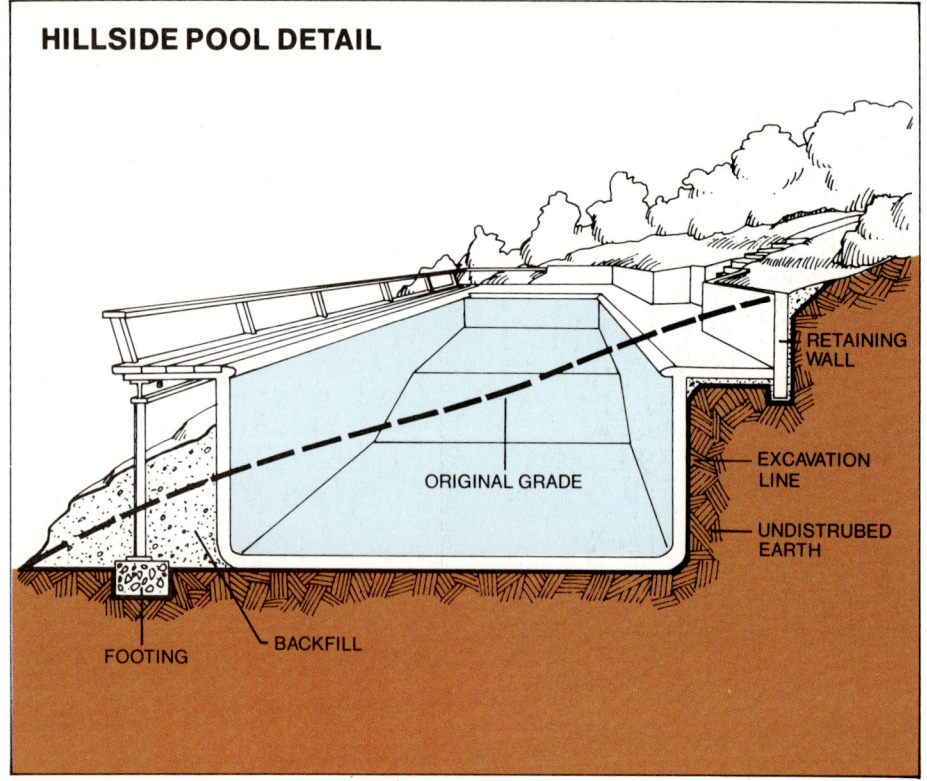

Hillside pools must rest on firm, undisturbed earth.

the same. Building sequences and techniques will depend on the builder's experience, the talents of the crew, the type of pool and its location, and the type of work assigned to subcontractors.

The following descriptions are for typical installations of sprayed-concrete, vinyl-lined and fiberglass pools. The sequences of steps listed are those most often used to prepare the site and install the pool.

SPRAYED-CONCRETE POOLS

Much of the preliminary work involved in installing a sprayed-concrete pool is the same as for other types. Some details, such as providing access and locating underground utility lines, may have been taken care of during earlier visits from the pool builder.

If overhead utility lines must be relocated or fences removed to provide access, this will be completed before the crew arrives to begin building the pool.

Prior to installation, some or all of the materials needed for the job will be delivered to the site. Typical materials include rebar, backfill sand, wood for pool and deck forms, pipes, fittings and other plumbing materials, and any prefabricated items that are installed during construction, such as prefabricated steps. Support equipment might also be delivered before building begins. It is not necessary to have all materials on hand before initial work begins, as long as necessary materials are available for each phase when the workers need them.

Ask the contractor what materials will be delivered and when. Plan where you'd like them stored. Ask that materials be delivered when you are at home. Most pool builders will take care not to damage the lawn or plants. Materials delivered directly from suppliers may not be handled as carefully.

The talents of the workers who will appear on the job involve steel tying, carpentry, concrete application and finishing, plumbing, electrical work, tile setting and plastering. When the first members of the crew arrive, work will follow the steps outlined below. Every step may not be completed in exactly this order and work on some steps will be progressing simultaneously.

Step 1—Basic site work is completed. This includes leveling the site, locating the exact position of the pool and establishing excavation lines.

Digging lines can be marked with flexible benderboards, stakes and string or a can of water-soluble spray paint. Benderboard forms are often used to indicate finished pool elevation, as shown in the photo at right.

Any necessary grading is completed at this time. Gently sloping terrain presents few unusual problems. A steeply sloped lot can create more complicated problems. The pool site will need to be leveled. As a general rule, the pool bottom should rest on solid, undisturbed ground.

This means a cut into the hillside may leave the uphill side of the pool below the slope of the land. A retaining wall may be needed to protect the uphill side. The downhill side may leave the side of the pool exposed above grade. The most important consideration is to make sure the bottom of the pool rests on solid ground, not excavated fill. Situate the pool so its length runs parallel to the slope of the land. This will reduce the amount of earth excavated. See drawing at left.

Step 2—The first bites into the ground are taken by the backhoe. Normally, the backhoe operator will work with another crew member standing on the ground to supervise excavating.

Excavating will continue until the rough shape of the pool is established. An efficient builder will scoop out the earth and drop it directly into a dump truck so it can be hauled away as excavating continues.

Step 3—As the rough cut is completed, the crew hand-shapes the pool to final dimensions using shovels and other handtools. Hand-shaping should be done while the backhoe is still at the site so as much excavated dirt as possible can be removed mechanically.

Hand-shaping includes preparing cuts for prefabricated steps or forms for poured steps. If pool walls are unstable, the builder may coat them with a light coat of gunite to hold the shape. The photos on page 81 show basic excavation procedures.

Step 4—Once the excavation has been shaped and cleaned, plumbing lines to the main drain are roughed in. A trench is cut from the drain location to the support-equipment location.

Step 5—Next, a gravel bed is laid in the excavation, then tamped and contoured to the shape of the pool bottom. Gravel depth will depend

Exact location of pool is marked with water-soluble spray paint. Benderboard forms are erected to indicate pool elevation above grade.

Pool site is graded; trees may be removed at this time. Backhoe does rough excavation. Final shaping is done with handtools.

Plumbing trenches are dug. In this installation, a trenching machine is used to cut trench from pool to support-equipment location. Worker at right is digging trenches in pool excavation for main drain and jet heads for pool-cleaning system.

Plumbing lines for drain, skimmer and return inlets are laid, and steel reinforcing (rebar) is placed. Skimmer and light niche are positioned. Note how rebar is used to form a continuous bond beam around the pool perimeter. In this installation, additional plumbing lines for attached spa are roughed in after rebar is in place.

largely on the type of soil and other variable conditions. Loose gravel 1 foot deep that can be compacted to 6 inches is typical.

Step 6—When the pool bottom has been tamped and leveled, rebar is cut, shaped and tied to form a web in the shape of the pool. Rebar is relatively soft steel that can be bent with a special tool or by using a length of steel pipe. It is cut with long-handled bolt-cutters.

Most builders use a #3 or #4 rebar. The size of the rebar grid will depend on the weight of rebar used, stress points and other structural considerations. Medium-weight tie wire is most commonly used to tie rebar together. The wire is soft and has little structural strength. Its function is to hold rebar securely in place until concrete can be applied.

In addition to using the correct-size rebar, the key to a strong structure is in making sure rebar overlaps are long enough, and there is adequate and uniform clearance between rebar and excavation walls and floor. The minimum rebar overlap should be 40 times the diameter of the bars. Rocks or masonry blocks can be used to support rebar to raise it above the pool floor so concrete can flow underneath it. The photo above shows completed rebar installation, including forms and rebar for bond beam (step 8).

Step 7—When the rebar has been tied, the remaining plumbing for the skimmer and stubs for the vacuum and return lines are roughed in. The skimmer and lines are supported by rebar and wired in place.

Step 8—Forms are built for the bond beam and the rebar positioned. Rebar in the pool shell is tied to rebar in the bond beam. When finished, the pool will be bonded into a single unit.

Step 9—The main drain is tied in place and plumbed. Drain and skimmer openings are masked so they won't be clogged when concrete is applied.

Step 10—Niches for underwater lights are wired in place and conduits

How Pools Are Built 81

Gun operator sprays initial coat of concrete underneath rebar, and a second coat over it, so the rebar is firmly embedded in concrete. This is the most exacting step in construction. The shell must be uniform in thickness with no voids.

Workers use mason's floats and trowels to do final shaping of sprayed-concrete shell.

are attached. The niches are masked to protect them when concrete is sprayed. Hardware used to attach pool ladders or other accessories to the shell is wired in place.

Step 11—When rebar and fittings are in position, gunite or shotcrete is sprayed through and around the rebar to form a solid pool shell. Depending on climate and soil conditions, the layer of gunite or shotcrete for pool walls is 4 to 6 inches thick. A thicker layer is often applied to coves and other stress areas. The same material is used to form a continuous bond beam around the pool perimeter. The average thickness for a bond beam is 12 to 14 inches. Shotcrete application is shown in the photo at left.

Step 12—Excess concrete is removed from around drains, skimmer, lights and other openings.

Step 13—If the pool is to be painted, the surface is troweled smooth. If the pool is to be plastered, the concrete is troweled with a wood or sponge float and left slightly textured to make a good bonding surface for the plaster.

Step 14—Tile is applied to the shell at the waterline. At this time, tile may be applied to steps, raised bond beams or any additional areas specified in the contract.

Step 15—Coping is installed. Coping can be precast concrete, stone, brick, tile or poured concrete. The coping for the pool being built here is poured integral with the deck. Polystyrene forms are placed when the deck is poured to form an overhanging lip around the pool perimeter. This sequence is shown in the photos on page 91.

Step 16—When the concrete shell has cured sufficiently to permit plastering, the finishing coats of plaster are applied to the inside of the pool. If the interior is to be painted, it may take several weeks before the concrete has cured well enough to paint.

Step 17—Before the deck is added, plumbing and wiring in and around the pool should be completed. Ground wires for underwater lights, pump motor and electric heater, if one is installed, are often tied to a projecting piece of rebar in the pool shell. All metal pool equipment—ladders, handrails, diving board—is also grounded this way. Once these steps have been taken, the support equipment can be installed, plumbed and wired independently of the work schedule on the pool.

Before plumbing trenches are filled, the plumbing may be tested for leaks. Depending on the job, plumbing and electrical inspections may be made at this time.

Step 18—Forms for the deck are completed and hardware for anchoring the diving board or pool ladders are positioned. The deck is poured or installed. The photo at right shows the deck installed and being given a coat of a concrete surfacing material, called *Kool Deck*. For more information on installing decks, see pages 92-94.

Step 19—When all plumbing and wiring are connected to the pool and stubbed out, the support equipment is set up and connected. Support equipment for all types of pools is installed and tested in much the same manner. See page 95.

Step 20—When the plaster has set, the pool is filled with water. The plaster will continue to cure after the pool has been filled. Plaster that hardens underwater is less likely to crack or check. When the pool has been filled, the support equipment is tested.

Step 21—The diving board and pool ladder are attached, if they have been included. Then the pool is manually cleaned to remove as much foreign material as possible before beginning the filtration cycle. A sprayed-concrete pool with a plaster finish will have more sediment and particles in the water than a vinyl-lined or fiberglass pool.

Step 22—Unless the builder is contracted to do any additional work, the final step will be to clean up the site around the pool and make a final test of the system to make sure everything's operating correctly. A good builder will make one or two follow-up calls after the pool has been in operation a few weeks.

When the pool is completed and filled with water, run the filter for an extended period of time. If a cartridge filter is being used, it may be necessary to replace the cartridge once plaster dust and other construction material have been filtered out of the pool water. Specific information on operating the filter and other support equipment is included on pages 134-135.

When the water is free of dirt and

Pool deck is poured. Tile is set around the waterline and in other areas specified in plans. Here, workers are applying concrete-surfacing material to deck.

Fittings for drain, return inlets, skimmer and light are installed. Pool shell is plastered. When plaster has set, pool will be filled with water and filtration system run to remove plaster dust and debris. The plaster is allowed to "cure" underwater for several days. Pool water is then chemically balanced and pool is ready to use. *Photo series courtesy of Patio Pools, Tucson, AZ.*

How Pools Are Built 83

Layout and excavation for vinyl-lined pools is the same as for other in-ground pools, except a shelf is cut to support sidewall panels. Here, excavation is complete and sidewall panels are being erected.

Sidewall braces are installed. Depending on soil conditions, braces may be set on concrete footings to provide additional support.

debris, add pool chemicals. You'll find directions for initial maintenance on pages 134-135.

VINYL-LINED POOLS

There is little difference in the basic techniques used to install the various types and shapes of vinyl-lined pools. Vinyl-lined pools differ only in design, type, and quality of materials and workmanship. They are all built on the same principle.

The site is excavated and contoured. Prefabricated wall panels of metal, wood, fiberglass or plastic are bolted together. A waterproof vinyl liner is installed. Filters, pumps and heaters are plumbed and wired. A deck is installed around the pool.

There is no agreement among pool builders as to the single best material to use for wall units. Some manufacturers offer a choice of panel materials to be ordered with the pool. Metal, fiberglass, plastic and pressure-treated wood are the most common. The advantages and disadvantages of each material are discussed on pages 26-27.

Once the pool has been ordered and contracts signed, a pool-company representative will arrive to evaluate the site. Some of this preliminary work may have been completed by the person negotiating the details of the sale and contract.

The purpose of the visit is to check access requirements, locate underground utility lines and sources for power and water. The representative will also make sure there is nothing obvious that can delay work when the crew arrives.

Before work begins, the pool will be delivered to the site. It will probably arrive strapped to a wood pallet. The disassembled components of even a large pool take up surprisingly little room.

One pallet may include all the components for a complete installation, including accessories and support equipment. If you are buying a separate pump, filter and heater from a pool dealer, these items may be delivered later. Other materials required for the job, such as backfill material, additional pipe and pool accessories, may also be delivered before initial work begins.

These are the steps that are usually followed to install a vinyl-lined pool:

Step 1—The exact location of the

pool on the property is determined. The site is leveled and digging lines established.

Step 2—Excavation begins. A backhoe is used to roughly shape the pool excavation. A backhoe operator and supervisor on the ground will work together to excavate to the depth and dimensions specified in the pool contract. For vinyl-lined pools, it is important that the depth and contour of the pool bottom be correct.

Because the pool sidewalls are erected independently, it is not essential that the excavation walls conform exactly to the pool shape. Room must be left behind the sidewall panels to provide access for panel assembly. During excavation, a trench is dug from the main drain location to the support equipment.

Step 3—If the pool will have a deep end, a shelf is cut around the perimeter of the excavation to support the sidewall panels. This work is usually done by hand. Soil in the shelf area should be firm and undisturbed.

The shelf for the panels should be leveled. This is a critical step. The panels should not slope. Also, if the shelf is too high or too low, the finished pool will not be flush with the finish grade level. The top photo on page 84 shows completed excavation for a vinyl-lined pool.

Step 4—If all or part of the sidewall will not sit on firm ground, concrete blocks are placed under the panel supports. If soil is unstable, a continuous concrete footing may be necessary to provide a firm shelf for the pool wall.

Step 5—Once a suitable base has been prepared for the walls, panels are bolted together and the step units positioned. Specific details for panel installation will vary, depending on the panel design. No two manufacturers design sidewall panels and other components exactly the same way.

Panels for most pools are supported by diagonal braces. These are usually installed at panel joints. Some manufacturers recommend panels be secured by setting the braces in concrete. Your pool dealer should be able to provide printed assembly instructions for your specific pool. The above photo shows a completed sidewall assembly.

Step 6—When the walls have been erected and secured, the bottom of the excavation is precisely contoured

When sidewalls are erected, plumbing is roughed in for drain, return inlets and skimmer. Skimmer and light niche are installed. Panels usually have cutouts for these fittings. Pool bottom is smoothed. On this installation, a thin layer of concrete is used to provide solid base for liner. Sand is also used.

Liner is installed. Installation details vary, depending on pool manufacturer. In this installation, liner is held in place by rigid-vinyl coping.

How Pools Are Built 85

Liner is smoothed tight against sidewalls. White hose at right is a vacuum. It is used to remove wrinkles between liner and sidewall.

The pool is filled with water. As water level rises, excavation is backfilled to equalize pressure on both sides of walls.

to the shape of the liner ordered.

Step 7—Plumbing is roughed in for main drain and skimmer. Most pool manufacturers provide wall sections with cutouts for underwater light niches and skimmer. These should be added before the liner is installed.

Step 8—When all rough plumbing is installed, the pool bottom is smoothed out. Rocks and other sharp objects that could puncture the liner are removed. Most manufacturers recommend placing an even layer of sand across the bottom. The depth of the layer will depend on the type of soil at the bottom of the excavation and how well it was contoured—2 to 4 inches of sand is usually sufficient.

Some builders prefer troweling an inch or two of cement or mortar evenly across the pool bottom, or pouring a concrete base. A relatively thin layer of mortar or concrete has little structural strength. Its purpose is to provide a hard, smooth and even base for the liner and to hold the main drain and other plumbing in place. A pool with a hard bottom won't show footprints and other indentations.

If a ground-water problem exists, a reinforced-concrete pool bottom will resist hydrostatic pressure that could deform or damage the vinyl liner. See pages 77-79 for information on soil and ground-water problems.

Step 9—After the pool bottom has been prepared, the liner is installed. A large, heavy liner can require the assistance of up to four helpers. It is spread over sidewalls and lowered into the pool. See photo on page 85.

Step 10—After the liner has been positioned, it is secured to the top of the pool wall. The system for attaching the liner varies from one manufacturer to the next. In some systems, a metal or plastic coping strip locks the liner in place. Some liners have a bead strip along the top edge that is clamped into the coping.

Some metal or plastic coping is designed to become an integral part of the pool deck when it is poured. Some systems use a plastic or polystyrene coping form to make an integral concrete coping. After the deck has been poured and the concrete set, the plastic form is removed, leaving the exposed concrete edge. Polystyrene coping forms similar to the one shown on page 91 are available for vinyl-lined pools.

Step 11—When the vinyl liner is in

position, irregularities and wrinkles are smoothed out. Some builders seal openings in the pool walls and use a heavy-duty vacuum to extract air from between the liner and walls to remove wrinkles. The liner can also be smoothed by hand as the pool is filled with water.

Step 12—When the liner is firmly in place, faceplates are attached through the liner to the main drain, skimmer, underwater lights and returns. The vinyl inside the openings is then cut out.

Step 13—When all plumbing and electrical lines are connected to the pool, the support equipment is installed and hooked up.

Step 14—The pool is filled with water. As the pool fills, the area behind the walls is backfilled. Backfill is firmly tamped as the water level rises. This helps equalize the pressure exerted on both sides of the pool walls, so the pool is less likely to collapse during the backfill process. Material used for backfill will vary, depending on soil conditions. In most cases, sand or clean fill is used.

Before trenches for plumbing lines are filled, the plumbing may be tested for leaks. Depending on the job, a plumbing inspection may be made at this time.

Step 15—When earth behind the pool walls has been leveled and final grade established, forms are completed for adding the deck. Some panels are designed to tie structurally into a poured pool deck. Panel braces have slots for placing rebar for deck reinforcing.

Step 16—When the deck forms are completed, the deck can be poured. For most vinyl-lined pools, the deck is an integral part of the pool and adds strength to the pool-wall structure.

Step 17—When the pool has been filled with water and the deck is completed, the support equipment should be tested. Testing is similar for all types of pools. See page 95.

Step 18—The pool site is cleaned up. Cleanup work can be done by the pool installer or the homeowner, depending on prior arrangements. Unless you've contracted additional landscape work with the installer, his job is through. The basic installation is now complete.

Step 19—If all the equipment is in order, the filter is turned on for an extended filtering cycle to remove dirt and debris from the pool water.

Forms are erected for pool deck and reinforcing mesh laid. Ladders, handrails and other permanent accessories are placed at this time.

Deck is poured. In this installation, concrete deck is poured flush to vinyl coping and interlocks with it. Support system is run to remove dirt and debris from water. Pool water is chemically balanced and pool is ready to use. *Photo series courtesy of Heldor, Morristown, NJ.*

Step 20—Once the water is free of construction dirt and dust, the filter is cleaned and chemicals added to the water. For details on initial maintenance for a new pool, see pages 134-135.

Pool site is excavated. A layer of sand is spread evenly across excavation bottom. Pool is delivered to site.

Crane lifts pool into excavation. On this pool, main drain and return inlets are preplumbed to pool shell with flexible PVC pipe.

Skimmer is attached and connected to preplumbed drain. Excavation is backfilled, keeping sand level even with water level as pool is filled with water. Sand is "flowed" into excavation, using water from garden hose.

Pool plumbing is attached to support equipment. Backfill is completed and site is graded. Forms are erected for pool deck.

Reinforcing wire for deck is laid. Permanent accessories are positioned and deck is poured. In this installation, the only accessory is a pool slide. No ladders or handrails were installed. Brace across pool keeps pool walls from bowing in while concrete cures.

Support equipment is run to remove remaining dirt and debris from water. Pool water is chemically balanced and pool is ready to use. Simulated brick pattern was applied to concrete deck for this pool. *Photo series courtesy of Swim Factory, Marietta, GA.*

ONE-PIECE FIBERGLASS POOLS

A one-piece fiberglass pool is the closest thing the swimming pool industry has to an instant pool. Site preparation is similar to work performed for sprayed-concrete pools. The pool builder will check the site for potential problems, locate underground utility lines, arrange for equipment access and take care of building permits, pool contracts and all other pre-installation details.

Any materials required for the job—except the fiberglass shell—are delivered to the site before the crew arrives to begin work. This may include support equipment and related plumbing. Plan where you want to store materials.

Once preliminary work has been done, the site is excavated. Then the installation crew arrives and the shell is moved to the site. It arrives in one piece ready to lower into the ground. An experienced crew can install the shell in a few hours. It often takes more time to install support equipment and pool accessories than it does to actually install the shell.

These are the basic steps that will be followed to install a one-piece fiberglass pool:

Step 1—The pool's exact location on the property is determined, the site leveled and graded, and digging lines established for the excavation.

Step 2—A backhoe is brought in to begin excavating. The cut for a fiberglass pool should be as accurate as possible. The pool should fit the excavation with a minimum of clearance and a minimum of backfill area.

Step 3—After the backhoe has completed the rough excavation for the pool, final shaping is done with shovels and other handtools. Hand-shaping the excavation is more exacting than for other types of pools. Extra care should be taken to remove rocks or other sharp objects that could puncture the fiberglass shell. The bottom of the excavation should be smoothed out to conform to the shape of the shell.

Step 4—A trench is dug from the main drain location to the support-equipment location and drain plumbing is roughed in.

Step 5—Sand or pea gravel is spread in the bottom of the excavation and contoured to the shape of the pool. Depending on soil conditions, the sand or gravel layer is 3 to 6 inches thick.

Step 6—The shell is lifted from the truck and lowered to the ground next to the excavation. Most fiberglass pools are *preplumbed* before they are lowered into the excavation. Lights, skimmer and pool fittings are attached to the shell. Skimmer and return lines are plumbed with PVC pipe. The plumbing lines are stubbed out on the shell to match the location of the trench leading to the support equipment once the shell is installed. Plumbing details vary with different models.

Step 7—The shell is lifted by the crane and lowered into the excavation. It is then leveled and adjusted to grade. On some installations, the shell is supported by wood braces to hold it in position.

Step 8—The main drain is attached to the drain plumbing. If the pool was not preplumbed, drain, skimmer and return lines are connected and stubbed out. The pool interior should be kept as clean as possible while the crew is working inside the shell.

Step 9—When the pool-shell plumbing has been completed, plumbing and electrical lines are run from the pool to the support-equipment location. Some builders may do this before backfilling begins, or after the excavation is backfilled up to the level of the plumbing stubs. At this point, support equipment can be set up and connected at any time, independent of the pool work schedule. A plumbing inspection may be required before the equipment trench is backfilled.

Step 10—The excavation around the pool is backfilled. Sand is usually used to backfill the gap between pool and excavation walls. As the sand is poured into the excavation, a light stream of water is used to flow the sand into voids around and under the pool. This is the most critical step in the installation. Any voids left under the shell can result in subsequent cracking and leaks. Using too much water should be avoided as it can cause the pool to shift or float in the excavation.

Most manufacturers recommend filling the pool shell with water as backfilling progresses, keeping the water level inside the pool and the backfill outside the pool at the same level. The pool should be cleaned before being filled with water.

Step 11—After backfilling, final plumbing and wiring is completed and all support equipment connected, if not already done. When the pool is full of water, the support equipment should be tested.

Step 12—Final backfilling and tamping is done. The area around the pool is smoothed, leveled and graded for pouring the pool deck. The deck is installed. If you're using a deck material other than poured concrete, some manufacturers recommend pouring a concrete collar around the pool to protect the backfill from the elements and facilitate water runoff.

Step 13—If the support equipment is operating correctly, it should be set for an extended filtering cycle.

Step 14—When the water appears clean, pool chemicals should be added and regular maintenance begun.

FIBERGLASS-SIDEWALL POOLS

The installation procedures for installing a fiberglass-sidewall pool are similar to those for installing a vinyl-lined pool. Excavation is essentially the same. The main differences are that the fiberglass-sidewall pool has a waterproof concrete bottom and the sidewall panels themselves form a watertight shell. No liner is required.

Preliminary site preparation and material deliveries are similar to those required for vinyl-lined pools. Sidewall panels and related pool accessories will be delivered by truck. Ask the pool builder how much storage space materials will require and when they'll be delivered.

Ready-mix concrete will be delivered by truck as the pool bottom is being poured. A typical pool takes four to six truckloads. The trucks will be arriving every 45 minutes or so, as the bottom is being poured.

Extra care must be taken in providing access for concrete trucks. They are much heavier than other trucks and equipment used for pool building. Fragile walks and patio areas should be avoided, or reinforced with planks.

How Pools Are Built **89**

1. Pool is located on site and excavated. Shelf is cut to support fiberglass sidewalls.

2. Fiberglass sidewalls are placed, braced and leveled. This pool uses rebar stakes for bracing. Reinforcing wire is placed in preparation for pouring concrete bottom. Plumbing for main drain is roughed in.

3. Concrete bottom is poured and hand packed to conform to final pool shape. Concrete is troweled to a smooth surface. Skimmer and return inlets are plumbed, skimmer and light niche installed in sidewalls.

4. Excavation is backfilled and permanent accessories are positioned. Deck is poured. Lengths of rebar tie sidewalls into concrete deck.

5. Concrete bottom is either plastered or given a coat of waterproof epoxy paint.

6. Pool is filled with water and filtration system is run to remove remaining dirt and debris. Water is chemically balanced and pool is ready to use. *Photo series courtesy of Hallmark Acrylic-Fiberglass Pools and Spas, Rolling Meadows, IL.*

These are the basic steps that will be followed to install a fiberglass-sidewall pool:

Step 1—The pool's exact location on the property is determined, the site leveled and graded, and digging lines established for the excavation.

Step 2—A backhoe digs the excavation to the approximate shape and size of the pool. The depth and contour of the pool bottom must be precise. The sides of the excavation are overdug by a specified amount to permit erection of the sidewalls. If the pool will have a deep end, a shelf is cut in the excavation wall to support the sidewall panels. The shelf must be level and at the correct height.

During excavation, a trench is dug from the main-drain location to the support-equipment location. Space is cut in the excavation for installing skimmer, underwater light and return inlets.

Step 3—Plumbing for main drain is roughed in and main drain is positioned. A layer of gravel is evenly spread over the pool bottom in preparation for the concrete.

Step 4—Reinforcing wire mesh is placed in the excavation up to the level of the sidewall location. One pool manufacturer recommends #10, 6x6" wire mesh.

Step 5—Skimmer, light niche and inlet fittings are attached to the sidewall panels. The sidewalls are then placed in the excavation, leveled and bolted together. Temporary braces may be installed for leveling purposes.

The sidewall panels will be embedded in about 6 inches of concrete when the pool bottom is poured. The sidewall panels are designed so they can be suspended slightly above the shelf. This allows concrete to flow under and behind them when the floor is poured. Usually, a length of rebar ties each panel to the concrete floor. Another piece of rebar ties the top of the panel into the concrete deck. Panels may require temporary bracing while concrete is poured.

Step 6—When the walls are assembled, the drain, skimmer and return inlets are plumbed and stubbed out at the support-equipment location. The underwater light is wired and grounded. Forms are built for concrete steps or prefabricated steps are installed.

Step 7—The concrete bottom is poured. This is the most critical step in building the pool. The first concrete truck will arrive and pour concrete into the pool bottom. The crew will then spread and *hand-pack* the concrete to conform to the desired shape of the pool bottom, using shovels and other handtools.

The concrete must be applied in an even layer and correctly tamped to remove all air bubbles in the mix. Typically, the concrete is 6 inches thick.

Where the floor meets the sidewalls, concrete is packed underneath and behind the walls, so about 6 inches of the wall is embedded in concrete. The skimmer and light niche are encased in concrete. The concrete pad for the support equipment is poured.

Step 8—The space behind the sidewalls is backfilled. Pea gravel or 1/2-inch crushed stone is recommended. When the excavation is backfilled to the correct level, prefabricated coping is attached to the sidewalls. Hardware for diving board, ladders and other permanent accessories are positioned in preparation for pouring the deck. All metal hardware components are grounded to the pool shell.

Step 9—The support equipment can now be set up and plumbed to the pool independent of the remaining work schedule on the pool. When the equipment is set up, plumbing and equipment is tested and inspected by the building inspector.

Step 10—The area around the pool is leveled and graded, and forms are installed for pouring the deck. The pool deck is then poured. The fiberglass sidewalls and prefabricated coping are designed to interlock with the concrete deck. Each panel is usually connected to the deck with a length of rebar.

Step 11—When the concrete in the pool bottom has set, it is coated with a waterproof, cement-base or epoxy sealant. Suitable sealants are recommended by the manufacturer. Some sealants can be applied as soon as the concrete as hardened; others can't be applied until the concrete has cured for a week or two.

Step 12—When the concrete bottom has been sealed, the pool is finished. Either you or the builder can fill the pool with water at this point. Unless the builder has been contracted to do additional landscaping work, the job is

Polystyrene coping forms (left) are used to make integral poured-concrete deck and coping. The finished deck is cantilevered over the pool edge. Photo at right shows worker troweling concrete surfacing material to provide textured finish. *Photos courtesy of Mortex Mfg. Co., Tucson, AZ.*

complete. The builder should make a final inspection and equipment test after the pool has been filled with water.

When the pool has been filled, run the filter for an extended period of time to remove construction dirt and debris from the water. If a cartridge filter is being used, it may be necessary to replace the cartridge once debris has been filtered out of the pool water.

When the water is free of dirt and debris, add pool chemicals. You'll find directions for initial maintenance on pages 134-135.

ADDING COPING

Coping is the cap on the pool wall that provides a finishing edge around the pool. Coping for sprayed-concrete pools is usually attached to the top of the bond beam. The pool deck is finished flush to the outside edge of the coping.

Concrete coping can be formed in place or ordered in a variety of prefabricated shapes, sizes and colors. Precast coping is usually porous and provides a good grip for swimmers and secure footing for diving. Precast coping units are set with mortar on top of the pool's bond beam, then the deck is laid or poured up to the coping.

Formed-in-place coping creates a cantilevered edge when the concrete deck is poured. To assure a perfect edge, prefabricated forms for pouring coping are available from pool suppliers. See photos above. An integral poured-concrete coping can be used on some types of vinyl-lined pools to create a more permanent appearance. Check with pool manufacturers to see if their pools have this option.

Vinyl-lined and fiberglass-sidewall pools come with prefabricated coping of extruded aluminum or heavy-gage rigid-vinyl. For most vinyl-lined pools, coping is an integral part of the system that secures the vinyl liner to the top of the pool wall. The deck is poured or formed to the edge of the coping. Installation varies, depending on the pool manufacturer. Some of these copings include a ceramic-tile strip glued onto them with waterproof mastic or silicone seal.

In practically all cases, the coping is installed before the deck is poured. *Bullnose* coping and similar designs are made so a concrete deck can be poured up to the edge of the pool. The coping often has a slight lip to prevent water from running back into the pool. For drainage, the deck is built with a slight slope away from the pool edge. This keeps rainwater, standing water or splashed-out water from draining back into the pool.

Other masonry materials can be used for coping. Brick and flagstone

Forms are also available to make integral poured-concrete copings for vinyl-lined pools. *Photo courtesy of Mortex Mfg. Co., Tucson, AZ.*

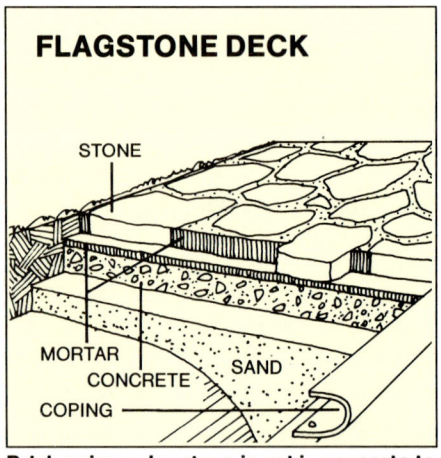

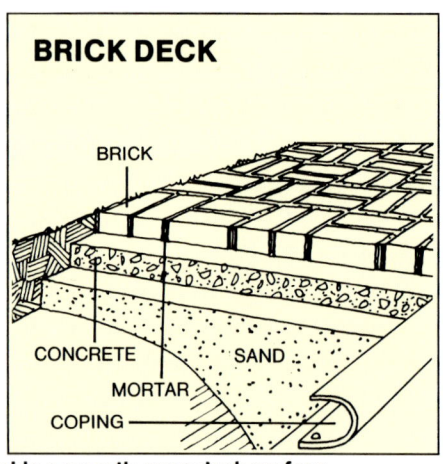

Brick or irregular stone is set in concrete to provide a smooth, even deck surface.

are two popular materials. If these materials are used as coping, they should not have sharp edges and should provide a suitable grip for swimmers climbing out of the pool. The material should be thick enough and the overhang designed so the coping will not break off.

ADDING THE DECK

Regardless of the type of pool you install, you have many options in deck designs and materials. Pool designers recommend a deck area at least equal to the surface area of the pool. Minimum deck width around the pool should be 3 feet.

A minimum-size deck makes it possible to walk around the perimeter of the pool without picking up grass or dirt that can be tracked into the pool. It provides firm footing for anyone cleaning or otherwise maintaining the pool.

How much space you wish to devote to a deck depends on the room you have around your pool and the type of activity you plan for the deck area. The amount of space allowed for adjoining decks or patios is also a consideration. A table and four chairs needs an area of about 10x10'. A lounge chair or sun bather needs at least 3x6' of deck space. Allow 3 additional feet between each lounger.

Extra room is required for a diving board. The National Spa and Pool Institute recommends a minimum 2-foot clearance behind a diving board. A standard board can extend 10 feet onto the deck area. In this case, the deck at the diving-board end of the pool should be at least 12 feet wide. See page 57.

Pool slides come in many different sizes. Curved slides that can be anchored to the deck parallel to the water take up as little as 3 feet of deck space. Straight slides need as much as 14 feet. An additional 2 feet of deck space along the sides and to the rear of the slide is required for walking room.

Just as you have many choices in deck size and design, there are many materials that make serviceable and attractive decks.

CONCRETE DECKS

Poured concrete is the most common and versatile deck material. Forms are relatively simple to build. In most areas, premixed concrete can be delivered to the site by truck, to eliminate on-site mixing. A properly reinforced concrete deck requires little maintenance and can be expected to last many years.

Some fiberglass and vinyl-lined pools are designed with a poured-concrete deck as an integral part of the pool structure. The deck adds strength to the pool walls.

The concrete surface can be finished in many different ways. A smooth-troweled finish can be too slick. It can be dangerous when it is wet. A rough broom finish may be too abrasive. It provides good footing, but can cause scrapes when falls occur.

Concrete finished with a wood float can be a happy medium—enough texture for good footing, but not too abrasive. Other troweling techniques, such as sprinkling salt over the fresh concrete and troweling it, make a smooth but skidproof surface.

Exposed aggregate is one of the most popular finishes for concrete decks. The pebble effect is attractive, and provides a good non-slip, low-glare surface.

Surfacing Materials—Concrete surfacing materials are manufactured under several different trade names. One popular brand is called *Kool Deck*. The material comes in several colors. It is applied like plaster over a finished concrete slab. It has a porous, non-skid surface that feels cooler underfoot than concrete and most other masonry materials. Concrete-surfacing materials are popular in hot climates where other masonry materials can burn bare feet.

OTHER MASONRY MATERIALS

Though concrete is the most common deck material, brick, stone or tile may also be used. When used for a pool deck, these masonry materials are best laid on a level concrete slab. The slab provides a solid, clean base and facilitates water drainage away from the pool.

Brick—There are a number of types and colors available. Brick can be laid in many different patterns to form

Large multilevel deck provides ample room for poolside activities. *Design: Gary Pools Inc., San Antonio, TX.*

Exposed-aggregate concrete provides a slip-resistant, non-glare deck surface. The surface is obtained by brushing and hosing poured concrete surface as it cures. This exposes the aggregate, or gravel, in the concrete. *Design: Barnett-Hendricks Pools Inc., Cherry Hill, NJ.*

Several manufacturers make concrete surfacing materials that are cooler underfoot than most other masonry materials. These materials come in several colors and provide a slip-resistant deck surface. The material used for this pool is called *Kool Deck*. *Design: Patio Pools, Tucson, AZ.*

Brick is a popular deck material because of its versatility. It comes in many colors and can be used in many ways. Here, brick blends pleasingly with natural stone to create striking pool surroundings. *Design: Aquatic Pools, Sherman Oaks, CA.*

pleasing designs. It can be laid with or without mortar joints. The specific type of brick used will depend on the local supply.

Half-size bricks, called *pavers,* are often used for pool decks and patios. They are half the thickness of ordinary bricks and are usually less expensive.

Stone—Flagstone, slate or similar natural materials make attractive deck surfaces. Stone in irregular sizes can be fitted with a minimum of cutting and shaping. Stone is also available in precut squares or rectangles in standard thicknesses.

Because natural stone is difficult to find in perfectly uniform pieces, a concrete slab is poured to provide a solid base. Then individual pieces of stone are laid in wet mortar to compensate for irregularities. See drawing on page 92.

The type of natural stone and its cost vary widely from one geographical area to another. Much of the expense of using flagstone or slate is in shipping. Stone acquired locally will be much less expensive than stone shipped from any distance.

Tile—This material is the most ver-

How Pools Are Built 93

Flagstone is one of the most beautiful—and expensive—materials for pool decks. It can be rough on bare feet, depending on the type of stone used and how it's laid. Flagstone decks are often cantilevered over the pool edge to eliminate coping. The stone should be laid so pieces won't break off around the pool edge. *Design: Johnson Pool & Construction Co., Huntsville, AL.*

Wood can be used for a pool deck if pressure-treated with wood preservative. This wood deck fits well into its woodsy setting. *Design: Town & Country Pools, Sringfield, VA.*

Unglazed quarry tile is a perfect choice for a Spanish or Mediterranean look. Ceramic tile for pool decks should be slip-resistant and made for outdoor use. In cold areas, unglazed tile should be treated with a water sealer to prevent cracking due to freezing and thawing. *Design: Boca Pool Lab Inc., Boca Raton, FL.*

satile for a deck surface. It can also be the most expensive. Use a slip-resistant unglazed or semiglazed tile manufactured for outdoor use. Outdoor tiles include quarry tile and patio tile, and are available in many colors and designs.

Tile used for a pool deck must be set in mortar on a solid concrete base. Any movement in the deck will cause tile to crack. Unglazed tiles must be sealed to resist moisture, especially in cold climates where freezing can crack the tiles.

If you choose to use tile on a deck, order additional tiles for replacement purposes. One of the disadvantages of tile is that it is brittle. It can be broken if struck by a heavy object. Tile colors vary and individual designs can't always be duplicated. If you have extra tile available, it will make repairs simpler.

WOOD DECKS

Wood can be incorporated into a total pool design, but is seldom used exclusively as deck material. The obvious problem with wood is splintering. Wood exposed to sun and weather requires regular maintenance. One advantage of wood is that it is slower to absorb heat and it holds heat for a shorter time than masonry materials. This makes it cooler underfoot on hot days.

Wood decks should be designed for good drainage. Use a naturally decay-resistant wood, such as redwood, or a wood that has been pressure-treated with a wood preservative.

In planning the deck, your pool builder will be able to suggest a number of options in deck materials. Your final choice may be largely for esthetic reasons. The deck should complement other patio or deck areas, walks, walls and the house itself. A well-designed deck will integrate the pool design into the landscape and enhance the general appearance of your home.

Pouring or laying a masonry pool deck requires the same techniques as laying a patio. Although pool contractors often include a minimal deck as part of the pool installation, it can be a do-it-yourself project. A helpful guide to laying different kinds of decks and patios is HPBooks' *Patios & Decks, How to Plan, Build & Enjoy,* by Michael Landis and Ray Moholt.

SETTING UP SUPPORT EQUIPMENT

The pool's pump, filter and heater can be positioned and the components plumbed together at any time during the pool installation, provided the equipment site has been prepared. When the equipment is actually plumbed to the pool depends on the installation. Refer to the building sequence in this chapter for the pool you're installing. Most often, the equipment is set up after all trenches have been dug to the equipment location.

Practically all modern systems use 1-1/2-inch or larger diameter PVC pipe. The only part of the system that must be metal pipe is a code-required section of the return line from the pool heater outlet. In colder climates, all exposed pipes are usually insulated against freeze damage. Local pool dealers will be able to recommend other winterizing measures for the equipment.

LOCATING THE EQUIPMENT

If you haven't already chosen a location for the equipment, choose one now. The closer the equipment is to the pool, the more efficiently it will operate and the less costly it will be to plumb. See page 46.

The equipment will require a solid, level foundation. A 2-inch-thick pad of poured concrete or 2-inch-thick precast concrete patio blocks is adequate for most standard equipment. The pad should be laid on a 2-inch bed of sand. The top of the pad should be several inches above ground level to allow water runoff. Depending on your pool design, you may want to encircle the equipment with a patio or the pool deck, build a wall around it, or enclose it in a shed. This work is best done after the equipment is plumbed to the pool.

Some pump manufacturers recommend that the pump be installed so the water inlet is below the water level of the pool. Ask the pool dealer if the pump you bought requires this, and locate equipment accordingly.

BASIC INSTALLATION

The following steps outline the procedure for setting up and plumbing a basic support system—single pump, filter and heater. A number of variations exist, depending on the type of equipment and accessories you've chosen.

As you add accessories, such as auxiliary pumps for waterfalls or fountains, a spa, an automatic pool-cleaning system, solar heating, automatic chlorinator and programmable controls, plumbing and wiring the support system become increasingly complex. These and other options are discussed in the chapter, *Selecting Pool Equipment,* pages 43-57. A diagram of a basic support system is shown on page 43.

Once the site is prepared, the equipment is generally installed as follows:

Step 1—During excavation, trenches are run from the pool excavation to the equipment location and from the equipment location to gas and electrical hookups.

Step 2—Pump, filter and heater are arranged on the equipment pad so they can be easily plumbed together. They are then mounted on the pad, according to manufacturer's instructions. Smaller pools and above-ground pools may use equipment with pump, filter and heater preplumbed as a single unit, eliminating steps 3 and 4 below. Such preplumbed equipment is called a *skid pack*. A skid pack has the advantages of easy installation and matched components.

Step 3—The pump is plumbed to the filter, from the pump outlet to the filter inlet. A valve may be installed at this location for draining the pool or backwashing sand or DE filters.

Step 4—The filter is plumbed to the heater. A line is run from the filter outlet to the cold water inlet on the heater, if the pool will have a one. A check valve is often installed between the heater and filter so heated water won't flow back into the filter and ruin it.

Step 5—If the support equipment includes an active solar-heating system, a line is run from the filter through the solar collectors and back to the equipment location. If the solar collectors aren't generating enough heat to sufficiently heat the water, an automatic valve diverts the filtered water directly to a backup heater, if the system includes one. A diagram of a typical solar-heating system is shown on page 62.

Step 6—Plumbing lines are run from the pool's skimmer or skimmers and main drain to the pump inlet. Regulator valves may be installed in the line near the pump inlet to balance water suction between skimmer and drain, or to operate an automatic vacuum, if the pool has one. Additional regulator valves will be required if the pool has an attached spa using the same equipment.

Step 7—Return lines are run from the heater outlet to the water-return inlets in the pool. Many heaters are installed with an automatic bypass so water won't flow through the heater when it's not in use. Some brands of automatic chlorinators are installed in the return line, downstream of the heater. Valves may be installed in the main return line to regulate water flow through branch lines to pool inlets, automatic pool agitator, or to an attached spa.

Step 8—Electric lines are run from the support-equipment location to an electrical subpanel, which includes a switchbox and time clock or programmable timer to operate the equipment. Underwater lights and other electric pool accessories are also wired to this location. The subpanel is then wired to the main-service panel at the house. If the equipment includes a gas heater, a gas line is run from the heater to the gas meter. All electrical connections should be made by a licensed electrician. All circuits should be protected with a ground fault circuit interrupter (GFCI).

Step 9—When all final connections have been made, the plumbing is tested for leaks. The gas line is pressure-tested and equipment is tested to make sure it's connected correctly.

Step 10—When all tests are completed, plumbing and electrical inspections are made by the local building department. Trenches are filled and the pool deck can be installed.

Above-ground pools adapt well to hillside locations. *Design: Jerry L. Pollak, Sherman Oaks, CA.*

CHAPTER 7

Above-Ground Pools

Almost half of all swimming pools in the United States are above-ground pools. There are several reasons why so many families have chosen to install this particular type of pool.

The basic above-ground pool is usually a third to half the cost of an in-ground pool of comparable size. It requires minimal site preparation. It can be a do-it-yourself project, which can save additional money. Pool kits include complete assembly instructions.

Most above-ground pools are portable. If you're not satisfied with where the pool has been installed, you don't have to live with your mistake. The pool can be dismantled and moved.

Early above-ground pools were often built of low-quality, lightweight materials that did not stand up to heavy use. Significant improvements in structural design, vinyl liners and quality of workmanship have produced sophisticated pools that can provide many years of service. Pumps, filters, ladders and other support equipment are manufactured to the same standards as equipment sold for fine in-ground pools.

Lower initial cost is the primary reason homeowners buy above-ground pools. There are other advantages that are only marginally related to cost.

Pools available in kit form can be purchased and installed in a few days. For a family anticipating a future move or the sale of a house, an above-ground pool offers a reasonable alternative to installing a permanent in-ground pool.

For families renting a home, an above-ground pool makes it possible to enjoy a temporary swimming facility that can be moved at a later date.

An above-ground pool can be a practical solution to difficult installation problems. You can install an above-ground pool in locations where rocky terrain would make excavating excessively expensive. An above-ground pool is also suitable where a high water table requires expensive solutions to drainage problems.

There are a few disadvantages to owning an above-ground pool. The pool, usually 3-1/2 to 4 feet deep, will be a dominant feature of any backyard. Diving is not possible in many above-ground pools. Suppliers of these pools attach "no diving or jumping" signs to their pools.

Because the pool bottom rests on the ground, an above-ground deck makes landscaping more challenging. It isn't easy to blend an above-ground pool into the scenery.

Landscaping for most above-ground pools installed on flat ground consists of planting flowers and shrubbery around the pool. Pool exteriors are available in many styles. Skirts designed to hide the below-deck structure and equipment are usually metal or plastic. They are available in many designs and patterns. Lattice work also makes a good pool screen.

An above-ground pool is more costly to heat than an in-ground pool. It is more difficult to prevent heat loss through the sides of a typical above-ground pool. A few models are available with insulated walls that will help prevent heat loss. Solar blankets and pool covers can greatly reduce heat lost to the air.

In colder climates, many manufacturers recommend that the pool be drained and the support equipment stored for the winter. The pool owner should follow the manufacturer's recommendations.

An above-ground pool has a limited lifetime and its value will not appreciate like an in-ground pool, which is considered a permanent addition to a home. The value of an in-ground pool will rise or fall in proportion to the value of the home. An above-ground pool may or may not contribute to home value, depending on the pool's condition and its popularity with prospective buyers when you sell the house. Above-ground pools are more popular in some areas of the country than others.

In most communities, an above-ground pool is not considered a permanent addition and is not taxed as a home improvement. It also won't

Above-Ground Pools

Pool must rest on firm, undisturbed soil.
EXISTING GRADE

Deck for above-ground pool allows swimmers to enter pool without use of ladder. Safety railing is required for hillside installations like this. Check local code requirements. Some excavating will be required to provide flat area for pool (see inset).

add to the appraised home value. It can be an asset in a home sale if the buyer wants to have the pool included in the sale. Or, you can dismantle the pool and take it with you when you move.

CHOOSING A SITE

Planning the installation of an above-ground pool involves many of the same steps necessary to plan an in-ground pool. Most steps are less complicated. The major difference in planning and installation is that most above-ground pools sit on the ground and are considered temporary structures.

LEGAL RESTRICTIONS

Code restrictions and zoning limitations for temporary above-ground pools usually aren't as specific as for in-ground pools. In some communities, requirements for above-ground pools are not included in building codes. In other areas, building covenants adopted by local homeowner's associations or deed restrictions that may allow in-ground pools will not permit above-ground installations.

Before buying your pool, check with your local building department to see if a building permit is required and if there are local code restrictions that may apply. Your local pool dealer will also be able to provide general information on restrictions or limitations in your area. Restrictions on water use or waste-water disposal may be the same for above-ground pools as for in-ground pools.

In selecting a site on your property, make sure the pool will not be placed directly over water and utility lines, a septic tank or leach field. A full pool is heavy. One cubic yard of water weighs 3/4 ton. A pool filled to 4 feet in depth has a downward pressure of 250 pounds per square foot. The weight could damage underground lines.

Don't place the pool directly beneath overhead utility lines. If there is no acceptable alternative site, the utility lines should be relocated.

THE PERFECT SPOT

The site itself should be perfectly level. If there is a slope, plan to remove enough earth to make a flat, level area for the pool. Don't place the pool on loose fill as it will compact the earth and cause a pressure imbalance on the pool's sidewalls. Provide natural drainage away from the pool.

Sharply sloping land may actually be more suitable for an above-ground pool than an in-ground pool. Above-ground pool walls are structurally designed to withstand the outward pressure of water in the pool without the opposing support of backfill or an integrated concrete deck.

An above-ground pool built on a slope makes it possible to build a deck on the uphill side so the pool can be entered without climbing steps or a ladder. An above-ground pool can be made to look like an in-ground pool when seen from the uphill side. The exposed structure on the downhill side can be screened with a fence, lattice, decorative siding or plants.

Because the sidewalls of an above-ground pool are exposed, it is harder to insulate them from heat loss due to wind. A house can provide some wind protection. A pool built next to a house will usually be more esthetically pleasing.

Other site considerations that are desirable for in-ground pools are equally useful in picking a site for an above-ground pool. Review the information on choosing a pool site, starting on page 9.

Situate the pool so it gets maximum exposure to the sun. This takes advantage of natural heat gain and can extend the swimming season. Most above-ground pools are chosen for summer use only. Because of their low initial cost, most are not equipped with heaters. Regular use of a pool blanket or solar cover will trap the sun's heat during the day and help hold the temperature at comfortable levels overnight.

When possible, avoid placing the pool under or near trees. Falling leaves make it difficult to keep the pool clean. The elevated pool walls will help keep blown debris out of the pool.

THE PRIVACY PROBLEM

The height of the pool walls make it difficult to provide privacy. It may be possible to locate the pool so the nearby house or another existing building blocks the view of neighbors or from the street. High fences, walls or screens that meet local codes may be capable of hiding the pool, but can be unsightly in themselves.

One solution is to accept the fact that swimmers may have little privacy entering and leaving the pool. A ground-level deck or patio area can be built near the pool to provide privacy for sunning and relaxing. Trees or tall shrubs can be selectively placed to block views of the pool from outside the property. They can also make the pool less obtrusive in the yard. For more on poolside plantings, see pages 107-108.

CHOOSING A POOL

In choosing a pool, the first step is to find a dealer. The second step is to decide what specific type of pool to buy. Many options are available.

Above-ground pools are available

98 Above-Ground Pools

from pool dealers who sell and install several different types of pools. They are available through some hardware and department stores. It's possible to order a pool from a mail-order catalog. Above-ground pools come in several styles and shapes, with a variety of accessories and in many different price ranges.

WHERE TO BUY

There are at least as many outlets for above-ground pools as for in-ground pools. Begin by asking for specific recommendations from friends or neighbors who have installed above-ground pools. How satisfied are they with their pools? Ask them about the dealer, the quality of the pool itself, and any specific problems they have had with the pool. An above-ground pool may cost less than an in-ground pool, but it can still be a major investment.

If you are unable to get recommendations from friends, check the Yellow Pages in the phone book for the names and locations of pool dealers. On request, the National Spa and Pool Institute will provide a list of participating dealers in your geographical area. Their address is 2111 Eisenhower Ave., Alexandria, VA 22314.

Some pool dealers will have sample pools installed that you can see. Dealers with no working samples should be able to arrange for you to see pools they have sold. All dealers should have samples of the materials used in their pools.

Pick up the available literature. If you have questions about installation, ask to see the instructions that come with the pool kit. Make sure you have a clear understanding of what components are included in the basic pool price. Which components are essential? Which are optional?

Check the quality of pool materials. Compare material thicknesses, weights and finishes. Sharp edges should be shielded. Precision-made components assure proper fit and simplify assembly. Check vinyl-liner thickness. The industry standard for vinyl liners is 20mm. A good-quality liner should carry at least a 10-year warranty.

The pool cost should be in direct relationship to the quality of materials. The least expensive pool may not be the best value. The investment

Privacy is often a problem with above-ground pools. This pool is completely enclosed by raised deck, railing and fence. Ample space is provided for poolside furniture. *Design: Aqua-Rama of Atlanta, Marietta, GA.*

equipment will be justified by longer pool life and minimal equipment problems. Check the availability of specific models and delivery times.

Before deciding to buy from a specific dealer, contact the Better Business Bureau to see if any complaints have been filed against the dealer. Reputable dealers welcome such inquiries.

Some national department store chains sell above-ground pools in their stores or through their mail-order catalogs. If you've been satisfied with the store's products and service in the past, you may want to buy your pool from them.

An advantage to buying from a large, established chain is that they will take care of problems arising from product defects. Local outlets or representatives will provide follow-up services or replace defective parts. If you hold a store credit card, this gives you a financing option.

Established pool dealers can provide the same services as national department stores. They also offer additional advantages. Dealers in the pool business are specialists with experience in servicing the pools they sell.

A pool dealer will also be able to recommend efficient and effective support equipment. A good dealer will also stock many of the accessories you would like to include in the original purchase or acquire later. Pool dealers also stock the necessary chemicals, water-quality test kits and cleaning equipment needed to maintain a clean pool.

Whether you buy from a retail chain or a local pool dealer, check the pool warranty. Warranties list individual pool components and the length of time each is protected. Typical components covered include pool walls and structure, the vinyl liner and support equipment.

Established dealers representing quality products can be expected to be in business to honor warranties for many years to come. Be suspicious of exceptionally long warranties offered by companies new to the pool business. They may not be around in a year or two to take care of warranty problems.

If you plan to install your own pool, a good dealer will provide technical advice or help if problems arise during installation. Many dealers provide installation service. Those who don't can usually recommend a competent installer.

Establishing a good relationship with a local dealer will help guarantee continuing follow-up service.

WHAT TYPE OF POOL?

All above-ground pools are similar in construction and design. They vary only in size and shape, and in the quality and type of materials.

Above-Ground Pools 99

Spacious deck addition provides separate lounging area, adds beauty to standard above-ground installation. *Design: Olympic Pools, Toledo, OH.*

Rectangular and oval pools come in stock sizes from 12x20' to 20x40'. Octagonal or round pool sizes run from 15 to 28 feet in diameter. For pools designed to rest on the ground, the most common depth is 4 feet. On-ground pools are available in depths up to 4 feet, 8 inches.

Round or Rectangular?—The first above-ground pools were round. The reasons for building round pools are still valid today. A round pool is less expensive to manufacture. It contains the greatest volume of water with the smallest surface area. Outward pressure against the supporting walls is equalized so pool walls don't need complicated bracing. A cylinder is the strongest geometrical design for a container.

Oval and rectangular above-ground pools evolved out of a demand for more versatile pools and more esthetically pleasing designs.

Inherent structural weaknesses in rectangular and oval designs have been compensated for by using diagonal supports along the flat walls. Stronger bottom and top rails also contribute to stability.

Models installed as permanent pools may call for poured-concrete footings to secure the bottom rails. In some models, the surrounding pool deck is an important structural component in providing wall support. Well-designed rectangular and oval pools, properly installed, will provide years of trouble-free service.

Choices of Materials—Pool walls are prefabricated in panels of aluminum, galvanized steel, wood and reinforced fiberglass or plastic. They are similar to the panels built for in-ground vinyl-lined pools, described on page 27.

Higher-quality metal pools use extruded aluminum for walls. It is stronger than rolled-aluminum sheet. Galvanized steel panels should be protected with a rust-inhibitive primer and finished with baked-enamel paint. Wood panels should be pressure-treated with a non-toxic wood preservative.

Plastic and fiberglass panels are relatively new. They are lightweight and corrosion resistant. Panels are being made with insulation to help reduce heat loss.

Sidewall panels come in many different colors and designs. Simulated wood, wood shake and solid colors are the most common. Although individual manufacturers may produce pools with a variety of panels, most models come with a specific type and color of wall panel. Choices are limited.

Significant improvements in vinyl liners have extended the life of above-ground pools. Modern liners are more resistant to ultraviolet light and pool chemicals. They are also more flexible and capable of conforming to pool-bottom irregularities. They are less affected by cold and are less likely to tear or crack.

The quality of the liner will be reflected by the manufacturer's guarantee. A good-quality liner should be guaranteed for at least 10 years.

Pools With Deep Ends—A few manufacturers of above-ground pools offer models that include a deep end for diving. They are installed similarly to other above-ground pools except that the deep end, or hopper area, is below ground. This requires excavating and shaping the deep end to accept the pool's vinyl liner. The pool's sidewalls and structural components are installed at ground level.

While these pools do offer the option of diving, they defeat some of the initial advantages of installing an above-ground pool.

CHOOSING SUPPORT EQUIPMENT

Larger above-ground pools use the same basic equipment as in-ground pools to provide clean water, free of contaminants and debris. The primary difference is most above-ground pools aren't equipped with heaters.

The basic reasons for selecting one system over another will be the same for above-ground pools as for in-ground pools. Complete details on selecting a specific pump, filter, heater and skimmer start on page 43. Many above-ground pools come with a basic package of preplumbed, matched support components, called a *skid pack*.

Pool suppliers can recommend pumps and filters with specific capacities, based on size of the pool and number of users. Pumps, pump motors, filters and heaters will usually carry their own warranties.

Most above-ground pool packages are sold without heaters. The same basic heaters that are used to heat in-ground pools can be adapted to the support equipment of an above-ground pool. Heaters for above-ground pools are sized and selected the same way as for in-ground pools. See page 50.

ACCESSORIES

The accessories included in the basic price of a pool vary from manufacturer to manufacturer. Determin-

Round pools usually require no bracing. Sidewalls come in many colors and patterns. Solar blankets are also available for heating pool water. *Photo courtesy of Cantar Corp., Carlstadt, NJ.*

Many above-ground pool kits come complete with surrounding deck and railing. On this model, railing is an extension of braces used to support sidewalls. *Design: Olympic Pools, Toledo, OH.*

ABOVE-GROUND POOL LADDERS

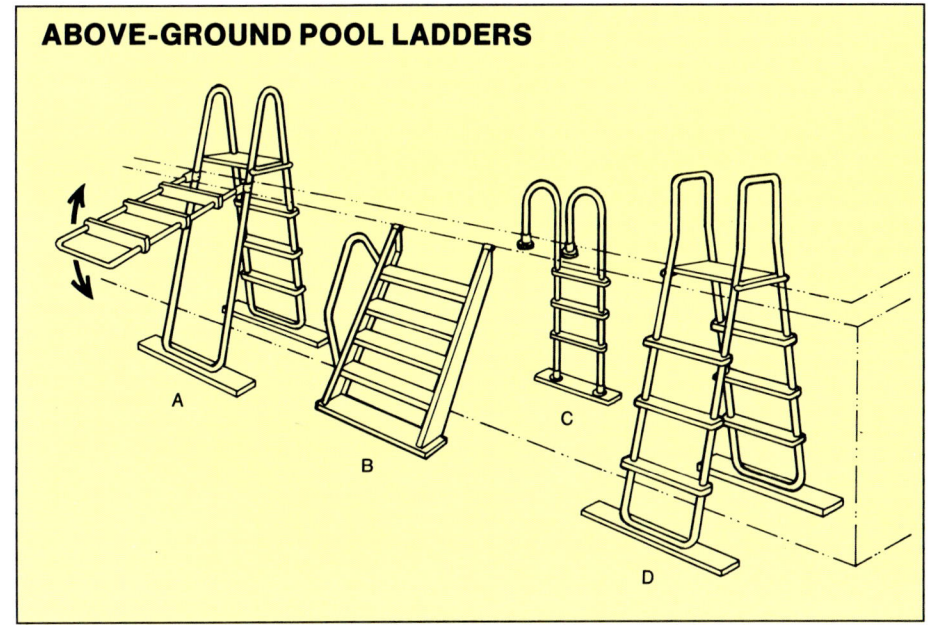

Pool ladders for above-ground pool include: A. Limited-access ladder; B. Deck ladder; C. In-pool ladder; and D. Double-access ladder.

ing the price of a pool is similar to buying a new car. You start with the basic model and select the optional items you would like included in the delivered package. In defense of the manufacturer, few pool buyers would agree on exactly which components are necessary to make the perfect pool.

When comparing pools, find out which items each manufacturer includes as standard equipment in the basic pool package. Items offered as standard equipment will vary between manufacturers. Make sure that standard items include all components necessary to build the pool and use it. For instance, a ladder or other means of entering the pool may be listed as optional equipment, but should be figured into the basic price.

For above-ground pools larger than wading-pool size, basic support equipment—pump, filter, skimmer and related plumbing—is standard. Beyond that, there is a long list of options and accessories. The most common are heaters, ladders, decks, fences and pool covers.

More exotic extras include automatic pool vacuums, automatic skimmers, underwater lights and automatic water chlorinators. A wide variety of games and pool toys is also available.

Basic safety equipment and safe pool use are the same regardless of the type of pool. Follow the basic pool safety rules described on pages 149-152. Above-ground pools have one safety advantage over in-ground pools. The high pool walls make it unlikely small children can tumble into the pool by accident.

To prevent unauthorized swimmers from entering the pool, install a removable access ladder that can be drawn up or stored when the pool is not in use. Above-ground pools with fenced decks can be closed off with a gate. Deck-level fences satisfy most safety codes. Check with your building department to verify local code requirements. A local pool dealer will also be aware of applicable codes in your area.

HOW TO INSTALL YOUR POOL

Pool manufacturers provide detailed, illustrated instructions with each pool. Specific instructions will vary depending on the pool model, size and structural design. A majority of pools will be built as described in the following text.

SITE PREPARATION

When you've chosen a location for the pool, the site is leveled. Remove rocks, stones, roots and other debris. An inch or two of sand provides an

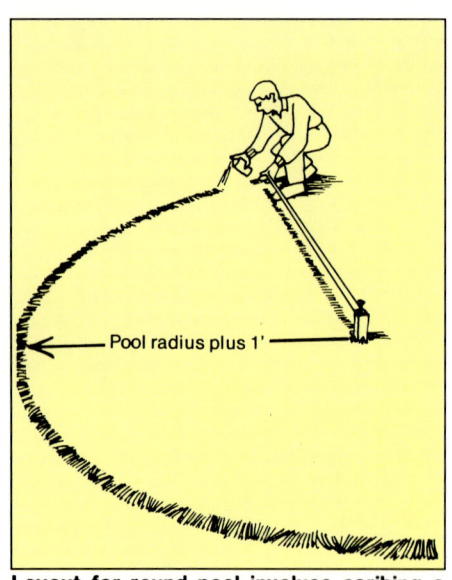

Layout for round pool involves scribing a circle and marking with spray paint.

ideal cushion for the vinyl liner. Porous sand will allow some drainage. The area around the pool should be graded or contoured so surface water will flow away from the pool.

Remove sod and soil to the lowest point in the pool area. Don't level the site by filling in low spots. The pool's weight will compact the earth. An uneven site can rupture the liner or buckle pool walls. Loose topsoil should be tamped and compacted. You can rent a hand-operated or power tamper at a tool-rental company.

One of the advantages in installing an above-ground pool is that you needn't worry about subsurface soil conditions that make excavating for an in-ground pool a problem. Extreme conditions, like springs or underground water that make soil soggy or unstable, may require special drainage provisions. See pages 78-79. If you suspect the soil at the site will not support the weight of the pool, have a soils engineer conduct a soil test and recommend a solution to the problem.

If excavation involves removing more than a few inches of soil, such as on a hillside, you may want to hire an excavation company. They will have the right equipment to do the job quickly and accurately. It will save you time and labor.

Once the basic pool area has been cleared and leveled, the site should be staked and marked out for the pool.

Round Pools—To prepare a site for a round pool, drive a stake in the ground at the centerpoint of the pool location. Using the stake as a pivot point, attach a line or tape measure and scribe a circle approximately 2 feet larger than the inside diameter of the pool. Example: For a 20-foot pool, measure a radius of 11 feet from the center stake to make a circle of 22 feet. A can of water-soluble spray paint can be used to mark a highly visible circle.

Use a long straightedge and a carpenter's level to help level the site. The uncut edge of a sheet of plywood provides a good 8-foot straightedge. Cut a strip 6 to 12 inches wide along the length of the sheet. Use the uncut edge as the straightedge. Long lengths of dimensional lumber, such as 1x4s or 2x4s usually don't make good straightedges for this purpose. They are not rigid enough and are seldom perfectly straight.

The site is leveled in much the same way you would prepare a site for pouring a concrete slab. Light surface dirt can be leveled with a *screed*—a straight board pulled across the site to level high spots. Loose dirt should be tamped firm.

Rectangular Pools—The quickest and most accurate method of establishing the site for a rectangular pool is to establish the pool outline with stakes and string, and square the four corners where strings intersect. To make corners square, use the *3-4-5 right-triangle method*. Any triangle with sides measuring 3, 4 and 5 feet or multiples of these numbers will form an exact 90° angle. See the drawing on page 103.

Drive the first stake at one corner of the pool site. Pick a corner closest to the house or some other fixed object on the property. Tap a nail into the top of the stake, with the nailhead protruding 1/2 inch or so.

Tie or loop a line to the nail and stretch it along the short dimension of the pool site. Drive a stake at the second corner, tap a nail into the top of the stake and secure the string.

From either stake, measure the long distance of the pool, drive a stake at the third corner and attach a string between the second and third stakes.

Measure 12 feet along the short edge of the pool—or any appropriate distance that is a multiple of 3—and mark the string at that location, using chalk or a short piece of string.

Measure 16 feet—or the corresponding multiple of 4—along the length of the pool and mark the string at that point. If the diagonal distance between the two marks is 20 feet—or the corresponding multiple of 5—the two strings at the second stake form an exact 90° angle. If the distance between the two marks is not 20 feet, adjust the string marking the long side of the pool until the diagonal measurement is exactly 20 feet.

Once the angle has been set correctly, use the same method to square up the other three corners of the pool site.

If the two long sides are parallel, the distance between the stakes of the first short-side measurement should be equal to the second short side. As a final check, measure diagonally from one corner stake to the other. Then measure the opposite diagonal. The two measurements should be the same. If they're not, adjust the stakes until the corners are square.

Once the pool dimensions have been established, erect a set of *batter boards* 3 or 4 feet behind each corner stake, as shown in the drawing on page 103. Stretch a line from each batter board across the tops of the corner stakes to the opposite batter board. These lines will provide reference points for preparing the ground for the pool and squaring the sides of the pool when you assemble the sidewalls.

POOL ASSEMBLY

Above-ground pools are delivered as a complete package. The dealer will try to include all accessories and other items ordered in one delivery. A complete set of assembly instructions should be included.

Most tools required to assemble the pool are standard household tools. A list of necessary tools should be included with the instructions. An inventory list should also be included that identifies and describes each of the pool components.

Separate operating and service manuals will be supplied for the motor, pump and filter. Warranties for support components are usually provided by the manufacturer, not the pool dealer.

Unpack the pool and check the parts against the inventory list to make sure everything has been delivered in good condition. If any piece is missing or damaged, notify the pool dealer immediately so you can quickly replace the part.

Many of the assembly steps can be accomplished by one person. A helper or two will speed the work. Extra help will be necessary to position the vinyl liner.

The following steps describe the installation of an average above-ground pool. No two pools are exactly alike. Always follow the manufacturer's instructions.

Arrange Bottom Rails—Check the strings that outline the pool location to make sure they are still square. Use the 3-4-5 triangle method to adjust strings on the batter boards to make 90° angles at intersecting corners.

Using the strings as guides, lay the bottom rails around the pool circumference with the post supports and the pieces needed to connect the bottom rails.

Check the soil where each section of bottom rail is joined. If the earth is not stable, rest the joint on a leveled concrete block. For maximum strength and stability, you can pour a concrete footing. Connect the bottom rails. Check to see that they are correctly aligned.

Some pool manufacturers recommend setting the bottom rails in concrete. After the walls have been erected, concrete is poured over the protruding bottom rail around the entire perimeter of the pool. This makes a more stable pool, but it is no longer portable. If you intend to install a pool temporarily or have plans to move it at a later date, avoid a pool that must be set in concrete for stability.

Erect Wall Panels—Once the bottom rail is secure, place the wall panels and connecting posts. Panels are normally attached with bolts. Don't tighten the bolts until you have all the panels in place. If any panels are out of alignment, they may still be shifted into position. For most oval and rectangular pools, diagonal braces are required for some of the connecting posts between straight panels.

Add Base Cove—Position the cove around the bottom perimeter of the pool as described in the manufacturer's instructions. The base cove prevents water pressure from forcing the liner out under the bottom rail.

Level Pool Bottom—This is the last chance to clear the pool site of stakes or any debris that could damage the pool's vinyl liner. If sand has been used on the bottom, screed it smooth

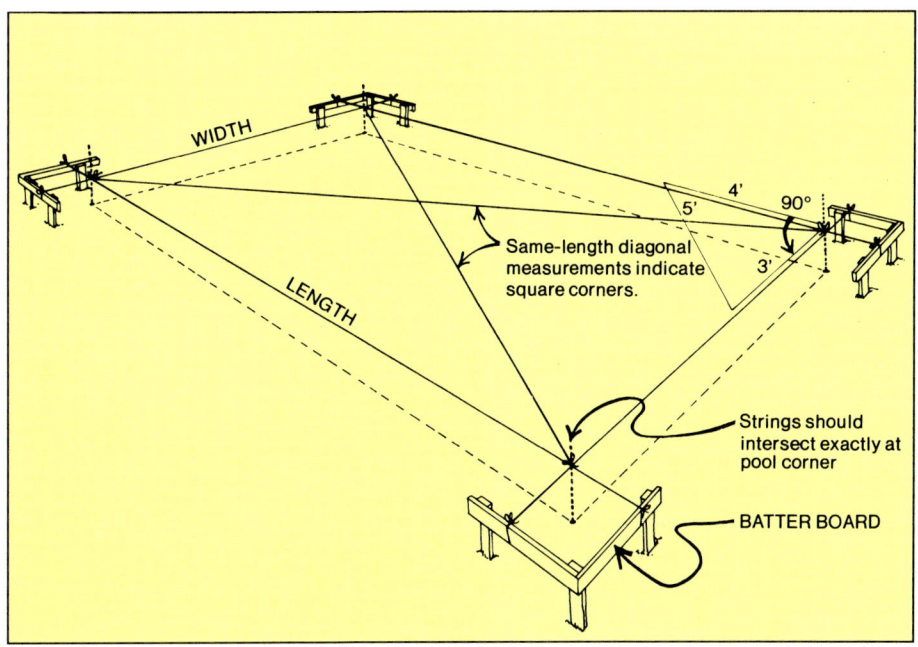

Use string and batter boards to lay out position of rectangular pools. Batter boards allow string to be adjusted to form exact 90° angles at corners.

before you install the liner.

Position Liner—Instructions for this step will vary for different types of above-ground pools. Normally, the liner is draped over the edge of the pool walls, then lifted with the help of assistants across the pool and lowered into place.

When the liner is in place, some manufacturers will recommend adding several inches of water to hold it in position. There are several different systems used to secure the liner to the top edge of the pool. Follow the manufacturer's instructions to complete these final steps. In all cases, the liner must be free of wrinkles, once installed.

Install Plumbing Fixtures—Some panels will be marked for inlet and outlet connections and for skimmer and lights, if included. As the pool is filled, adjust the liner so it is stretched uniformly along the walls. The liner should be perfectly positioned before cutting any openings for attachments.

Connect Wiring—Most local codes require that a waterproof outlet be installed within 3 feet of the pump motor. The circuit should be used strictly for the pump. Additional circuits will be required for electric heater and pool light, if included.

Have a licensed electrician do the wiring for all electrical equipment to be used with the pool. Electricity and water are a dangerous combination. If possible, find an electrician experienced in pool hookups. Most codes require a ground fault circuit interrupter (GFCI) be installed on each circuit servicing the pool.

Gas Heaters—If a gas or oil heater is installed, a line must be run to the heater to provide fuel. This step should be handled by a licensed plumber. Local building codes will cover the technical requirements for an outside gas or oil line.

Connect Plumbing—If a standard support-equipment package is furnished with the pool, it will be preplumbed prior to delivery and need only be connected to the skimmer and return line. Instructions will be supplied by the pool manufacturer.

If separate components have been selected, they will have to be plumbed together and to the skimmer and return line. Support equipment is usually located near the pool and set on a concrete pad. Components are usually plumbed with PVC pipe.

Setting up and plumbing support equipment is discussed on page 95. Do not attempt to plumb the equipment without complete instructions provided by the equipment manufacturer or pool dealer.

No two pool installations are exactly the same. Don't hesitate to ask your local pool dealer for advice. The pool manufacturer may also be able to help solve special problems. Thousands of above-ground pools are installed every year and dealers acquire additional knowledge that can be used to help you.

Above-Ground Pools **103**

Landscaping is an important part of any pool installation. The goal is to create a pleasant, relaxing environment for using your pool. *Design: Wildwood Pools, Fresno, CA.*

104   Pool Landscaping

CHAPTER 8

Pool Landscaping

Low maintenance landscape includes deck that's easy to clean and hardy plants that require little care. *Design: Patio Pools, Tucson, AZ.*

The most appealing pool installations feature a pleasing combination of landscape elements. These include patios and decks, walks, fences, outdoor buildings and plantings. All combine to provide an attractive and relaxing atmosphere. Whatever elements you choose to complement your pool, they should work well together to create the environment you imagined when you first considered building it.

The photos in this book offer many excellent examples of pleasant, functional pool installations. They represent a variety of tastes and a wide range of costs. Each one has its own distinct features.

When considering landscaping, there is no better place to start than by looking through these photos for ideas. Imagine how individual examples can be adapted to your pool site. Keep geography in mind. An appealing Southwest look might not be practical for a pool in Vermont. A pool with large, open decks in a mild climate might not work in hot climates where poolside shade is important.

If you have friends or neighbors with pools, take time to look at what they have done. Ask questions. How functional is the pool and its surroundings? What would the owners have done differently if they had a chance to do it over? How do your family's needs compare with theirs?

MAKE A FINAL PLAN

When you start planning a pool, think in terms of the total pool environment. The original site plan created as the first step in pool planning should include the entire pool area. See page 9.

You can design your own pool area or work with a landscape architect or landscape designer. Many pool builders and dealers also offer landscaping services, or have a working relationship with local landscapers.

If you want to hire an independent landscaper, it makes sense to select one in much the same way you have chosen a pool builder. Ask friends and neighbors with pools for recommendations. There is a good deal of personal taste involved in landscaping a pool area. Consider landscapers who have done projects that appeal to you.

Before you start, decide how involved you wish to become in planning and executing the landscape project. A landscape architect or designer can assume responsibility for the whole project. This includes arranging for building permits, if required, negotiating with subcontractors, including electricians and plumbers, and selecting the nursery that will supply the plants. All you need do is tell the designer what you want, pay the price, and you'll have a finished project.

You may decide to have the project designed and do the work yourself. You can do any amount you want and hire outside contractors to do the rest. Certain phases, such as wiring, should be left to licensed individuals.

Whatever your decision, begin your landscaping project with a complete site plan. Sketch in house, plantings, walks, decks, pool buildings, fences, patios, lighting and all other physical features you intend to include. This is the time to experiment with various ideas. Make several drawings to visualize different plans.

Plan in advance any earth-moving or contouring needed to prepare the site for landscaping. You might be able to save time and money by having this work done at the same time the pool site is being excavated. Equipment and operators will already be at the site. Excavated earth may be needed for fill. Excess earth from pool and landscape excavations can be removed and hauled away at the same time.

Contouring is an important part of landscaping a hillside pool. This site was contoured to preserve the appearance of a natural slope. Ground covers help prevent erosion. Design: Aquarius Pools, Sacramento, CA.

Flowering plants add color to the landscape. Consider using flowering annuals to dress up the landscape while waiting for major plantings to mature. Design: Aqua-Rama of Atlanta, Marietta, GA.

All elements of a completed pool should be in scale and work together. While the pool itself is the focal point, it is still only a part of the whole.

Adopt a final plan early, rather than making landscaping improvements a series of unrelated steps. As a budget consideration, not all work in an overall plan need be completed at one time. The area surrounding the pool can be developed over a period of months.

An ambitious project could take several summers. Your final plan may include an extended work schedule that lists various phases and projects in order of importance. Less important phases can be postponed until time and money allow you to complete them.

Pool building requires special skills and equipment. There aren't many opportunities to reduce pool costs by doing some or all of the actual installation yourself. But there are many opportunities to save money by handling all or part of the landscaping as a do-it-yourself project.

LANDSCAPING ELEMENTS

Landscaping can be broadly defined as the creation or improvement of the total environment surrounding your home. Landscaping is not restricted solely to plantings. Pools, patios and decks, garden structures and other man-made additions are part of a total landscaping plan.

Most pool owners spend much more time relaxing around the pool and entertaining friends than they do in the water. This makes developing a functional outdoor-living area as much a practical problem as an esthetic one.

The final design will reflect the needs and interests of you and your family. Make a list of the features and considerations most important to you. If you plan to entertain frequently, it may be important to have a large deck area and outside facilities for cooking or barbecuing. Terraced decks with built-in seating can create separate activity areas. Lighting will be important for both atmosphere and safety.

If privacy is a concern, fences, screens and plantings can be strategically located to provide privacy and an attractive pool setting.

If you enjoy gardening, you may want to include large areas for vegetable gardens and ornamental plants, as well as for greenery around the pool area. If you simply want to enjoy your pool and spend as little time as possible on upkeep, plan a low-maintenance pool area. Include easy-to-clean patios, decks and walks, and select plants that require minimum care. Your local nursery can suggest low-maintenance plants that grow well in your area.

CONTOURING

The first step in landscape planning is to determine if your pool site requires more than minor grading. A gently sloping lot may be satisfactory as is. A step or two, a low retaining wall or raised planters may be all that

106   Pool Landscaping

A formal landscape like this requires a lot of care, but the effect is well worth the effort. Carefully placed shrubs and trees create an attractive privacy screen. When choosing and locating plantings, consider their size and shape when mature. *Design: Ken Nelson Aquatech Pools, Turlock, CA.*

is needed to take care of small terrain changes.

A steeper grade requires planning more steps and terracing to create usable space. A multilevel area actually offers some interesting opportunities to create separate activity areas with decks and patios.

A steeply sloping lot may create more complex problems. Steep banks require high retaining walls and planting ground covers to control erosion. Steps may be needed to reach the pool. Drainage requirements become more complex.

Often, the only way to create a flat space on a steep slope is to install an above-ground wood deck around the pool. Above-ground pools are often best adapted to steep sites. See pages 98-99.

PLANTINGS

Lawns, ground covers, flowering and ornamental plants, shrubbery, vines and trees serve many useful purposes in the pool area. Aside from creating a natural, colorful setting, a careful selection of plants can create privacy, serve as windbreaks, block unwanted views, serve as dividers, hide support equipment and soften harsh architectural lines.

Trees and tall shrubs help to cool the pool area and provide shade. Nearby lawns and ground covers will help reduce glare. Select plants suitable for your particular climate. The area surrounding a pool will have higher-than-normal moisture and humidity.

Several landscaping and garden books published by HPBooks will be useful in planting and plant care around the pool area. Included are *Western Home Landscaping* by Ken Smith, *Lawns & Ground Covers* by Michael MacCaskey, and *Hedges, Secreens & Espaliers*, by Susan Chamberlin. Other HP titles offer specific advice on such gardening topics as roses, fruit, nut and citrus trees, annuals, bulbs, vegetables and other types of plants.

Plant selection and placement will influence the amount of maintenance required in the pool area. A primary concern of most pool owners is keeping the pool free or leaves, seeds, fruit, grass and other plant debris that can be blown or carried into the pool.

Lawns—A lawn near the pool area can create some direct problems. Grass clippings carried into the pool by wind or on the feet of swimmers can clog the filtration system and make it difficult to maintain correct water balance.

If you want to include a lawn in your landscaping scheme, design the pool area so swimmers don't have to walk across the lawn to reach the pool. A low wall or planting strip on the pool-side of the lawn will help keep wind from blowing clippings in the pool.

Pool decks are designed to slope away from the pool. This is to keep water splashed from the pool from draining back into it. As a result, splashed pool water may wash across the deck into nearby lawns or planting areas. Chemically treated pool water can be damaging to lawn and plants. For solutions to this problem, see *Planting Tips* on page 108.

Flowering Plants—Annual and perennial flowering plants add color to the pool area. To protect plants and to prevent swimmers from tracking

Pool Landscaping 107

dirt into the pool, raised flower beds are the most practical. If the pool area is small, flowers planted in containers or in hanging planters can bring color into the area.

The climate around the pool can be considerably different than in areas away from the pool. When you choose plants for the pool area, allow for the added humidity and higher temperatures the pool will create. In some cases, tropical or subtropical species that don't ordinarily grow in your area may do well around the pool.

Shrubbery and Vines—These plants have multiple purposes in pool landscaping. Low shrubs can be trained as hedges to define or fence-in the pool area. Shrubs make good ground covers to provide contrast to a light-colored deck and to reduce glare and noise.

Tall, thick shrubs and hedges can be used as privacy screens, but not for pool security. Thick, evergreen shrubs make the best privacy screens. Vines can be trained on trellis structures to serve as privacy screens or windbreaks.

Avoid berry bushes that can stain decks and walks and add to pool debris. These will also attract birds. Avoid flowering shrubs and vines that attract bees and other insects. Keep roses, cactuses and other thorny plants away from the pool area. Thorns and barefoot swimmers don't mix.

Trees—These have several advantages and disadvantages in the pool area. On the positive side, trees can provide a strong visual addition to the area. They offer shade, act as windbreaks and help keep the area cool during the hottest months of the year.

The primary disadvantage of having trees too near a pool is that it is difficult to keep leaves or needles from getting into the pool. Evergreen trees contribute less debris than most deciduous trees that shed all their leaves every fall. Evergreen trees also provide year-round privacy and wind control.

Deciduous trees provide more shade than evergreens during the summer and allow sun to enter the pool area during early spring and late fall months. There are usually more varieties of deciduous trees available than evergreens.

There are several ways to avoid some of the annoying problems caused by poolside trees. The problem of falling leaves or needles can be reduced by planting trees downwind and away from the pool. Not all deciduous trees shed their leaves at the same rate. If possible, select deciduous trees that drop their leaves over a short period of time.

Plant larger trees far enough away from the pool so roots from maturing trees won't damage the pool deck or the pool itself. Avoid planting trees near buried plumbing and utility lines, septic tanks or leach fields. Avoid selecting trees with shallow, spreading root systems, such as elms or poplars. Roots of these trees are more likely to invade plumbing lines and damage the pool's masonry deck. Your nursery will be able to recommend safe planting distances for specific trees you buy.

Fruit trees create more problems in a pool area than they're worth. Dropping fruit will clutter the lawn and can stain decks and walks. Fruit trees also attract birds and unwanted insects.

Planting Tips and Plant Care—Here are some additional tips to protect both plants and pool:
- Lawns and planting areas should slope away from the pool. If possible, install a low, watertight edging or wall on the pool-side of the lawn or planting area. This protects plants from splashed pool water and prevents dirt and fertilizers carried by wind or water runoff from entering the pool. Another precaution is to provide drainage between the pool and surrounding planting beds. Drainage can be accomplished by contouring or by installing a gravel-filled drainage area.
- Give trees frequent, deep waterings so they will develop deep, compact root systems. Underwatered trees are more likely to develop shallow, spreading root systems that can damage plumbing, deck and pool walls.
- To reduce the amount of plant debris entering the pool, locate major plantings downwind of the pool. Low, solid walls around the pool area will also help keep plant debris out of the area.
- Do not mow or water lawns immediately before using the pool. Grass clippings and debris are more likely to be tracked into the pool area. Always rake up and dispose of grass clippings after mowing the lawn. Discourage children from playing on the lawn or in planted areas while using the pool.

ROCKS

Rocks and boulders—real or simulated—are often used in conjunction with native plants to create a natural-looking pool and surroundings. The key to creating a realistic pond or pool is to use rocks and plants native to your area. As extreme examples, a pool owner in the desert should not try to recreate an alpine pool, nor should a pool owner living in the Rocky Mountains try for a tropical-paradise effect.

Aside from being appropriate, locally quarried rocks and boulders will be less expensive than those that must be shipped any distance. If appropriate rock is not available in your area, search for a pool builder or landscaper who is able to simulate rocks.

One of the pools shown on page 109 incorporates "boulders" made of gunite sprayed over wire forms and textured with colored plaster. The boulders are an integral part of the sprayed-concrete pool structure. The plaster finish was custom mixed to match the color of the desert mountains beyond the owner's property.

Also available are simulated boulders that are prefabricated and hauled to the site. They are usually much lighter than the rocks they simulate. Local landscape architects and designers can suggest local sources for real and simulated rocks and boulders.

A truly natural-looking pool is designed with partially submerged rocks around the pool perimeter. Because of the texture and porosity of real and simulated rocks, they tend to form a white crust where they meet the pool's waterline. This is due to scale buildup and other effects of chemically treated water. In most cases, the rough-textured surface is more difficult to clean than tile or other masonry materials. But rocks in natural stream or lakeside environments often have a similar crust. Consider if you like this effect before you decide to incorporate rocks into the pool itself. Dark-colored rocks will emphasize it.

FENCES, WALLS AND SCREENS

There are several reasons for building fences in the pool area. The most important reason is safety. Local codes may specify the type of fence and its location in the yard.

Simulated boulders were sculptured on site by spraying concrete over mesh forms and coating with colored plaster. Plaster color was carefully blended to match color of mountains in background. Real and simulated rocks usually form a white crust at the pool's waterline, due to calcium and other chemicals in pool water.

Granite and dwarf pines transform a flat yard into a miniature mountain paradise. Landscape design reflects Japanese technique of space illusion. *Design: Wildwood Pools, Fresno, CA.*

Rocks can be used to imply nature as well as recreate it. Here, the effect is more tactual than visual. Swimmers entering the pool enjoy the sensation of walking into a natural stream or lake. *Design: Eriksson, Peters and Thoms, ASLA, Pasadena, CA.*

Rocky hillside has been visually extended to pool's edge. To create a naturalistic pool, use rocks native to your area. *Design: Wildwood Pools, Fresno, CA.*

Wrought-iron pool fence is more open, less confining than a solid fence or wall. Low plantings help soften lines of fence. *Design: Boca Pool Lab. Inc., Boca Raton, FL.*

Wood fence provides security, wind control and privacy. Alternate board design makes better wind screen than a solid barrier would. *Design: Heldor, Morristown, NJ.*

In terms of esthetics, some people feel the best fence is one you can't see. A required fence can be made less obtrusive by growing plants on or around it, as shown here. Open designs using wrought iron, chain link or wire mesh are best for this purpose. *Design: Boca Pool Lab. Inc., Boca Raton, FL.*

Fences also serve as windbreaks or provide privacy from neighbors or traffic on adjacent streets. Fences offer an effective way to break up space in a large yard.

Security Fences—Code requirements for pool-security fences vary from one community to another. Check codes in your area. For residential pools, some codes require a separate fence around the pool area, even if the pool is in a fenced yard. Pool-area fences should allow a walking area at least 3 feet wide between the pool edge and the fence.

Some codes only require that the property or yard be fenced. Your final decision on fence type and location will be a combination of code requirements and your own preferences.

Families with small children may prefer to enclose the pool area within the yard, or build a fence between the house and pool, even if not required to do so by existing codes.

Fences designed to keep children from entering the pool area have these characteristics in common: The minimum height is usually 4-1/2 feet. The fence material should be some form of mesh, wrought iron, spaced slats or other material that allows an unobstructed view into the pool area. Wire mesh should be a tight enough weave to prevent a child from gaining a foothold. Any fence used for child protection should be difficult to climb. All gates should be self-closing and self-latching with latches near the top of the fence beyond the reach of small children.

A security fence between house and pool can be designed to be removable. It can be erected when friends with small children are visiting and removed for your personal convenience.

Wind Control—Fences can be designed to be windbreaks or baffles. Solid fences offer little protection from wind beyond a distance about equal to the fence's height. Fences can be designed with louvers or baffles to direct wind along a desired path.

Fences using spaced slats, lattice or basketweave designs will act as a baffle to break up strong wind currents into smaller eddies. Such fence designs are more effective wind screens than solid barriers.

Decorative Fences—A number of materials are used for fences. Wood is the most common and versatile material. Attractive fences can be built with glass or plastic panels, wrought iron, wire or plastic mesh, or reed and bamboo. Other than for safety reasons, the final choice is largely personal preference.

Walls—There are as many types of walls as there are fences. Your final choice will be based on a combination of safety, cost, esthetics, materials and ease of construction.

Low masonry walls make excellent retaining walls for sloping yards. They are also ideal for breaking up flat expanses of yard or for boxing in flower beds. A 6-foot-tall solid wall meets most code requirements as an acceptable safety fence—except between the house and pool where unrestricted vision is usually required.

Solid walls are effective in blocking sounds originating from outside the pool area. But walls also reflect and amplify sounds within the same area. Vines or shrubs against the wall will help mute sounds reflected by masonry walls and decks.

Screens—Bamboo, canvas, reed, plastic and wood are the materials used most often for screens. They can be built to set off private sunning areas, for windbreaks, for decoration or to enclose changing areas and showers.

Except for meeting safety-code requirements, choosing a screen design and materials is strictly a matter of esthetics. Because screens are usually light in weight, they make excellent patio and deck dividers where heavier walls or fences would be out of scale.

Screens differ from fences and walls in that they are usually taller and lighter in weight. They are primarily used to provide privacy, shade and wind control. Screens can be free-standing or attached to another structure; movable or permanent.

HPBooks' *Fences, Gates & Walls,* by S. Chamberlin and J. Pollock, is an excellent source for detailed planning and building information for poolside fences, walls and screens.

DECKS AND PATIOS

There are two types of *decks* usually associated with swimming pools. One is the *pool deck,* usually concrete or other masonry, that is installed around the immediate perimeter of the pool. This is the deck that provides a walkway, base for a diving board or slide and space for poolside furniture and lounging. Basic pool decks are covered on pages 92-94.

In landscaping terms, a deck is an elevated wood floor used for lounging and other outdoor activities. Its masonry equivalent is called a *patio.* Outdoor patios and decks often incorporate some sort of overhead structure to provide shade.

Patios and decks should be designed to tie in with the overall use of the pool and surrounding area. Multilevel decks and patios can define separate activity areas and break up a flat landscape. Patio and deck materials should complement those used for the pool deck.

A patio or deck can adjoin the pool deck or be located in another part of the yard to provide a separate activity area.

Installing a patio or deck can be a do-it-yourself project. Photos in this book show many examples of patios and decks incorporated into the poolside environment. For instructions on how to build masonry patios and wood decks, see HPBooks' *Patios & Decks, How to Plan, Build & Enjoy,* by Michael Landis and Ray Moholt.

Patios and decks included in a basic

This pool deck is so large it could also be considered a patio. Grey flagstone was chosen to match color of brick house. Black-bottom pool stands in striking contrast to overall landscape. *Design: Carousel Pools of Wichita Inc., Wichita, KS.*

pool-landscaping plan will be similar to those designed for a comfortable outdoor area for any home. As part of a pool plan, give special attention to pool needs. A raised deck can be used to hide the pool's support system. Deck storage can be built for maintenance equipment, toys and games. Raised decks can provide flat space on a sloping site.

When designing a patio or deck, consider traffic patterns in and around the pool and from the house to the pool. Also consider privacy and multipurpose use for dining and entertaining. Deck size and materials will determine building costs.

WALKS

Walks or paths to and from the pool should be easy on bare feet. Walks can be made of the same material as the pool deck, or of a contrasting masonry material. Choose a material that is cool and smooth, but not slippery, underfoot.

Walks can be made of concrete, ceramic tile, brick or flagstone. Garden paths and walks often consist of gravel, bark chips or other loose aggregates. If using an aggregate for a

Wood deck enhances forest setting for this pool. Raised wood platform behind pool offers a shady retreat. *Design: Classic Pool & Patio, Indianapolis, IN.*

Ceramic tile carries formal design of this classic Roman-shape pool. Spacious pool deck/patio and low plantings emphasize panoramic view. *Design: Ken Nelson Aquatech Pools, Shrewsbury, NJ.*

Large poured-concrete steppingstones help prevent grass from being tracked into pool area. Steppingstones, patio and terraced pool deck are exposed aggregate. *Design: Ken Nelson Aquatech Pools, Shrewsbury, NJ.*

Raised wood decks are often the least complicated way to gain flat space on a steep hillside. *Design: National Pools of Roanoke Inc., Roanoke, VA.*

walk or path, choose one that is least likely to get tracked into the pool area. Locate aggregate paths and walks away from the pool for the same reason.

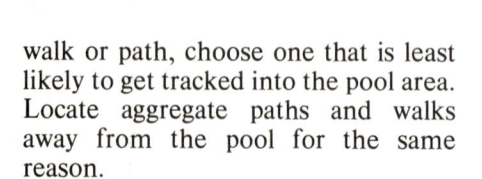

LIGHTING

The first consideration in lighting the pool area is safety. The priority is to see that steps, walks and the pool deck are illuminated so swimmers can walk safely around the pool area at night. If the pool is used for night swimming, underwater lights should be placed so all parts of the pool are illuminated.

Once the practical considerations have been made, lights can be used to enhance the poolside atmosphere and highlight the most attractive features. Low voltage, non-hazardous outdoor lighting can be used to illuminate trees, shrubbery and planting beds. The most effective outdoor lighting is low key and soft.

Lights for paths and walks are usually 6 to 18 inches above ground level and shaded to direct light on the pathway. They should not shine up in your eyes.

There are a number of light fixtures to provide different effects. Spotlights or bullet lights at ground level can be directed up to highlight trees, garden sculptures or architectural features in the yard. Many fixtures have inter-

112   Pool Landscaping

changeable filters to provide different light colors.

Floodlights are placed high above the ground to illuminate large areas and provide general illumination. A more subtle approach is to use high-level, directional lights—spotlights or bullet lights—to illuminate specific areas or objects, such as the diving board, slide, pool gate or poolside dining area. High-level lights can be mounted on the house, nearby pool buildings, walls or fences.

Tasteful lighting will enhance the entire pool area and surroundings. Bright, glaring lights can be disturbing. Leaving dark areas in the yard beyond the pool helps create an intimate atmosphere and offer swimmers a sense of privacy.

For safety, position lights so they do not shine in the eyes of divers and others in the pool area.

POOL BUILDINGS

Poolside structures can add convenience and versatility to the pool area by providing places for entertaining, dining, changing, sunbathing and relaxing. Pool houses, gazebos, cabanas or lanais need not be complicated structures to be useful. Most are wood-frame structures using a number of different siding and roofing materials. They can be built by anyone with basic do-it-yourself skills.

Whatever structure you build near your pool, it may be difficult to identify as a specific type of pool building. A gazebo is usually distinctive, but many pool owners use terms like *cabana* and *lanai* interchangeably.

Some pool buildings referred to as lanais bear little resemblance to the original Hawaiian open-air porches or rooms called lanais. The name is less important than the usefulness of the structure.

If your initial plans include a pool building, check with your local building department when you first investigate code or zoning restrictions. Find out early in the planning stages what codes and restrictions apply to poolside structures.

Pool Houses—These are usually multipurpose pool buildings. A basic pool house usually includes a storage area for chemicals and maintenance tools, an enclosure for support equipment and one or two changing rooms. Many have showers.

A more elaborate pool house can in-

Lighting within the pool can be dramatic as well as providing safety. Low-level lights illuminate surrounding planting beds. Spotlights on house provide general lighting around pool area. *Design: Peri-Bilt Aquatech Pools, Carmichael, CA.*

Here, creative lighting goes beyond use of ordinary outdoor fixtures. No matter how you light the pool, make sure fixtures will withstand outdoor use. *Design: Lifescapes, Costa Mesa, CA.*

Pool Landscaping 113

Elaborate pool building is designed to match house architecture. Pool house has all comforts, including fireplace. **Design: Jay Davis Pools, Inc., San Antonio, TX.**

clude a recreation room, toilet and bath facilities, kitchen, bar and even a guest bedroom or two.

Typically, most homeowners add a pool house for convenience, to provide storage and a changing area, and to isolate pool activities. The main purpose of a pool house is to keep barefoot swimmers in wet bathing suits from tracking in and out of the house. A pool building can be particularly useful if the pool is some distance from the house.

Gazebos—One of the simplest pool structures is the familiar free-standing gazebo. Another is the basic lanai. These structures provide a shady retreat for swimmers.

The gazebo is a traditional garden structure. It has survived not because it's highly functional, but because it provides a cool, attractive retreat. An imaginatively designed gazebo is simply nice to look at. These free-standing structures usually have solid roofs and open, latticed sides. The floor is raised a step or two above ground level and has benches around the perimeter. Gazebos can be square, round, hexagonal or octagonal. They come in sizes from 6x6' to as much as 12x12' or more. A traditional gazebo is shown in the photo on page 115, top left.

Smaller gazebos don't need an elaborate foundation. The structure can be supported by a basic wood and concrete-pier foundation. The floor can be a raised wood deck, or a brick or masonry patio.

You can design a gazebo to include room for a table and several chairs. Built-in storage under benches and pegs to hang wet towels make them useful pool additions.

Some lumber dealers and home-improvement centers sell gazebo kits. These include all the lumber—much of it pre-cut—and hardware necessary to build a gazebo. Often you have a choice of two or more models. Local dealers who don't stock kits may be able to order a kit for you.

If you don't want to buy a stock gazebo, you may enjoy designing one of your own. There are no design rules to follow, other than meeting local code requirements. Gazebos have been built in hundreds of different shapes, sizes and styles.

Cabanas—The original cabanas were seaside or poolside shelters designed to provide privacy for changing or lounging. Cabanas are usually built of wood. They usually take the form of an enclosed or semienclosed building with a connected roof extension or overhead to provide shade. Cabanas provide a handy place to change and keep towels. They offer storage for pool accessories. More elaborate cabanas may include showers, toilet facilities and a small kitchen.

The primary function of a cabana is convenience. Close to the pool, it is a relaxing spot for those supervising children playing in the pool. It can be a cool place to serve a poolside lunch. A cabana can be designed to fit your personal and social needs.

Lanais—The original Hawaiian lanai was a semienclosed room with an open roof, free-standing or attached to a house, where family and friends could gather protected from the sun. Its open design allowed breezes to circulate through walls and roof.

Modern lanais are still built of wood posts and beams—some with open roof and sides. The wall and roof coverings can be lattice, canvas, glass or plastic panels, woven reed or bamboo. Many incorporate roll-up vertical shades to control the amount of sun entering the lanai at various times of the day.

The lanai design is based largely on climate, desired privacy and its proximity to the pool or house. In areas with frequent spring and summer showers, a solid roof makes the lanai a shelter from the rain. In areas where there are annoying insects, a fully screened lanai provides protection while permitting air to circulate.

A lanai can be built free-standing near the pool or it can be attached to the house or garage. The design is largely a matter of taste and utility. There is also no limit to size. Simple post-and-beam construction allows you to cover a large area at a relatively low cost.

Traditional Victorian gazebo rests directly on brick pool deck. Includes bar and ample seating. *Design: Walt Young, Landscape Architect, Northridge, CA.*

Redwood gazebo is integral to pool-landscape design. Semienclosed design offers privacy from nearby neighbors. *Design: Aquarius Pools, Sacramento, CA.*

Multipurpose pool house includes changing rooms and pass-through snack bar. Design fits well into forest setting. Extended overhang provides shade. *Design: Heldor, Morristown, NJ.*

Polynesian influence on architecture might classify this structure as a lanai. Solid roof provides shade, protection from rain. Lath overhead connects lanai to house. *Design: Wildwood Pools, Fresno, CA.*

Pool Landscaping 115

CHLORINE
3.0
2.0
1.5
1.0 IDEAL
0.6
ADD CHLORINE
0.4
pH & ACID DEMAND
TOTAL ALKALINITY
pH
8.2
7.8
ADD pH DECREASER
7.6
IDEAL
7.4
ADD pH INCREASER
7.2
6.8

CHAPTER 9
Pool Care & Repair

The obvious advantage of maintaining a properly conditioned swimming pool is a limitless supply of sparkling clean water that offers an irresistable invitation to swim. In addition to keeping the water clear, good maintenance will guarantee pure and sanitary water and long life for your pool's support equipment.

When you think of pool maintenance, your first thought may be treating water with pool chemicals. Successful chemical treatment depends on an effective and properly working filtration system. Chemicals, filtration and manual cleaning work together as the three essential steps to good-quality pool water.

Maintenance also includes servicing the pump, pump motor, filter and heater. It includes keeping the deck, diving board, slide and ladders in good repair. Good maintenance means making necessary minor repairs to the equipment and pool itself, to keep everything in good operating condition.

Time spent maintaining your pool—2 to 8 hours a week when the pool is being used regularly—will prove worthwhile. A regular maintenance program will cut operating costs and help prevent major repair bills. With proper maintenance, you can expect many years of trouble-free service from any of the pool types being installed today.

Buying Pool Chemicals—There are several companies that produce and sell a complete line of pool chemicals and supplies. Many of these chemicals are generic, but individual companies identify their products with specific trade names. There may be slight differences in the strength and composition of chemical products from one company to another.

It is best to treat your pool with chemicals manufactured by the same company under the same brand name. If you change brands, make a complete switch to a line of products manufactured by that company. Each company's family of chemicals has been formulated to work most effectively with other chemicals in the same line.

You may be unfamiliar with some of the terms and the chemicals used to treat pool water. The first section in this chapter describes the most common chemicals used for pool maintenance and explains the basic steps you can take to keep your pool in good condition.

You don't have to be a chemist to learn the fundamentals of water chemistry. By monitoring just a few conditions and adding the recommended chemicals, it is easy to keep a clean and safe pool. Check the glossary on pages 126-127 if you are not familiar with the terms used here, or wish to review them.

Using a Pool Service—In areas where residential pools are common, there are pool-service companies that do basic pool maintenance. Service personnel will appear regularly to clean the pool, maintain the filter and other support equipment, monitor water quality and add necessary chemicals. Calls are normally two or three times a week during the swimming season and once a week or less in the off-season.

Even if you intend to have your pool maintained by a pool-service company, it will be useful to understand the steps that are necessary to keep your pool in top condition. You will be able to identify common water-quality problems and know when maintenance is being performed correctly.

Labor-Saving Devices—Automatic chlorinators, pool vacuums and pool sweeps will reduce the amount of time it takes to maintain a pool. This equipment is discussed in detail in the chapter, *Selecting Pool Equipment*, pages 43-57. Many of these labor-saving devices are surprisingly effective. This equipment will enable the pool owner to save time and carry out basic maintenance chores at less cost than by hiring a pool-service company.

Left: An accurate test kit is essential to maintaining good water quality.

Pool Care & Repair 117

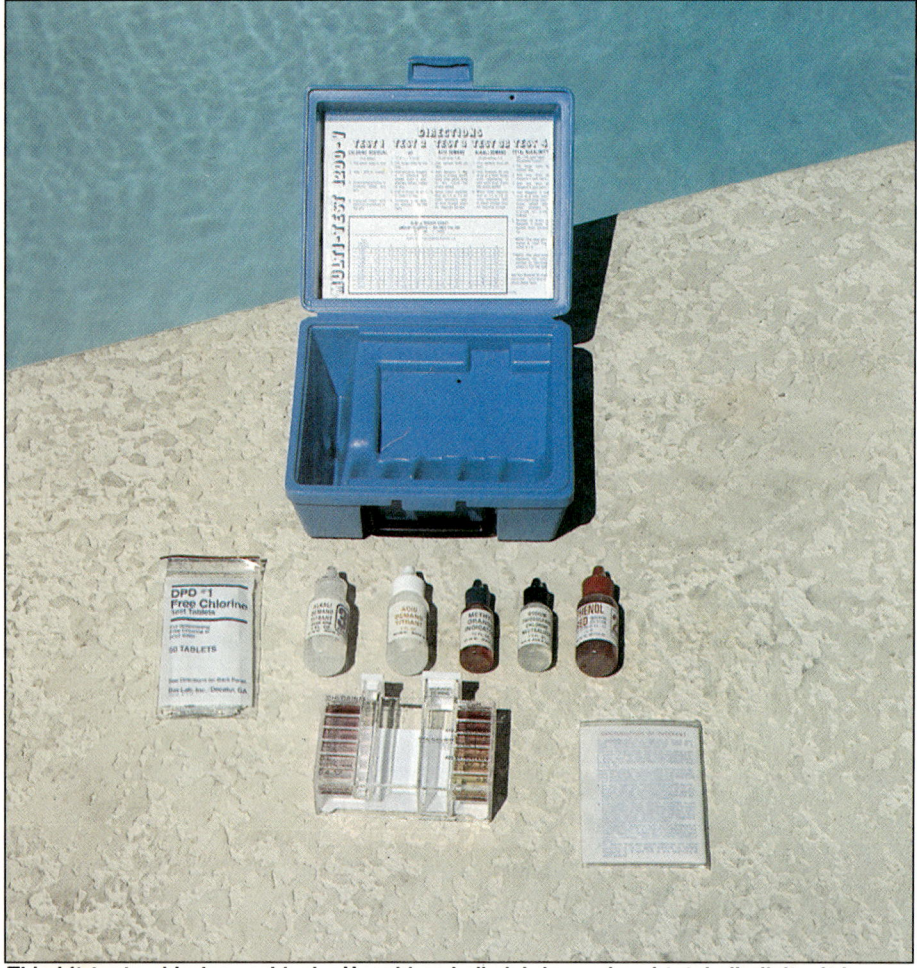

This kit tests chlorine residual, pH, acid and alkalai demand and total alkalinity. It is more sophisticated than simple kits that test only chlorine level and pH. It's a good all-around kit for day-to-day pool care. Kits like this cost around $20.

MAINTAINING WATER QUALITY

Most pools are filled from the same water supply that is piped into the pool owner's home. Yet water fit to drink isn't necessarily ideal for a pool. Tap water that is perfectly safe to drink may have high or low mineral levels. Such mineral imbalances occur naturally in the water supply and are determined by local conditions.

Excessively high or low mineral levels can prevent sanitizing chemicals from working efficiently and can lead to corrosion, staining and scaling. Fortunately, there are chemicals available to correct mineral imbalance. See page 121.

The ability to treat and recirculate pool water over a period of months is what makes residential pools practical. As most pools contain from 15,000 to 30,000 gallons of water, it would be wasteful and costly, if not impossible, to replace pool water often enough to keep it fresh. Tap water for home use is normally used once and directed as waste into the sewer system or septic tank. Pool water is used over and over again.

Skimmers, filters and manual maintenance can keep pool water free of dirt particles, leaves and other sediment blown into the pool. It takes chemicals to kill bacteria and prevent algae from growing. Filtration alone can't control or eliminate contaminants like pollen, perspiration, algae spores, rainwater and impurities that are blown into the pool or carried into it by swimmers.

MINERAL BALANCE

No two pools are exactly alike. What's right for treating water in your neighbor's pool may not be right for your pool. If you're putting a new pool into operation for the first time or opening your pool in the spring, the first step is to check the mineral balance. Imbalanced water leads to pool-chemical waste and makes it difficult to maintain sanitized water.

Test the Water—Test pool water for mineral balance at least once or twice each season. Based on test results and natural water quality, your pool dealer will be able to recommend how often testing is necessary.

Most pool dealers who sell chemicals and pool supplies are equipped to test and analyze pool water for minerals and solids. There is usually no charge for this service. Computer-run testing systems will examine the water and print the results with recommendations for correcting the problem. The dealer needs this information before selecting specific chemicals for your pool.

If there is no dealer available, you can buy a kit to perform some of the same tests. This kit will be more sophisticated and expensive than the simple kit you will need to check the pH reading and chlorine level as part of your routine pool maintenance. Testing for pH and chlorine level is described in the following text.

Collect A Sample—Use a clean plastic or glass container to collect a water sample to take to your pool dealer for testing. You'll need about a quart. Before taking the sample, clean the pool of debris and operate the filter system for 2 or 3 hours. Take the sample at elbow depth or about 18 inches below the water surface and away from the return lines emptying filtered water back into the pool.

The water will be tested for acid or base (alkalai) demand, chlorine, total alkalinity, calcium hardness, total dissolved solids, copper and iron content and stabilizer levels. With these complete test results, your pool supplier can recommend the right chemicals for the condition of your pool water. It's best not to chemically treat the water until you've received the test results and treatment recommendations have been made. The use of chemicals to correct mineral imbalance is discussed on page 121.

Self-Testing—If a local pool service isn't available to perform a water analysis, or if you prefer making the tests yourself, you will need a kit that will test for complete water balance, including mineral balance. The small kit sold to most pool owners produces only a pH reading and tests for chlorine residual—the only tests required for routine pool maintenance.

Specific instructions for using the kit and the required *reagents,* or chemicals used for testing, will be included in the kit. Once you've completed the following tests to obtain readings, refer to instructions on how to cure mineral imbalance beginning on page 121.

Test Procedures—To test for mineral imbalance, complete these tests:

Step 1—Check chlorine level to find out how much chlorine is in the water. Record the results. Don't attempt to adjust chlorine level until completing all the tests. The ideal amount of free (usable) chlorine is 1.0 to 1.5 ppm (parts per million parts of pool water). A reading below 0.6 means the water doesn't have enough chlorine. A reading above 3.0 means it has too much and you are wasting chlorine.

Step 2—Check and adjust total alkalinity. This is the measurement of alkalines in the water. Alkalines act as buffering agents to prevent big changes in pH and to prevent staining and corrosion. In plaster pools, a measurement of 80 to 125 ppm is ideal. In vinyl-lined, painted or fiberglass pools, a measurement of 125 to 150 ppm is ideal. Total alkalinity should be adjusted before adjusting pH balance. See page 120.

Step 3—Test and adjust pH. The pH reading measures the degree of acidity or alkalinity in pool water. The correct pH range for plaster-finished pools is 7.4 to 7.6. For fiberglass, vinyl-lined and painted pools, 7.6 is preferred. The right pH reading means chlorine will be able to work full strength and the pool will not be damaged by overly acidic or alkaline water. A new plaster pool will leach alkalines into the water during the first few weeks of operation and will usually require frequent pH adjustments before the plaster cures.

Step 4—Measure stabilization. This test is to determine the amount of stabilizer or cyanuric acid in the pool. It should be about 40 ppm. The stabilizer prevents sunlight from dissipating chlorine. If there is insufficient stabilizer, slowly add stabilizer through the skimmer while the pump is running. Stabilizers dissolve slowly, so don't backwash or clean the filter for 2 or 3 days after adding stabilizer.

Step 5—Check calcium hardness. To prevent etching of plaster and corrosion of metal equipment, make sure the calcium hardness is not too low. The desired range in plastered pools is 200-250 ppm. A slightly lower range of 175-225 ppm is right for fiberglass, painted and vinyl-lined pools. If calcium hardness exceeds 450 ppm, add a scale inhibitor or dilute the pool water with fresh water low in calcium. If calcium is too low, treat the water to increase calcium hardness, as described on pages 121-122.

Step 6—Retest free (usable) chlorine and pH. Make any necessary adjustments now. When you have a chlorine reading of 1.0 to 3.0 and a pH of 7.4 to 7.6, your pool can be used.

DEMAND AND BALANCE

Understanding the terms *demand* and *balance* is the key to understanding how pool chemicals are used to maintain good water quality easily and economically. Demand represents the pool's need for chemicals and sanitizers. A properly conditioned pool needs only small quantities of chemicals to maintain good water quality. After heavy pool use, chemical demand will increase, but it takes little effort to bring the pool back into adjustment.

If maintenance is neglected, demand will increase substantially. Potential damage to the pool's finish and equipment will also increase. Time-consuming and expensive procedures may be needed to bring the water back into balance.

When pool chemicals are all within recommended ranges, the pool is said to be *in balance.* This means chlorine, pH, alkalinity, calcium hardness and stabilizer are at acceptable levels. The chemicals work efficiently and the pool is easily maintained.

Through regular testing and maintenance, you can keep demand to a minimum and keep the water in balance. With stable pool water, problems that arise can be quickly corrected.

There is no set formula for the addition of specific chemicals. The amounts to be added will change as test results change. Water properties vary widely from one geographical area to another. The best way to determine treatment is to keep a detailed record of your maintenance program. Write down the dates water is tested, the test readings, the amounts and types of chemicals added and the results.

These records will help you determine a pattern for normal treatment. You won't be able to abandon regular testing. You will be able to identify abnormal conditions and treat them immediately.

pH TESTING

The test to determine pH balance takes little more than 30 seconds to complete. The test is simple. It's also the most important test. Fill the two tubes of the kit with pool water. Add the recommended amount of regeant,

---

TESTING TIPS

No matter what brand of testing kit you have purchased, the testing procedures are very much the same. Here are the guidelines that will enable you to produce accurate results:

- Always conduct the test before adding any chemicals.
- Rinse the vials with pool water before and after each test. When taking water samples, fill all vials at the same time. Most simple test kits have two vials molded into a single testing unit.
- Some kits include a chlorine neutralizer that makes it possible to test for acid if the chlorine level is above 1.0. If there is no neutralizer, don't test for acid above 1.0 because the reading will be invalid.
- If liquid reageant is being used, hold the test vials and dropper bottle vertically to assure uniform drops. Add the solution slowly and mix after each drop. Don't cover the vial opening with your thumb or finger to mix, because chemicals or contaminants on your fingers can affect the test results.
- Read test results immediately.
- Compare colors against a light background, but out of direct sunlight.
- After conducting tests, do not empty vials into the pool.
- Store the test kit in a cool, dark place away from chemicals. Pool chemicals can emit vapors that will neutralize the reagents.
- Replace the reagents at the beginning of each season to make sure they are fresh. Most liquid reagents have a 1-year shelf life.

Take care handling acid. Use glass or plastic measuring cup to pour acid in pool. Pour acid away from pool edges and close to water surface to avoid splashing.

supplied with the kit. Gently mix the water and it will turn a shade of color from light yellow to dark red or purple. Compare the color to the chart provided with the test kit.

One color scale will give you the pH reading. Neutral is 7.0. The ideal range is between 7.4 and 7.6. The other color scale will tell you the amount of free chlorine in the water. The ideal range is 1.0 to 1.5. Complete information on chlorinating your pool starts on page 122.

WATER BALANCE

The pH scale measures the acid-alkaline balance of the pool water. The higher the number, the higher the alkalinity. The lower the number the greater the acidity. If the pH falls below 7.0, the water becomes corrosive. It can damage pool equipment, etch and stain pool plaster, damage vinyl liners and corrode metal fixtures. Also, it can irritate eyes and noses of swimmers and dissipate chlorine and other disinfecting chemicals.

If the pH rises above 8.0, high alkalinity prohibits chlorine from working effectively. The chlorine is less effective in destroying bacteria and algae. The water will turn cloudy. A high pH can cause scale buildup on plaster, in the water lines and in the pool-heater coils.

During normal pool operation, testing two or three times a week is sufficient. Daily testing is required for a few days after the pool has been filled with water or reopened in the spring. Test daily when the pool is receiving heavy use. Make daily tests for several days after a heavy rain. Even rainwater falling directly in the pool carries contaminants that can disrupt the pool's water chemistry. However, water runoff during a heavy rain is more likely to contaminate pool water than rain falling into the pool.

Frequent testing is necessary because a pool is a relatively unstable environment. Climatic and chemical conditions change the water constantly. Test results one day can be completely different from tests a day or two earlier. Testing is the only reliable method of determining water quality. A judgment on water quality can't be made by appearance of the water. A clean-looking pool can still be unsanitary because of chemical imbalance.

ADDING CHEMICALS

Several major chemical companies produce chemicals specifically for use in residential swimming pools. These pool chemicals are sold under different brand names and in different forms.

Each supplier includes specific instructions on the container for the use of each product. Always follow manufacturer's recommendations. Some manufacturers provide charts that give recommended dosages for specific readings on the pH scale. Dosage is also determined by the number of gallons of water in the pool. If you don't know the water capacity of your pool in gallons, see page 44.

Raising pH—If the pH reading is under 7.2, add soda ash (sodium carbonate) while the filtration system is running. Soda ash is inexpensive. It's sold in powder or granular form or in cakes. A 1/2-pound cake will dissolve in 3 or 4 hours.

Sprinkle granular soda ash over the water surface or premix it with warm water in a plastic bucket. With the filtration system running, pour the mixture into the pool away from the suction lines. If you have no specific recommendation for dosage, start by adding about a pound of soda ash. After an hour, retest the water. If it is still under 7.2, add another pound of soda ash and take a second reading after an hour. Repeat the process until the reading is in the desired range.

Lowering pH—Acid, used for reducing alkalinity and lowering the pH level, comes in liquid or granular form. The most popular liquid acid is *muriatic acid*. It stores easily and a small amount will make major changes in the water balance. If it is incorrectly used, it can be damaging.

One quart for every 10,000 gallons of water will drop alkalinity sharply. In adjusting the water, begin by adding no more than one pint at a time. Wait an hour. Retest the water, then repeat the dosage, if necessary.

With the filtration system on, pour the acid into the water away from the suction lines. Don't add it through the skimmer. If you must dilute concentrated acid, pour the acid into water to make the solution. *Do not pour water into the acid concentrate.* Handle muriatic acid carefully.

If you splash or spill the acid, immediately wash it away with clear water. Treat all pool chemicals with respect. For additional information on handling chemicals, see page 121.

Sodium bisulfate (dry acid) is recommended for all pools that require small dosages of acid. It is easier to store than liquid acid. Premix the acid with water before adding. Spread it evenly around the pool surface. Again, always add acid to water. Never add water to acid.

Follow instructions on the container for the correct dosage. If there are no instructions, don't buy the chemical. Test the water an hour after adding acid and repeat dosages until the water balance is in the correct range.

TOTAL ALKALINITY AND pH

Total alkalinity is the amount of *soluable salts*—carbonates, bicarbonates and hydroxides—present in the pool water. Alkalines act as buffering agents, preventing large fluctuations in the pH. The reading obtained by measuring total alkalinity indicates the water's resistance to change in pH.

The correct alkalinity level is what helps keep the pH in the 7.4 to 7.6 range. Too much or too little alkalinity can cause serious problems that can be expensive to remedy. In plaster pools, a measurement of 80 to 125 ppm is ideal. In vinyl-lined, painted and fiberglass pools, it should be from 125 to 150 ppm.

In some areas of the country, excessive alkalinity levels are present in normal tap water. Where this occurs,

CHEMICAL SAFETY

Pool chemicals can be dangerous when incorrectly handled. Read the labels on chemical containers and carefully follow instructions. Different chemicals may be packaged in similar-looking containers with similar labels. Assign the responsibility for using pool chemicals to an adult. Don't delegate this work to children.

Concentrated chlorine compounds are oxidizing agents. They are capable of causing a fire or an explosion if they come in contact with reactive organic materials like turpentine, kerosene or some swimming pool algaecides. When these materials burn, they usually emit toxic gases.

Here are a few basic tips for handling pool chemicals safely:
- Read instructions and use the exact amounts specified. Don't overdose. More is not better. Underdosing will not save money. Don't experiment.
- Never mix pool chemicals together unless specified on container directions. If you have to add more than one chemical to pool water, add them individually.
- Use separate measuring devices for each chemical. Measuring devices can be cups, spoons or scoops made of plastic, glass or enamelware. Metal spoons or cups should not be used. Rinse and dry measuring cups and scoops after using.
- When adding pool chemicals, hold the container close to the water surface so liquids won't splash and dry chemicals won't be blown by the wind.
- If a chemical is to be mixed with water, don't add water to the chemical. Add the chemical to the water. This is especially important with acids that can react violently with small amounts of water and spatter.
- Keep chemical containers closed when not in use. Exposure to air and humidity can reduce the chemical's effectiveness. To avoid contaminating chemicals, place the right cap on the right container.
- Store chemicals and cleaning agents in a locked, cool, dry, well-ventilated place. Keep out of the reach of children.
- Don't store chemicals in the same enclosed room with the pool's support equipment. Chemicals may emit corrosive fumes that can damage equipment. Chlorine is corrosive and shouldn't be stored near metal equipment like lawnmowers, bicycles or cars. Do not store chemicals in the same place as the test kit.
- Avoid inhaling fumes or letting chemicals contact eyes, nose or mouth. Always wash your hands after handling pool chemicals.
- If any chemical is swallowed, follow emergency advice on the container. Call a doctor or contact your local poison-control center.
- Don't smoke around chemicals. Some chemical fumes are highly flammable.
- Don't use empty chemical containers for storing other materials. Dispose of them as soon as the contents have been used.

---

it is necessary to adjust the alkalinity range after the pool is filled. Newly filled pools must be monitored frequently and adjustments made until the alkalinity drops to acceptable levels.

If alkalinity is too high, the pH will not stabilize. It may be necessary to add acid daily for a month or more. Check frequently to see that the pH does not drop below 7.2 at any time. It will take time to correct the imbalance. If alkalinity is allowed to remain at high levels, scaling will occur.

In some areas, tap water may have an extremely low alkalinity—in the 10 to 70 ppm range. This will also cause pH instability—pH could fall below 7.0. If the alkalinity level is below 80 ppm, it can be raised by adding bicarbonate of soda (baking soda). It will take 1-1/2 pounds to increase total alkalinity by 10 ppm in 10,000 gallons of pool water. Water with low alkalinity is corrosive and will etch plaster and damage pool equipment.

To control alkalinity, add acid while the filtration system is on. Never add more than 1 pint of muriatic acid per 10,000 gallons of water within a 24-hour period. If tests show the water is over-acidic, shut off pool equipment immediately. Add soda ash to raise the pH to the desired range. Once the pH is over 7.2, vacuum any residue and clean the filter before activating the system.

Add chemicals to the pool in the evening or early morning. Distribute them in water away from pool walls, suction or return lines. Use dosages recommended by the chemical manufacturer. Once alkalinity has been brought within the correct range, it will take a minimal amount of treatment to maintain good water quality.

TREATING HARD WATER

Calcium, magnesium and similar minerals won't evaporate. They tend to build up in pool water over a period of time. A high hardness level combined with high alkalinity will cause scaling on pool walls and in plumbing and heater coils. Normally, the hardness level doesn't increase rapidly.

One or two water tests a year will usually be enough to monitor calcium hardness. Most pool dealers will be able to test for calcium hardness if you provide a water sample. If testing through a dealer isn't possible, you can buy a kit to do the job.

The preferred range of calcium hardness in plastered concrete pools is 200 to 250 ppm. For vinyl-lined, painted and fiberglass pools, a range of 175 to 225 ppm is ideal. Some chemical suppliers suggest that a range of 100 to 300 ppm is acceptable. If the hardness level reaches 500 ppm, use a scale inhibitor or partially drain pool and refill with fresh water.

Test tap water before using it to fill the pool. Some areas of the country have extremely hard water. That makes it necessary to take the special step of adding soft water while the pool is being filled. Check with your pool dealer or local water department for a source of soft water. Ask the dealer how much soft water the pool will require.

TREATING SOFT WATER

Soft water—0 to 90 ppm calcium hardness—is extremely corrosive and must be tested to determine the mix necessary to bring the hardness level of pool water within the recommended range.

Start filling the pool with hard tap water. When the pool is approximately 1/4 full, begin adding small amounts of soft water. The amount of soft water must be metered to control the volume. As you add soft water, agitate it with a pool brush or some similar device. Soft water is too corrosive to attempt to mix it by turning on the pump and running it through the filtration system.

Test the water as the pool is filled to keep the mix within the recommended range. Don't operate support equipment until water quality is acceptable.

If hardness remains below 100 ppm, add calcium chloride, a hardening agent, to raise the hardness level. Four pounds of calcium chloride will raise hardness approximately 40 ppm for 10,000 gallons of water.

It is more difficult to reduce the hardness level. The solution to unacceptable hardness levels is to add a liquid mineral control, dilute hard water with carefully measured amounts of soft water or drain and refill the pool.

WORKING WITH CHLORINE

Chlorine is the one chemical most swimmers can identify whether they own a pool or not. In its various forms, it is the most common disinfectant used in public and residential pools to control algae and kill bacteria carried into the pool by swimmers. A basic test kit measures free (usable) chlorine in the water, as well as pH level. The ideal range of free chlorine is between 1.0 and 1.5 ppm. See page 119 for information on how to test for free chlorine.

Chlorine is available in solid, liquid or gas forms. Solid forms include tablets, sticks, cartridges or granulated chlorine. Chlorine can be hand-fed or distributed into pool water automatically or semi-automatically. Chlorine products sold for sanitizing pool water are available in two basic forms.

Inorganic Chlorine—Liquid bleach (sodium hypochlorite) and inorganic chlorine granules (calcium hypochloride) are readily available. The disadvantage of using chlorine granules is that they don't dissolve completely. They leave a residue that can cloud the water and form scale.

Liquid bleach is unstable, has a short shelf life and loses its sanitizing power rapidly. Both types of inorganic chlorine raise the pH level rapidly and reduce the chlorine's effectiveness.

Slow-dissolving chlorine sticks and tablets are placed in skimmer basket or floating dispenser.

Inorganic chlorines are not stabilized and quickly break down in sunlight.

Organic Chlorine—Stabilized chlorines have a longer life and resist decomposing in sunlight. Chlorine combined with cyanuric acid filters out ultraviolet rays. That adds to the length of time chlorine is effective. Tablets, sticks or cartridges used in automatic or semi-automatic chlorinators can last from a few days to several weeks.

Chlorine Gas—There are two basic methods of treating pool water with chlorine gas. One is to hire a pool maintenance company to *gas* the pool on a regular basis during the swimming season. The chlorine gas is injected into the pool through a hose connected to a pressurized tank. This is an effective way of superchlorinating a pool, page 124, but chlorine gas dissipates rapidly. Frequent applications are required if this method is used as a regular chlorine treatment. This service is relatively new, and may not yet be available in your area.

The second method is to install a chlorine generator in the support system. This device generates chlorine gas by electrolysis and injects it into the pool through the return line of the support system. Sophisticated models have sensors that monitor chlorine demand and add the correct amount of chlorine when needed. Chlorine generators are discussed in detail on pages 55-56.

CHLORINE RESIDUAL

When chlorine is added to a pool, some of it will be consumed in the process of destroying bacteria, algae and other oxidizable materials.

The amount of chlorine needed to keep the chlorine level, or *chlorine residual,* above 1.0 ppm is called the *chlorine demand* of the water. The chlorine residual is the remaining disinfectant that isn't used destroying impurities. It is important to maintain a certain minimum free chlorine residual level. Only a small amount is needed to fight bacteria carried into the pool by swimmers or through the air in dust or rain.

Chlorine by itself is almost odorless. If there is a chlorine odor to the water, the residual level is too low. The strong odor often associated with chlorine occurs when it is combined with ammonia to form *chloramines.* An odor will be particularly noticeable when pH level is low. Chloramines

122 Pool Care & Repair

Liquid chlorine is poured directly into pool water. Follow label instructions for use.

Floating chlorine dispenser uses dry chlorine tablets. Tablets dissolve slowly, releasing small amounts of chlorine in water over a long period of time. This dispenser can be adjusted to meter amount of chlorine fed in water.

are responsible for itchy or burning eyes and skin irritation.

Pool water contains ammonia-nitrogen compounds. These nitrogenous compounds are produced primarily by urine in the water and fertilizers used near the pool. Such compounds use up chlorine. Heavy pool use dramatically increases chlorine demand. Test the water daily during periods of high pool activity.

ADDING CHLORINE

There are three ways to add chlorine to your pool—manually, semi-automatically or automatically. Any of these chlorinating methods will produce satisfactory results. Methods of installing chlorine gas are discussed on page 122.

Manual Feeding—Liquid bleach or liquid chlorine (sodium hypochlorite) and dry chlorine (calcium hypochloride and sodium dichlor) are the most common chlorines used to hand-feed a pool. Liquid chlorine mixes quickly in the water. Its disadvantages are that it has a low chlorine content and loses its zest if left on the shelf too long. Also, it dissipates more quickly in the pool than dry chlorine.

Dry chlorine in granular or tablet form dissolves more slowly than liquid chlorine and contains only about 65% available chlorine. Granular chlorine can be fed directly into the pool. Its disadvantages are that it may leave calcium residue in the water that can clog filters, or cement grains of sand together in sand filters and cause milky water.

Add both liquid and dry chlorine granules to the pool by sprinkling around the edges. Add chlorine in the early morning or evening.

Semi-Automatic Feeding—Chlorine sticks or tablets that dissolve slowly will steadily leach chlorine into the water. Two basic systems are used. Tablets or sticks are placed in the pool's skimmer basket or in a plastic dispenser that floats on the surface of the water. Some of these dispensers can be manually adjusted to control the amount of chlorine fed into the water.

Tablets or sticks offer uniform chlorination with little effort and with little or no investment in special equipment.

The advantage in semi-automatic chlorination is greater convenience of maintenance. Pool water still needs frequent testing for pH levels and available free chlorine level.

Automatic Feeding—Several pool suppliers manufacture automatic feeders that vary widely in cost and sophistication. Most are designed to be installed as a component of the support system, usually on the return line between the heater and the pool. There are also models that can be added any time after the system has been installed and is operating.

Automatic feeders adjust to control the flow of chlorine and other chemicals. Most semi-automatic feeders do not. Automatic feeders use chlorine tablets, sticks or canisters specifically designed for individual units. The manufacturer will recommend the type and form of chlorine to use.

The most sophisticated and expensive systems include sensors that monitor pH and free chlorine in the

Pool Care & Repair 123

return line. They automatically feed chlorine, acid or soda ash into the system as needed. The computer-controlled models are used widely in commercial pools. Smaller units are available for residential pools and spas.

SUPERCHLORINATION

No matter how carefully chlorine residual is maintained, combined chlorine (chloramines) and contaminants will build up in the pool. Combined chlorine is not effective in killing bacteria and controlling algae. Ammonia that combines with chlorine to form chloramines is added to the water by small children who are not "pool trained" and from lawn and garden fertilizers that find their way into pool water.

To break up chloramines or ammonia compounds, the pool usually must be superchlorinated or *shocked* every week or two during the swimming season. If outside temperatures rise above 85 degrees and the pool gets heavy use, it may have to be superchlorinated once a week.

This involves using a heavy dose of chlorine to raise the chlorine-residual level above 10.0 ppm. Unstabilized chlorine in liquid or granular form is commonly used. A gallon of liquid or a pound of dry chlorine is recommended for each 10,000 gallons of pool water.

Add chlorine after sundown. This prevents chlorine from being destroyed by ultraviolet rays and gives the pool time to recover before it can be used again. The pool is ready for use when chlorine residual drops below 3.0 ppm.

Superchlorination is also needed for algae control when filtration or pool-water circulation is not adequate. This step is necessary when the chlorine residual level drops to zero. At this level, the reading rapidly becomes negative. This occurs because at a zero chlorine residual level, bacteria accumulation, algae growth and buildup of organic matter cause the chlorine demand to increase. If the zero reading exists for a day or two in hot weather, water will turn cloudy or green.

An alternative to superchlorination is shocking with a non-chlorine oxidizer. This process also breaks chloramines. The oxidizer contains no chlorine and remains in the water longer to improve the retention of chlorine in its free form.

ALGAE INHIBITORS

Algae are microscopic forms of plant life that exist in the air and water. They grow explosively. When you can see algae, you will have about 30 million algae per ounce of pool water.

Algae can exist in a pool in a controlled state and remain invisible. When permitted to grow, algae will turn the water a green or mustard-color, or will appear on the walls of the pool as dark green or black spots.

In addition to creating an unpleasant appearance, excessive algae can clog the filter. This results in downtime for the pool and the need for expensive chemicals to correct the problem.

Regular pool maintenance will usually prevent algae buildup. But abnormal heat or rainstorms can upset the balance quickly enough to permit algae to grow. If you have a dark-bottom pool, an algae problem will be more difficult to spot. These pools must be checked more frequently to spot potential algae problems before they get out of control.

If algae becomes a problem, it may be necessary to add a supplemental algaecide, or algae inhibitor, to keep algae under control. An inhibitor is designed to penetrate pores in pool walls and into corners, favorite places for algae to grow. You can get algae inhibitors at pool-chemical suppliers.

TROUBLE-SHOOTING

Regular testing, correct use of pool chemicals and diligent care will help you avoid most pool problems. This includes mechanical problems that are caused by corrosion and water imbalance. When a problem does occur, it is usually possible to trace it back to its source.

When any water-quality problem occurs, a logical first step is to have the water analyzed by a pool dealer or product supplier who offers laboratory testing. These tests will provide a more detailed analysis than is possible with the average pH test kit used by most pool owners. These are the most common problems you are likely to encounter:

CLOUDY WATER

Correctly maintained pool water should look clean, clear and sparkling. If the water looks cloudy or hazy and lacks sparkle, check the following:

Water Filtration—Check the filter to see if it needs cleaning. Backwash sand or DE filters, or clean cartridges in cartridge filters. See pages 130-131. Increase time of filter operation until water clears—to 24 hours a day, if necessary.

Adjust pH—If you're using a high-pH chlorine, such as liquid bleach or calcium hypochlorite, switch to an organic chlorine that requires less acid to maintain pH balance. See page 122. Adjust pH to between 7.4 and 7.6., following instructions on page 120.

High Alkalinity—Test for alkalinity. If too high, add muriatic acid or dry pH reducer to lower alkalinity and correct pH balance. See page 121.

Superchlorinate—If there is a buildup of swimmer wastes that produces ammonia and chloramines, shock the pool with a heavy dose of chlorine, as described at left.

COLORED WATER

If maintenance is neglected in newly filled pools, water may take on various shades of reddish-brown, black or blue-green.

Reddish-Brown Water—A reddish-brown color results from iron particles in the water. Correct the discoloration by adjusting pH. Run filter continuously. Vacuum the pool bottom to pick up settled material. If the water remains colored, superchlorinate to help oxidize remaining iron. Metal chelating agents are also available to correct this condition.

Grey-Black Water—Manganese with traces of iron will cause water to appear dark or grey. *Floc* the pool or sand filter with alum or metal-removing compound. Floc is the gel-like substance formed when a coagulant is combined with suspended alkaline matter in the pool. Don't floc DE or cartridge filters. Check pH. Vacuum bottom of pool. If water remains colored, superchlorinate.

Blue-Green Water—Traces of copper or small amounts of iron will give the water a blue-green tinge. The cause can be poor filtration, incorrect pH balance or algae. Clean filter and run filter continuously. The pH balance or alkalinity is probably too low. Check pH balance and bring to 7.4 to 7.6.

Correct pH by adding soda ash or sodium bicarbonate. Vacuum the swimming pool. If water remains colored, superchlorinate.

ALGAE

These simple, single-cell plants can be the most troublesome problem in pool maintenance. They are easily identified. If they are the floating type, called *green algae*, the water will take on a greenish or mustard-colored tinge. If they are the clinging type, called *black algae*, black or dark green spots will appear on the bottom and sides of the pool. Black algae will initially collect in cracks and pool corners.

Algae can make the pool surface slippery. They will consume chlorine, making it difficult to hold an effective chlorine level. The longer the condition is permitted to exist, the more difficult it is to correct.

Chemical Treatment—Test for total alkalinity. If it is not between 80 and 120 ppm, adjust to the correct range. Adjust pH to 7.2 to 7.4. Add algaecide prescribed for type of algae in pool. One hour later, superchlorinate the pool using at least 1 gallon of liquid chlorine or 1 pound of dry chlorine for each 10,000 gallons of water. Turn off pump for 24 hours.

Manual Cleaning—With the filter off, use a stiff, stainless-steel algae brush to clean algae from sides and bottom of a plaster-finished pool. For fiberglass, painted or vinyl-lined pools, use brush with nylon bristles. Vacuum away dead algae. Clean filter. When algae have been removed, resume filtration.

Initial cleaning may destroy only the top layers of algae. Persistent algae on the pool sides may be killed by pouring liquid chlorine directly around the edges of the pool.

Difficult spots of algae on plaster can be removed with a hard pumice stone. The stone attached to the end of a brush pole will remove surface algae. It won't remove deep-seated algae. Pool suppliers carry all the items needed for manual cleaning.

Continue treatment cycles until pool water is clear. Do not permit swimming while algae treatments are continuing. Test and adjust water to proper pH balance before using pool again.

If algae conditions persist, use an al-

Pumice stone is used to remove stains and scale deposits from pool plaster. Stone can also be used to remove stubborn scale deposits on tile. Too-frequent use of stone on tile can scratch glazed tile surface.

gaecide or algae inhibitor on a regular basis to condition the water.

STAINS

Stains not traceable to minerals or algae can be caused by foreign matter in the pool. Hairpins or other metal objects left on the pool bottom will rust and stain. Leaves will also stain the pool bottom. Small metal items can be picked up from the pool bottom with a magnet attached to a skimmer net or brush pole.

Maintaining a proper pH balance, an adequate filtration cycle and regularly vacuuming or sweeping the pool will prevent or eliminate most stains.

On painted, fiberglass or vinyl-lined pools, stains can be removed with a chlorine solution or detergent. Most pool manufacturers produce or can recommend a suitable cleaner for their specific pools.

Some stains on plaster pools can be removed by brushing with fine, waterproof sandpaper. Badly stained plaster-finished pools may have to be drained and the surface washed with an acid solution. Stain-removing solutions are sold by pool suppliers.

After treating stains, test pool for

WATER CHEMISTRY GLOSSARY

The following list is intended to clarify the basic terms used in conditioning pool water.

ACID: Muriatic acid, sulphuric acid and sodium bisulphate are chemicals used to lower pH and alkalinity in pool water.

ACID DEMAND: The amount of acid required to reduce pH and alkalinity to the correct range.

ALGAE: Microscopic plants that propagate by airborne spores that enter the pool in rain, wind and dust. Some species are free-floating (green algae); others attach themselves to pool walls and surfaces (black algae). Free-floating, green algae turns the water a green or mustard color. Black algae appears as green or black splotches on pool walls.

ALGAECIDES: Also called algae inhibitors, these chemicals prevent or control algae. Some algaecides prevent growth; others are formulated to kill specific types of algae.

ALKALI: A hydroxide or base that neutralizes acid. Used to raise pH when conventional chemicals won't work.

ALUM: A coagulate used to settle suspended impurities in pool water. When alum combines with suspended alkaline matter in pool water, it creates a gel-like substance called *floc*. See COAGULATE.

BACTERIA: Undesirable unicellular germs with the potential to contaminate a pool and cause disease. They are introduced into the pool by swimmers, dust, rain and wind. Chlorine is used to control bacteria.

BACKWASHING: The system of cleaning sand and DE filters by reversing the flow of water through the filtering elements.

BAKING SODA: See SODIUM BICARBONATE.

BREAK POINT: In pool water, the point at which chlorine demand is neutralized and free chlorine becomes available to sanitize the water. Water with an excessive chlorine demand is superchlorinated to reach the break point. This is sometimes referred to a *break-pointing* a pool. See SUPERCHLORINATION.

BROMINE: A water disinfectant, usually a solid, used as a substitute for chlorine. Bromine is primarily used in spas and hot tubs.

BALANCED WATER: Water with the correct ratio of mineral content and pH level that prevents it from becoming too acidic (corrosive), or too alkaline (causing scaling). A pH reading between 7.2 and 7.6 is considered the ideal chemical balance.

CALCIUM HARDNESS: The amount of dissolved calcium in pool water. High hardness levels cause cloudy water and scaling. Low levels can harm the pool and pool equipment. The calcium level should be maintained between 175 and 250 parts per million (ppm) depending on the pool-shell finish.

CALCIUM CARBONATE: Crystalline compounds formed from calcium in the presence of high alkalinity.

CALCIUM HYPOCHLORIDE: Disinfectant compound of calcium and dry chlorine used as a shocking agent or for treatment of yellow or green algae.

CHLORAMINES: Compounds formed when chlorine combines with nitrogen from fertilizers, perspiration, skin proteins, urine and other impurities. The result is an ineffective disinfectant. Chloramines can cause eye and skin irritation and an unpleasant odor.

CHLORINE: The most widely used and effective sanitizing chemical for controlling bacteria and algae in pool water.

CHLORINE DEMAND: The amount of chlorine necessary to destroy germs, algae and other impurities in the water. The term *demand* refers to the amount of it required before chlorine can be made available to continue sanitizing pool water.

CHLORINE NEUTRALIZER: A solution of *sodium thiosulfate,* used to neutralize excessive chlorine in test water to obtain accurate pH and total-alkalinity readings. It is also used to counteract the bleaching effect of chlorine.

CHLORINE RESIDUAL: The chlorine level after chlorine demand has been satisfied. As available chlorine oxidizes new organic material coming into the pool, the residual drops until more chlorine is added. This is the reading obtained with the basic pool test kit.

COAGULATE: A chemical compound, usually alum, used in pool water to collect suspended matter. Commercial coagulates are available at pool suppliers. See FLOC.

COMBINED CHLORINE: Chlorine that combines with other chemicals in pool water to form chloramines and other chlorine compounds. Combined chlorine is not free to sanitize the water. See FREE CHLORINE.

CONDITIONER: A chemical holding agent or buffer that retards the dissipation of chlorine in sunlight.

---

pH balance and adjust water before resuming use of the pool.

SCALE

Rough deposits that coat pool walls and clog pipes, filters and heaters can cause serious equipment damage. Extreme cases of scale can all but shut off water flow through support equipment and cause the pump motor to labor. There is no simple solution to scaling.

This problem can occur in new in-ground plaster-finished pools if water balance isn't maintained while the new plaster is curing. High calcium hardness, usually combined with high total alkalinity and a high pH reading, is most often the cause of scaling in all pools.

If scaling is detected, don't use the pool heater. Test and correct the pH balance. Test for total alkalinity. Refer to *Total Alkalinity and pH,* page 120. If the calcium content and total hardness are excessive, the steps described on page 121 may be necessary to return water to an acceptable quality level.

The percentage of minerals and salts in pool water increases in minute amounts daily as pool water evaporates. As this buildup increases, pool chemicals work less and less effectively.

This condition can be controlled by monitoring the water and adding soft water when necessary. Soft water is corrosive and should be metered carefully. There may be no alternative, other than to drain the pool, scrub the pool walls with an acid wash and refill. If you live in an area with naturally hard water, a chemical scale inhibitor will slow scale buildup.

ELECTROLYSIS

When two different metals come in contact with chemically treated water, a small electric current may flow between the two metals. The current is barely detectable, but can corrode metal. This is called *electrolysis.*

If you notice electrolytic corrosion

126 Pool Care & Repair

CORROSION: The chemical reaction that causes the deterioration of metal. Water turns corrosive when the pH level drops below an acceptable level, making water acidic.

CYANURIC ACID: The chemical *trihydroxy triazine*. It is a stabilizer or conditioner that helps prevent sunlight from dissipating chlorine strength. It is used to stabilize water before starting routine pool maintenance.

DPD: The chemical, *Diethyl-p-phenylene Diamine,* used as a reagent to test free chlorine in pool water.

DRY ACID: A granular material, *sodium bisulfate,* used to lower total alkalinity or pH in pool water.

ELECTROLYSIS: The flow of electrical current created by electrochemical interaction between two dissimilar metals plumbed together. It can also be caused by power lines too close to the pool. It can cause black stains around metal fixtures or on plaster pool walls.

FREE CHLORINE: Usable chlorine in pool water available to kill algae and bacteria. This is the chlorine left after the water's chlorine need has been met. Free available chlorine should be maintained at between 1.0 and 1.5 ppm to destroy contaminants carried into the pool. See CHLORINE RESIDUAL.

FLOC: The gel-like substance formed when a coagulant, usually alum, is combined with suspended alkaline matter in pool water.

JUNK: Pool industry term for organic matter or protein materials in pool water, such as leaves, perspiration, body oils, suntan lotion, hair, lint, and so forth. Junk in the water increases chlorine demand.

HARDNESS: The quantity of minerals, primarily calcium and magnesium, dissolved in water. See CALCIUM HARDNESS.

MICRON: One-millionth of a meter. Used to describe particle sizes that filters are capable of trapping.

MURIATIC ACID: Commercial term for a diluted solution of hydrochloric acid. It is used to lower pH level or total alkalinity in pool water. Also used to clean scale from pool plaster and equipment.

NEUTRALIZER: See CHLORINE NEUTRALIZER.

OTO: The chemical, *orthotolidine* used as a reagent to test total and combined chlorine in pool water.

OXIDIZER: A non-chlorine shocking agent that removes the buildup of contaminates and chloramines in pool water without raising chlorine levels.

pH: The measurement of acidity and alkalinity in pool water. pH means *potential hydrogen,* and refers to the concentration of hydrogen ions present in the water. A pH of 7.0 is neutral. Below 7.0, the water is acidic and can corrode pool equipment and damage the pool finish. Above 7.8, the water is too alkaline and can cause cloudiness and scale formation. The ideal range for pool water is between 7.2 and 7.6. Improper pH affects the sanitizing power of chlorine.

PPM: The abbreviation for *parts per million,* the common measurement by weight for minerals and chemicals in pool water. One pound of material to 120,000 gallons of water is 1 ppm.

PHENOL RED: The chemical reagent used for testing pH level.

REAGENTS: The chemical agents or indicators used to test various aspects of water quality.

SCALE: A buildup of solid calcium carbonate deposits caused by high mineral content. Scale can form on pool walls, in pipes and in heater coils. Excessive scale can damage the pool finish and support equipment.

SODA ASH: *Sodium carbonate,* the most common chemical solution used to raise pH level and correct an over-acidic condition.

SODIUM BICARBONATE: Baking soda used to raise total alkalinity of pool water with little change in pH.

SODIUM BISULFATE: A dry acid that is mixed with water and used to lower pH and total alkalinity.

SODIUM HYPOCHLORITE: Liquid chlorine—an unstable chlorinating agent—used as a pool disinfectant. It contains more salt than other chlorines.

STABILZER: See CONDITIONER.

SUPERCHLORINATION: A large dose (5 to 10 ppm) of chlorine used to destroy ammonia buildup in pool water. A high level of chlorine is necessary to reach *break-point* chlorination, or converting weak *combined chlorine* to *free available chlorine.* Also known as *shocking,* or *breakpointing* the water.

TOTAL ALKALINITY: The amount of alkali salts (carbonates, bicarbonates and hydroxides) in pool water. Total alkalinity affects and controls pH. If total alkalinity is too high, pH is hard to adjust. If it is too low, pH will be unstable and difficult to maintain. Total alkalinity should be between 80 to 150 ppm.

TURNOVER RATE: The time required to pump the total volume of pool water through the filter. Also called the recirculation rate.

---

at joints where pipes of different metals meet, install a fitting called a *dielectric union.*

Experienced pool builders will avoid combining metals in plumbing or in support equipment likely to cause electrolysis. Take care not to use dissimilar metals in making pool-equipment repairs. Electrolysis will occur between iron or steel and copper. Blackened stainless steel is a sign of electrolysis.

EQUIPMENT MAINTENANCE

Most support equipment problems can be avoided if care is taken to maintain high water quality. A pump, filter and heater are basically simple pieces of equipment. They are designed to last many years with minimal maintenance.

No two pools are exactly alike and no all-purpose maintenance schedule will apply to all pools. How often a pump is serviced or a filter cleaned depends on how often the pool is used, the pool's location, weather conditions, the filter size, water quality and many other factors. The best maintenance schedule will evolve over a period of time, based on the pool owner's experience.

The most effective way to arrive at an ideal maintenance schedule for your pool is to keep a daily maintenance log. Write down the following items:

- Dates service is performed.
- When the water is tested and the test results.
- The quantity and type of each chemical added.
- When the filter is backwashed or the cartridges cleaned.
- The number of hours the filtration system is in operation.
- Any other miscellaneous notes on non-routine use or service.

The quality of pool water changes constantly. Over a period of time, you can determine the average amounts of

Pump strainer basket traps leaves and other debris that could clog pump. It should be checked and cleaned frequently.

chemicals necessary to maintain good water quality. You will also be able to establish the ideal number of hours to run the filtration system each day.

The goal is to maintain good water quality by using the fewest and smallest amounts of chemicals. The filtration system should be operated the fewest possible number of hours each day. If you can achieve this, you will be keeping a clean pool at the lowest possible cost.

PUMP AND MOTOR

Most pumps installed for residential pools are self-priming and have self-lubricating bearings, so they need little attention. Make sure you receive the owner's manual and warranty card packed with the motor when it is shipped from the manufacturer to the pool dealer.

The owner's manual will list specific maintenance steps to be performed and include the terms of the warranty. Mechanical problems covered by warranty must usually be resolved between you and the manufacturer. The pool dealer or builder won't be involved unless the problem is the result of an installation error.

Clean Strainer Basket—The most common maintenance performed on a pool pump is cleaning the strainer basket of hair, leaves and other debris sucked in from the pool. Debris buildup in the strainer basket can cause back-pressure in the plumbing system and shorten the life of the support equipment. See photo at left.

How often the strainer needs cleaning depends on how many swimmers have been using the pool and how much debris normally collects in the pool. An average may be about once a week. Steps to clean the strainer are as follows:

Step 1—Turn off the motor and power to the motor.
Step 2—If the pump is below water level, turn off the valves on lines leading to and from the pump. If you don't, water will flow out of the strainer pot when the lid is removed.
Step 3—Loosen the clamp or tee bolts holding the pot lid in place.
Step 4—Remove the basket and clean out debris. It will save time if you have an extra strainer basket to drop in when you remove the dirty one. You can then clean the strainer at your leisure.
Step 5—Check the 0-ring or gasket that seals the lid. Make sure it is still round and pliable and not cracked or damaged. Keep a spare on hand, because the ring will need periodic replacement.
Step 6—Lubricate the ring with a light coat of non-petroleum grease. The pump manufacturer may specify the type of lubricant to use.
Step 7—Replace basket, prime the pump—see below—replace and secure the lid, and turn on water supply, if it has been turned off.
Step 8—Turn on motor.
Step 9—If air bubbles appear in the pool, bleed off remaining air in the plumbing by opening the relief valve on the top of the filter tank. When water spurts out of the valve, turn it off and continue the filtration cycle.

If air bubbles continue to appear in the pool, check to see if the pump-pot lid is sealed tightly. A damaged ring can cause a leak. If the lid is tight, check to see if there is a crack in the lid. Check to see if the water level in the pool is below the skimmer inlet and not flowing into the system. Check the pressure gage on top of the filter tank. If pressure is zero, the pump may need priming.

Priming the Pump—Don't run any pump dry. Even self-priming pumps can run dry. If the pump continues to operate when no water is flowing through the system, the mechanical seal, which is water-cooled, will be damaged by friction and heat and the pump will leak. If the pump doesn't catch prime after 1 to 2 minutes, turn it off.

To prime the pump, shut off the motor. Remove the strainer-pot lid. Fill the pot with water and allow water to run back through the incoming line. Lubricate the seal, replace and secure the lid and turn on the motor. Release air through the relief valve on top of the filter tank. Close the relief valve when water spurts out.

If the pump still fails to catch prime, repeat the steps above. If that fails, put the nozzle of the garden hose in the skimmer line and turn on the water full force. If the pump still fails to catch prime, the problem may be a damaged impeller or a break in the system's water lines. Call a pool-service company to find and correct the problem.

Replacing Pump Seal—If the pump leaks, the seal may be damaged. Removing the pump and replacing the seal is not difficult.

Before taking this step, check the owner's manual to see if specific instructions are provided. You will need to know the brand, model and number of the pump to order a replacement seal. The pump gasket should also be replaced whenever the pump and motor are disassembled.

These steps will be similar for most pumps:

Step 1—Turn off the motor and shut off the circuit breaker or remove the fuse to cut off power to the pump.

Step 2—Loosen the four bolts that hold the pump assembly to the pump housing. Pull the motor straight up so bolt holes align and the motor can be removed.

Step 3—Remove the impeller. Most impellers are threaded onto the pump shaft. Some are held by allen screws. Check it for signs of wear. Clean debris from the impeller vanes. This will expose the water seal.

Step 4—Remove the old seal. Take care not to gouge or scratch the pump seating surfaces. Remember how the seal is positioned.

Step 5—Clean the pump shaft and surfaces that will be contacted by the new seal. Use a fine emery or crocus cloth to remove rust, scratches and burrs. Wipe the surfaces clean and lubricate with a medium-fiber marine grease, a light oil or soapy water. Lubricate the surfaces of the new seal that will come in contact with the metal surfaces of the pump.

Step 6—The white ceramic surface and the molded plastic surface are the faces of the seal that will be in contact with each other. Wipe these faces clean with a soft cotton cloth. Don't lubricate these seal faces. Be careful when handling the new seal as these surfaces are easily damaged.

Step 7—Install the new seal with the faces directed toward each other. Check the alignment to see that all the parts are in the right position. The seal must be evenly seated and the surfaces must meet exactly. Move the seal back and forth on the pump shaft to assure proper lubrication.

Step 8—Lightly lubricate the gasket and bolts with grease. Replace the impeller and reassemble the pump. Before turning on the motor, check to see that the pump shaft turns freely. If it doesn't, the impeller may not be correctly aligned. Disassemble the pump and check the alignment. Reassemble the pump.

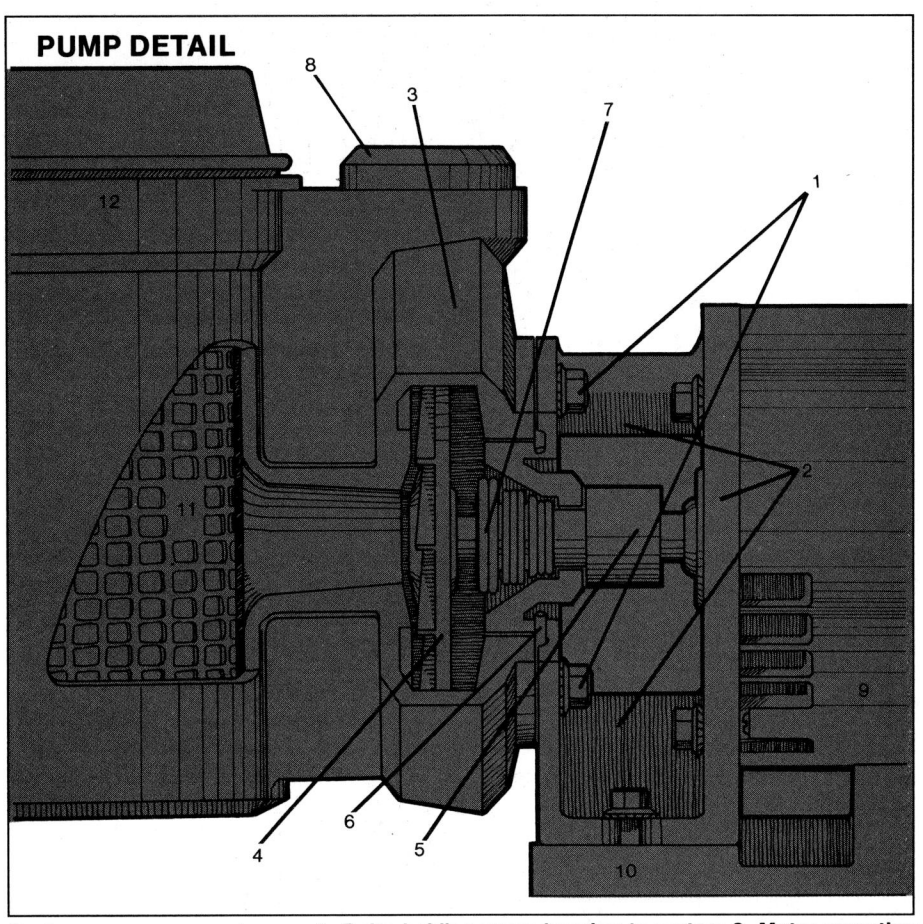

PUMP DETAIL

Basic pump components are: 1. Bolts holding pump housing to motor; 2. Motor mounting bracket; 3. Pump housing; 4. Impeller; 5. Pump shaft; 6. Gasket or O-ring; 7. Water seal; 8. Outlet port; 9. Motor; 10. Pump and motor support; 11. Pump strainer basket; 12. Pump strainer pot.

Step 9—Turn on the power to the pump and start the pump. If necessary, prime the pump as described in the preceding section.

Troubleshooting—During day-to-day operation of the filter system, stay alert for trouble signs from the pump. Catching a problem early may lead to a simple solution.

A motor that whines indicates that the bearings may be badly worn. Worn bearings can make the motor run hot and damage the armature and bearing seats.

Shut off power to the pump at the breaker box or remove the fuse. Shut off the water in the system. Loosen the bolts holding the motor in place and remove the motor.

Bearings can be replaced at a motor-repair shop or you can check with your pool dealer or the manufacturer to see if it can be returned for repairs. Check your warranty. Service may still be covered.

If the motor hums and won't start, check it immediately. When the motor is switched on, it may throw

Pool Care & Repair 129

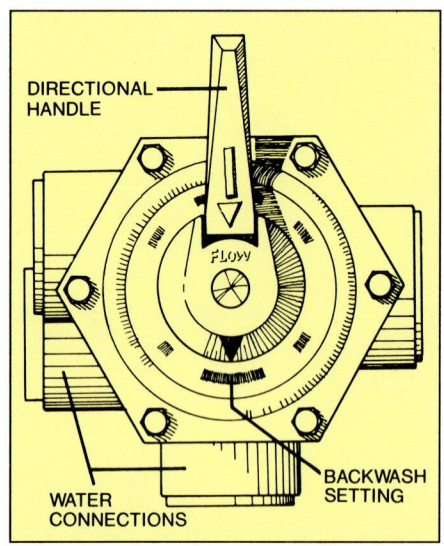

Water-direction valve on sand filter diverts flow for backwashing.

the circuit breaker or blow a fuse. This condition is usually caused by a faulty *capacitor*. If the motor won't start at all, the switch may be dirty or defective.

A switch or a capacitor is easy to replace. Check your owner's manual for instructions. An electric-motor supply house will be able to sell you the parts you need if you provide the brand, model and number of the motor. If you have difficulty finding a capacitor, you will have to order it directly from the pump manufacturer.

Never work on a motor unless the power is cut off at the breaker box or fuse box. It is dangerous to work on a motor around water with the power on.

If the capacitor is not the problem, the motor may be burned out. The only solution is to replace the motor. The motor is usually secured to the pump with four bolts. These bolts must be removed to free the motor. Your local supplier can tell you how to proceed. Information should also be included in your owner's manual.

Protect the Motor—The pump motor must be sheltered from water, sun, weather, dirt and other foreign matter. It's an air-cooled electrical appliance that needs protection.

A small shed or a custom-built enclosure designed to shelter the motor must have adequate air circulation to keep the motor from overheating.

Protect the motor from splashed pool water, rain or a soaking while washing the deck. A motor damaged by water, or burned out because of poor ventilation, is assumed to be neglect on the part of the pool owner. The manufacturer has no obligation to honor a warranty under these circumstances. When planning the pool, the motor should be located a safe distance from the pool and be well protected from the elements.

If the motor does accidentally get wet, allow it to dry thoroughly before restarting.

FILTERS

High-rate sand, diatomaceous earth (DE) and cartridge filters are the three commonly used filters for residential pools, and for good reason. All three effectively keep pool water free of minute particles of dirt and other impurities. The type of filter chosen is largely a matter of personal preference. Most major pool-filter manufacturers produce all three types. For additional information on choosing a filter, see pages 48-49.

All filters are cleaned in much the same way. Check the manual supplied with your filter for specific instructions. Once the filter has been installed and plaster dust or other construction debris has been removed from the water, the most important maintenance is keeping the filter clean. There are few, if any, moving parts in most residential pool filters.

Most pool filters are equipped with a gage that measures pressure buildup in the filter tank. As debris particles are trapped in the sand, diatomaceous earth, or cartridge pores, it takes an increasing amount of pressure to force water through the filter. This is the pressure that is measured by the gage. See photo on page 49.

The gage reading will indicate when it is time to backwash the filter or clean the cartridges. No two systems are exactly the same, so there is no specific reading to tell you when the filter needs cleaning. Take note of the pressure reading immediately after the filter and pump strainer basket have been cleaned and the system activated.

When the pressure rises about 10 pounds, it is time to clean the filter. Another method is to backwash or clean when the pressure rises 50% above the initial reading.

A less common method of determining when a filter needs cleaning is by reduced water flow. A flow meter located on the return line measures the number of gallons per minute flowing through the system. When flow decreases approximately 20% below startup gpm, it's probably time to clean the filter.

Regardless of the gage or flow reading, if the water is no longer clear, it's time to clean the filter. Unclear water could mean you are not running the system long enough each day. Off-color water can indicate serious water-quality problems. See page 124.

Cleaning may be necessary once a week or as infrequently as once a month. The weather, pool use and filter size will determine the cleaning cycle. The greater the filter's capacity, the less often it must be cleaned. It will only take a few months of operation to be able to anticipate when the filter needs cleaning.

High-Rate Sand Filters—As dirt particles and other solids become trapped between grains of sand, it takes increasing pressure to force water through the filter. The steps to clean the filter are as follows:

Step 1—Turn off the pump.
Step 2—Place the water-direction control valve in the backwash position and start the pump.
Step 3—Backwash for approximately 2 minutes or until clear water either runs out of the discharge line or can be seen in the sight glass. From 50 to 300 gallons of water will be used in backwashing. Some communities forbid discharging backwashed water into the sewer system. The only solution is to dig a dry well large enough to handle the discharged water.
Step 4—Shut off the pump.
Step 5—If the direction-control valve has a rinse position, restart the pump and turn the valve to rinse. This will direct the flow through the filter and directly into the waste line. This reduces the amount of unsettled dirt that will be sent back into the pool. Rinse 15 to 20 seconds.

If there is no rinse cycle, shut off the pump and return the valve to filtering position. Restart the pump and resume the filtration cycle. Backwashing may stir up fine grains of sand that will be noticed in the discharge. They may appear when the pump is restarted. This is a normal condition.

Once a year, inspect the sand inside the filter. Most filters have simple clamp rings that can be opened without tools. If the surface has a buildup of scale or other material not being removed by backwashing, remove the top layer of sand and replace it with new sand. Filter sand should be usable for several years without replacement.

DE Filters—Diatomaceous earth is the finest medium for pool filters. DE filters also require more care than high-rate sand filters. A series of fine grids, called *septa*, inside the filter tank are coated with DE. DE mixed with water, to form a slurry, is fed into the system at the skimmer. DE is drawn into the filter and distributed evenly over the septa.

The septa are intended only to support the filtering medium. The pump should never be run unless the septa have been coated with DE. The pores will become clogged and the septa permanently damaged. There are several types of DE filters; *vertical, spin* and *deck*. These terms refer to the configuration of the septa inside the filter. Check your owner's manual for instructions on cleaning and treating your specific DE filter.

In some filters, the septa must be removed for cleaning. The septa are cleaned manually, then replaced. In others, they are cleaned by backwashing—similar to a sand filter. Both of these methods make it necessary to reintroduce DE into the system after each cleaning to coat the septa.

In another type of filter, dirt and DE are jarred off the septa manually so they fall into the bottom of the filter tank. These are called *bump assisted* filters. When the pump is restarted, the septa are recoated. DE must be replaced after several recoatings.

An annual cleaning will help keep a DE filter functioning effectively. This involves removing the septa and using a brush to scrub them with a filter-degreasing compound.

After thoroughly rinsing the septa, soak them for 24 hours in a filter descaling compound. These compounds are available at pool suppliers. Rinse and scrub the elements before replacing them in the filter. An acid-soak once a year will lengthen time between cleaning cycles and extend the life of the septa.

When recoating the septa, use approximately 1 pound of DE for every 10 square feet of filter area.

Loose dirt in filter cartridges can be removed with a spray gun attached to a garden hose. More stubborn dirt and scale requires soaking cartridges in acid solution. See text below.

Water backwashed through a DE filter can be disposed of most effectively by using a *separation tank*. Contaminated water is washed into a reusable bag in the separation tank. DE caught in the bag can be deposited in the garbage, the bag rinsed and placed back in the tank ready for the next filter cleaning. Water remaining in the separation tank, cleansed of DE, can be disposed of as non-contaminated waste water.

DE filters use less water for backwashing and are more practical than sand filters in areas where water use is limited.

Cartridge Filters—The percentage of cartridge filters being installed by new pool owners has been rising. They are the least complicated filters to understand and maintain. When it is time to clean the filter, the cartridge or cartridges are lifted out of the filter tank, washed and replaced. No backwashing is required.

Plaster dust in the water of a newly built plastered pool may make it necessary to dispose of the start-up cartridges. Once construction dust has been removed, a properly cared for set of cartridges should last for 2 or 3 years. Some cartridge pool filters use several individual cartridges in one tank. The number of cartridges needed depends on the size and design of the filter.

Alternating two sets of cartridges is the most convenient system for maintaining a cartridge filter. A second set of filters increases the initial investment, but by alternating the cartridges, each set will have more than twice the life.

When the set of cartridges in the filter needs cleaning, shut off the pump, remove the dirty cartridges and replace them with a clean set. This will get the filtration system back in operation in a few minutes and make it possible to clean the dirty cartridges when it's convenient.

Cartridges can be cleaned using a special filter-cleaning compound available at pool suppliers.

Calcium deposits can be removed with a solution of 1 part muriatic acid to 20 parts water. Handle acid carefully. Always add acid to water. Don't pour water into acid. Soak the cartridges until they stop bubbling. Remove them and flood with clear water.

Pool Care & Repair   **131**

GAS HEATER DETAIL

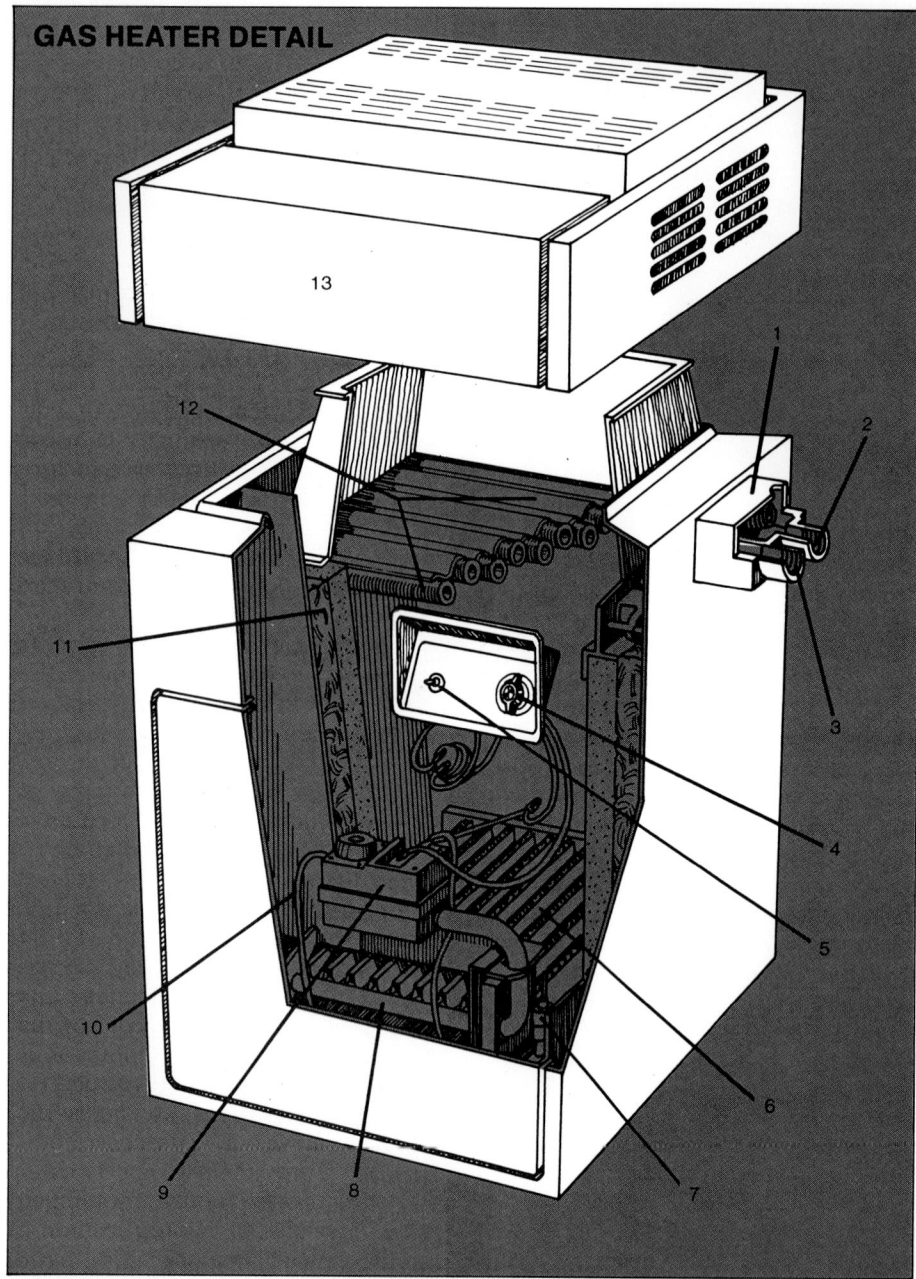

Shown are major components of a typical gas heater. They include: 1. Front water-header assembly (usually houses pressure switch, high-limit switch, automatic-bypass valve and temperature sensor for thermostat); 2. Hot-water outlet; 3. Cold-water inlet; 4. Temperature control (thermostat); 5. On/off switch; 6. Burners; 7. Pilot light or electric-spark ignition; 8. Burner manifold; 9. Automatic gas valve; 10. Pilot tube; 11. Fiberglass insulation; 12. Heat-exchanger tubes; 13. Vent-top assembly.

Slightly dirty filters can be cleaned by spraying them with a high-pressure nozzle on a garden hose. Moderately dirty filters can be taken to a coin-operated car wash and cleaned. Hot water under high pressure works effectively.

POOL HEATERS

Natural gas is the most efficient fuel for pool heaters. Where natural gas is available, gas-fueled heaters are by far the most common. If you have no natural-gas service, electric heaters or propane-fueled heaters are used. There are several companies manufacturing heaters designed specifically for residential pools. For more on selecting heaters, see pages 50-53.

Make sure you get the owner's manual for your heater and know the terms of the warranty. The following information on heater maintenance will apply to most gas and electric heaters. The heater manufacturer also may have specific service requirements necessary to keep your heater operating efficiently.

The heater is the most complex component of the support system. The key to trouble-free heater operation is maintaining good water quality. High pH, excess alkalinity and excessive calcium hardness can cause scaling in the heater tubes that lowers heater efficiency and can lead to serious damage. A consistently low pH will corrode heater tubes and other metal plumbing parts.

Heater Inspection—A regular inspection can help keep the heater running efficiently, avoid malfunctions and hold down pool-heating costs. The heater should always be examined before the swimming season begins and inspected periodically during the summer.

Check to see that the top area is free of leaves and debris. Examine the vent pipe on open-flame heaters to see that it is secure and free of leaks. If your gas heater is in an enclosed room, make sure vents to the outside have not been closed or obstructed.

Check inside the heater cabinet for leaves, spider webs, bird or rodent nests or other debris. Thoroughly clean the inside of the cabinet.

Each time you inspect or operate the heater, turn the thermostat switch up and down quickly several times to keep it free of dirt and corrosion. Set thermostat to desired temperature.

If you have a gas, oil or propane heater, check the burners for accumulated soot. You may need a mirror and flashlight to see. If soot has accumulated, follow the guidelines on page 133 for cleaning it and correcting the cause.

Heaters with Pilot Lights—The pilot light should be turned off when the heater is not in use. To light the pilot, follow manufacturer's directions. Instructions are usually written on the nameplate inside the heater, or included in the owner's manual. When the pilot is lit, turn the gas valve knob to the **ON** position. When the filtration system is turned on, the heater should come on.

Check the pilot light and burners to see that you have a full, clean flame—blue with little yellow or orange.

If you have difficulty lighting the pilot light, keeping it lit or holding a burner flame, turn off the gas supply to the heater. Call the gas company to

132   Pool Care & Repair

have the equipment examined by an experienced service representative. In most areas, the gas company will inspect gas appliances free of charge.

Solving Problems—Some common heater malfunctions can be easily corrected by tracing the problem to the source. Here are some examples:

Heater Won't Turn On—Often the heater won't come on because restricted water flow in the system will activate the heater's protective switch. Protective switches are designed to turn off the heater if there is too little water flow. The most common reason for low flow is a dirty filter. When the pressure-gage reading is high, it means the flow out of the filter is low. Often, the problem will take care of itself when the filter is cleaned. If the filter is not the problem, check the pump-strainer basket for debris and clean it.

Reduced flow can be caused by blockages in the main drain or skimmer. Make sure the pump is not airlocked or clogged. Check to see that all lines are clear. Check water valves, particularly the heater-bypass valve. See that they are all turned on.

If you have an electric heater, make sure the breaker is on. For gas heaters, make sure the gas valve is on. Make sure the pilot is lit and correctly adjusted. Make sure the thermostat is turned high enough.

Heater Won't Turn Off—A heater can be severely damaged if it continues to operate with no water circulation. Also, hot water forced back into the filter can damage it. Never bypass a protective switch to permit the heater to operate. The purpose of the protective switch is to turn off the heater when there is little or no water flow.

Check to see if the pressure switch is clogged. If the switch isn't functioning, it won't turn off the heater when water flow is reduced. The pressure switch is oil filled. If you see oil on the switch, it is probably defective. Check for shorts in the electrical system. Make sure the gas valve is functioning.

If no immediate solution can be found, turn off the filtration system and the electricity or gas to the heater and call a service representative.

Heater Won't Raise Pool-Water Temperature—Check to see that the filtration cycle is long enough to heat pool water to the desired temperature. Adjust the time clock to increase the length of the filtration cycle. If the water is cold, run the system continuously until water temperature rises.

A dirty filter that reduces water flow will cause the heater to shut down quickly. Make sure the filter is clean and the water lines are clear.

Make sure the thermostat is set high enough and it is working correctly. Your owner's manual should include a method for testing the thermostat. If the thermostat is switching on and off too frequently, it will prevent proper heating. You may need to adjust the cycling mechanism that controls the temperature difference required to turn on the heater.

Check the automatic heater-bypass assembly. If it is malfunctioning, it may not be directing water through the heater. Inspect the bypass-spring assembly and clean the center shaft with crocus paper to prevent further sticking. Crocus paper is a fine emery-type paper that uses iron oxide as a polishing agent.

Soot Has Formed—Soot can be a problem in any open-flame heater. Remove light soot with a wire brush. Remove scale buildup to prevent further sooting. When removing soot, remove the exchanger tubes before you clean them. This keeps debris from clogging burner orifices.

The most common cause of soot is poor ventilation. Soot can also be caused by too much water flowing through the heater. This is caused by a faulty valve. Restricted gas flow or the wrong fuel for the heater will cause soot. Clean all the burner and air inlets.

Scaling—Cool water being pumped through the heater can cause extreme condensation. This leads to sooting, which contributes to scaling. If alkalinity and hardness levels are allowed to remain unbalanced or at high levels, scale will quickly form. A chlorinator installed on the wrong side of the heater may cause scaling.

A malfunctioning bypass valve that continuously directs water through the heater can also cause scaling. Scaling can also be caused by a defective pressure switch or high-limit switch that permits the heater to operate under low water flow.

Scale can be removed chemically or mechanically. Chemical removal involves soaking the heater tubes in a mild acid solution of 3 parts water to 1 part muriatic acid. This process will remove scale, but will also remove a small amount of copper in the tubes, shortening their life. When the tubes are clean, flush the exchanger with a soda ash solution. Coat steel plates with high-temperature, rust-inhibiting paint, such as that used for painting automobile engines. This method works best to remove light scale formations.

Mechanical removal involves taking the exchanger assembly out of the heater and cleaning the tubes with a carbide drill bit and brush attachment in a low-speed drill. Wait until the tubes are dry before attempting to clean. This method works best for heavy scaling.

After scale has been removed, replace the heater's gasket set before replacing the exchanger assembly. Follow manufacturer's directions.

POOL SKIMMER

Clean the skimmer basket daily when the pool is getting heavy use or when wind is blowing an excessive amount of debris into the pool. Cleaning is simple. It isn't necessary to shut off the system.

Remove the access cover, lift out the basket and dispose of leaves and other debris. Replace the basket and put the cover back in place. See photo above.

If cleaning the skimmer basket is neglected, it can clog, reducing water

In most pools, access to skimmer basket is through recessed cover in pool deck. Check basket frequently, especially during windy weather.

POOL REPAIR

There are many reasons why even a carefully maintained pool may need repairing. Problems can be traced to a variety of causes, such as defective materials, poor workmanship, earth movement, extreme temperatures or simply old age. Even the best-quality pool will eventually need a new liner or replastering.

Many minor structural or cosmetic repairs can be done by the pool owner. Most manufacturers of vinyl-lined and fiberglass pools sell repair kits to take care of small tears in vinyl liners or gouges in fiberglass shells.

When you have the option, select repair materials produced or recommended by the pool manufacturer. It is important to use compatible materials that will guarantee a good bond. Follow the manufacturer's instructions carefully. Pool shell repairs can be made by draining enough water to expose the damaged areas. Many simple repairs can be made underwater using epoxy putty or similar materials.

Minor repairs to concrete decks and gunite shells can be made using premixed patching materials. Before making any repair, find out what caused the original damage. Cracks that develop in a sprayed-concrete pool or a masonry pool deck could be the first signs of rising ground water or severe earth movement.

Solutions to water-quality problems are given in the trouble-shooting section on page 124. Problems that develop in heater, filter, pump or other support-system components are covered under their respective sections in this chapter.

Before taking on major repair projects, seek expert counsel. If you have maintained a good working relationship with the original pool builder or pool dealer, ask for suggestions. If your pool is relatively new, check to see if damage is covered by the original guarantee.

Pool dealers and builders often do pool repairs. Other companies that do pool repairs are listed under the heading, *Swimming Pool Service*, in the Yellow Pages of your phone book. Also, your pool-maintenance company or pool dealer may be able to give you the names of local companies with good reputations for doing good repair work.

If you are facing a major pool repair, select your repair company with as much care as you would in choosing a new pool builder. See pages 36-37. Structural problems caused by shifting earth or poor workmanship in the original installation may require greater technical expertise than building a new pool.

Some minor pool repairs that can be handled as do-it-yourself projects may be handled more economically by a pool-repair company. It may be more costly to acquire the necessary tools and materials to do a job than to turn the work over to a repair service with the technical knowledge and equipment needed to do the work quickly.

Unless you are sure you want to make the repairs yourself, take time to get two or three quotes from local companies before making a final decision.

COMMON POOL PROBLEMS

The basic pool types—vinyl-lined, sprayed-concrete, fiberglass and above-ground—are susceptible to slightly different problems that make minor repairs necessary. Earth movement that can cause serious structural damage to a sprayed-concrete pool, won't harm an above-ground pool. Objects that can puncture a vinyl pool liner will have little affect on a fiberglass or sprayed-concrete pool.

Vinyl-Lined Pools—The most common damage to a vinyl-lined pool is a split or tear in the vinyl liner. Small splits under 2 or 3 inches can usually be repaired using a kit recommended by the pool manufacturer. Repair kits should be available through the dealer that sold you the pool.

Most repairs can be made underwater, so draining the pool is often unnecessary. Larger tears can be patched. Kits are also available for this purpose.

Vinyl liners installed in new, good-quality pools are durable. They are not easily punctured in normal use, but can be under abusive conditions. Don't allow metal objects or toys with sharp edges in the pool area. A vinyl-lined pool is no place to practice with a spear gun.

Widespread cracking or tearing may indicate the liner needs replacing. New techniques for cutting liners make it possible to have a new liner custom-fitted to an old pool. Your local pool dealer should be able to help you order and install the correct size.

Buckling pool walls or cracks in surrounding deck are usually signs of earth movement or underground water problems. Under normal circumstances, pressure exerted by water in the pool offsets pressure exerted by backfill around the pool shell. Water leaking from the pool can cause soil to expand, as can extremely wet weather or existing ground water.

Such damage is less likely to happen if the pool is full of water, but it can in extreme cases. It may be necessary to call in the help of a soils engineer to analyze the problem and a pool builder to make the repairs.

Fiberglass Pools—Most damage to fiberglass-pools is cosmetic. The pool shell actually gains strength with age and remains flexible enough to absorb minor earth pressures.

Scratches in the pool shell are in-

---

flow. This will reduce the effectiveness of the whole filtration system.

OPENING YOUR POOL

If you have a new pool or have closed your pool for the winter, there are several steps you must take to put your pool in shape for swimming. Starting up a new pool requires preliminary cleaning to eliminate plaster dust or other construction debris.

New Plaster-Finished Pools—Take extra care with new plaster-finished concrete pools. These pools should be filled immediately upon completion. Use acid sparingly, if at all, during the first two weeks the pool is in use. This allows fresh plaster time to harden and the water to balance.

If total alkalinity is over 140 ppm, or if pH rises above 8.0, add small amounts of acid to lower pH to between 7.6 and 7.8.

Daily brushing with a wall brush will help remove fine sediment that has accumulated on pool walls and bottom. This condition will disappear in a few weeks.

Operate the filter during and after wall brushing. Don't attempt to use a evitable and do little harm to the function or the pool. Gouges can be repaired, but it is difficult to produce a perfect cosmetic match.

Discolored or scratched shells can be painted with a durable epoxy paint. Most fiberglass-pool dealers recommend making the cosmetic repairs without repainting. Even epoxy paint will not become as hard as the original gelcoat or acrylic applied at the factory.

Many pool manufacturers provide repair kits to touch up minor scratches and gouges. Kits include a gelcoat liquid that matches the original shell color. Because shell color of the pool tends to fade over a period of years, matching it will be difficult.

Shell discoloring can be minimized by keeping water chemically balanced and using a gelcoat conditioner available from pool suppliers.

Sprayed-Concrete Pools—Sunlight and pool chemicals will gradually cause plaster to deteriorate and flake. Over a period of years, the plaster will develop a rough surface and stain more easily than a newly plastered pool.

Plaster deterioration is referred to as *spalling*. Spalling plaster is not a serious structural problem. The pool should be replastered when it is cosmetically desirable. A well-maintained concrete pool should last about 10 years before it needs replastering. The exact life of the original plaster is determined by water quality, exposure to the sun and temperature fluctuations.

Localized spots of spalled plaster can be repaired by sanding off all loose material and patching with new plaster.

As an alternative to replastering, the pool shell can be painted with an epoxy pool paint. A sprayed-concrete pool with a painted shell will need repainting every 3 or 4 years. Once a pool has been painted, it cannot be replastered unless all the paint is removed by wear or sandblasting the surface.

Minor cracks in plaster can be repaired with epoxy putty or special caulking compound. Your local pool builder or pool supplier will be able to recommend a specific brand.

If serious cracks develop, check to determine what has caused the shell to crack. If there has been earth movement, call in qualifed help to examine the problem and to suggest solutions. Ask a soils engineer to make a soil test. The test results will tell you how serious the problem may be.

If there is an underground water problem, do not drain the pool to make repairs. Water pressure outside the pool will further damage the shell.

DECK REPAIRS

Cracks in a masonry deck are usually caused by one of two problems.

If the cracking occurs within a year or so of the initial installation, it may mean backfill was not tamped well enough and rain or pool overflow has caused earth settlement. If the deck has settled with the earth, resurfacing the deck to bring it up to grade may solve the problem permanently.

Cracks in the deck can be repaired. There are several different brands of patching materials for masonry decks. A local pool dealer or home improvement center can recommend a specific product. Serious damage may make it necessary to replace entire sections of deck.

If there is space between the deck and the earth, the void must be filled before the deck is patched or resurfaced.

A cracked concrete deck that is structurally sound can be covered with a new surface to hide the original damage. If the deck is stable, it could make a perfect base for quarry tile or other outdoor tile.

If minor cracks have been repaired and continue to widen, it is probably a sign of earth movement. This can be caused by underground water or continued settling of backfill. Call in help to determine the cause of the problem.

REPLACING AN OLD POOL

Most older pools are concrete and were installed before vinyl-lined pools and fiberglass pools became popular. Old pools age structurally and in design.

The options in replacing a pool are to remove the old pool and build a new one, or to refurbish the old pool. Breaking up and removing a well-built reinforced-concrete pool can be an expensive and time-consuming job. It may be easier to build a new shell inside the old pool.

An imaginative pool builder can take advantage of the support provided by the old structure. In other words, a new pool can be installed inside the old. The new pool will be limited to the basic shape of the original pool, or any shape that can fit inside it without appreciably reducing the size of the pool. The new pool will be slightly smaller. With new support equipment and plumbing, a new deck and new landscaping, the results can be pleasing and the cost considerably less than starting over.

Sprayed-concrete, vinyl-lined and fiberglass pools can all be installed within the old pool shell. Necessary modifications will depend on the type of pool installed. This is a job best left to a qualified pool builder.

A possible alternative to rebuilding the pool is to fit it with a vinyl liner. A new coping will be necessary, but little interior preparation will be needed. If a liner can't be ordered to fit the exact shape of the old pool, a few interior modifications may be necessary to form a shape that will accept a standard liner.

wheel-type vacuum at this time. The wheels may compress surface sediment into fresh plaster and cause stains that are difficult to remove. Take care not to gouge or score new plaster with the vacuum.

Before use, thoroughly clean the filter. For new plaster pools that use a cartridge filter, check the filter as soon as the water turns clear. The first cartridge or set of cartridges may need replacing. When accumulated dirt and debris have been removed and the water is balanced, you can start routine maintenance and water conditioning.

Spring Cleaning—Here are the steps to take in opening a pool that has been closed for the winter:

Step 1—Remove pool cover, sweep and clean. Store cover in a clean, dry place away from the sun. If rain water has accumulated on the cover, carefully remove the cover so rain water does not get into the pool.

Step 2—If the pool was drained, clean out any loose debris that might have collected in pool, drain or skimmer. Wash the walls and bottom with a mild muriatic-acid solution. Scrub down the diving board and ladders with a concentrated chlorine solution. Remove stains and tarnish from metal

POOL-CLEANING SCHEDULE

The key to maintaining a clean pool is adopting a maintenance schedule that is effective, practical and convenient. Once a routine program has been worked out, you need to stick with it. Some tasks, like vacuuming the pool or cleaning the filter, can be shared. Handling chemicals should be left to responsible adults.

Pool size, local water quality, support equipment, landscaping and climate are a few of the conditions that affect the cleaning schedule of your pool. No two pools are exactly alike. A maintenance program worked out for one pool may not work for another.

The following recommendations are general and work for cleaning most pools. You may have to make minor modifications to adapt them to your own pool.

EVERY DAY

Test daily for pH and chlorine levels in new pools, during periods of heavy pool use, in hot weather or after wind and rain storms. See page 118. If the pool is lightly used and daily readings are consistent, testing twice weekly may be sufficient. Add chemicals as tests indicate.

Use the skimmer net or leaf rake to pick out leaves or other organic matter that have blown into the pool. Check the pool daily for debris. Organic matter left in the pool not only makes the pool look dirty, it affects water-chemical balance.

Check skimmer basket daily and clean out any debris. A buildup of debris will interfere with water flow through the support system. It will reduce suction if you have a pool vacuum integrated with the system. A seriously clogged skimmer can cause pump damage.

To avoid accidents, pick up pool toys and other objects left on the deck or around the pool. Sweep or hose off the deck so swimmers won't track dirt into the pool.

EVERY WEEK

While taking care of routine daily maintenance, look for any unusual problems that may be developing. Weather or water conditions may require you to perform some service chores more often than weekly. If the pool is used infrequently, some cleaning jobs may be delayed if they are not necessary. The objective is to keep a clean pool with the minimum amount of work.

Clean Tile—The visible ring that forms on ceramic tile at the pool's waterline is usually a combination of oil and dust. Pool-supply companies sell tile cleaners specifically for pools. A fine-grit household scouring powder will work on ordinary dirt and stains. For vinyl-lined or fiberglass pools, use cleaners recommended by the swimming-pool manufacturer.

If the ring is difficult to remove, it may indicate a scale buildup. Remove light scale with a pumice stone or a solution of 1 part muriatic acid to 6 parts water. If the buildup is persistent or returns quickly, the pool water is seriously imbalanced. Have the water tested for total alkalinity and calcium hardness.

Brush Pool—Regular brushing prevents staining, discourages algae growth and dislodges dirt clinging to pool walls and bottom. A thorough weekly brushing is usually enough for normal pool use. More frequent brushing—even a few minutes every day—can cut down on the time it takes to brush weekly. An automatic pool sweep or agitator will help reduce brushing time.

Start at the shallow end and work dirt toward the main drain so some of the dirt will be pulled into the filtration system. Shut off or block water through the skimmer. First brush the walls, using light, overlap-

---

fittings with a common metal-cleaning compound.

Step 3—If the pool held water while it was closed, brush the walls and pool bottom and remove leaves and other debris in the water. Vacuum the pool if necessary.

Step 4—Check the pool for cracks, tears or other structural damage. Tighten loose bolts or screws on the diving board, ladders and other outside pool equipment. Make any necessary repairs.

Step 5—Refill the pool, or raise the water to the middle of the skimmer opening.

Step 6—Check the pump, filter and heater. Clean the skimmer basket and pump strainer. Examine the filter and heater. Turn on gas and electrical power to the support equipment. Start the filtration system. If the system does not function correctly, note the symptoms and check the troubleshooting section, starting on page 124. Minor leaks may be the result of dry gaskets. These leaks should disappear when the gaskets absorb water and expand.

Step 7—Run the system for at least 2 hours. If there is a pool dealer or pool-product supplier with facilities to test water, collect a sample and have it analyzed.

Most suppliers offer water analysis as a free service. If this service is available, obtain a complete analysis at least twice each season. Test kits used for routine maintenance will not analyze water for total dissolved solids, cyanuric acid, total versus free chlorine, calcium hardness, iron, copper and other minerals. If water analysis is not available locally, kits that perform these tests are available from pool-supply companies.

Step 8—Check reagents in your test kit to make sure they're not outdated. Replace old reagents. Dated reagents can give inaccurate results. This can result in costly and wasteful misuse of chemicals. Conduct basic tests.

Step 9—Based on water analysis results and your pH and chlorine-level readings, begin routine pool maintenance.

Step 10—If the heater is gas or oil-fired, light the pilot if necessary. Some gas heaters have electric-spark ignitions instead of pilot flames. Program timer for filtration system and turn on the system. Establish a regular water recirculation time.

CLOSING YOUR POOL

When you close your pool for the winter, or for any extended period of time, a simple maintenance program will protect the pool and equipment. It will make startup in the spring an easier job. It will help prevent stains, scaling and damage to pool equipment that could lead to expensive cleanup and repairs.

If you will be away for more than

ping strokes from the top of the wall to the bottom. Then brush the floor, working from the pool sides toward the main drain.

Clean Pump Strainer Basket—The debris that escapes the skimmer's strainer basket and is too large to be sent through the pump and filter will be trapped in the pump strainer basket. Weekly cleaning should be sufficient, depending on pool use. See page 128 for instructions on how to clean the strainer basket.

Vacuum Pool—Weekly vacuuming should be enough for a pool getting average use during good weather. If the pool has had heavy use or wind and rain have added excessive debris, an extra cleaning may be needed. Vacuuming is the major cleaning the pool will receive.

If your pool uses a vacuum tied into the filter system, make sure the filter is relatively clean before vacuuming. Clean the filter if necessary. A dirty filter restricts water flow and reduces suction through the vacuum head. When operating the vacuum, turn off the water flow through the main drain.

Attach the vacuum head to the telescopic pole, then attach the hose to the vacuum head. Make sure the filter hose is full of water before attaching it to the filter line. Avoid permitting air to enter the vacuum intake line. Keep the water level well above the intake. Don't lift the vacuum head out of the water once the hose has been attached.

The vacuum-head wheels should hold the head about 1/8th inch above the pool floor. Move the vacuum head *slowly* across the pool floor in overlapping passes. Avoid stirring up debris and clouding the water.

If the pool is exceptionally dirty, you should discharge dirt sucked up from the pool floor before it enters the filter. This is done by opening a valve between the drain and filter. If water is not run through the filter, resistance will be lower and greater suction obtained at the vacuum head. Follow instructions provided with your vacuum or support system. If water is discharged as waste, bring the water level back to normal before removing the water hose at the skimmer.

If you are using a jet vacuum system, turn off the pool pump. Attach the telescopic handle to the vacuum, and the garden hose to the vacuum head. Lower the head into the water and turn on the faucet. The higher the pressure and water flow from the faucet, the greater the suction at the vacuum head. Move the vacuum slowly over the pool floor in an overlapping pattern until the entire floor has been covered.

EVERY TWO WEEKS

Carefully monitor the water quality on your regular maintenance schedule. If your pool has received normal use, it will probably need to be superchlorinated about every two weeks. If the pool has had heavy use, shocking may be desirable every week or 10 days. See page 124 for information on shocking or superchlorinating the pool.

CONTINUING MAINTENANCE

In addition to a regular maintenance schedule, try to spot potential problems before they have a chance to become serious. Check bolts and screws on the diving board and keep the matting in good repair. Check pool ladders. Keep an eye on the support equipment to spot any leaks or malfunctions early.

How often you clean or backwash the filter will depend on filter capacity and pool use. There is no set cleaning schedule for filters. The pressure gage on top of the filter will indicate when the filter needs cleaning. See page 130. Tips on maintaining and cleaning the support equipment—pump, filter and heater—are on pages 127-133. Most pool problems are avoidable. A correctly maintained pool will provide many years of pleasure.

---

two or three weeks, employ a pool-service company to perform minimum maintenance while you're away, or find a volunteer you can train to look after your pool.

Regardless of climate, all pools should be covered in the off-season. A pool cover is an easy way to keep the pool clean. It also cuts chemical and electrical costs. A sturdy cover also provides safety. Pool suppliers sell cleaning agents that prevent vinyl covers from sticking and protect them from mildew stains.

WINTERIZING IN MILD CLIMATES

The major advantage pool owners have in areas where temperatures rarely fall below freezing is that the support system doesn't have to be drained or winterized. Here are steps to take to secure your pool in a mild climate:

Step 1—Thoroughly brush and vacuum the pool. Clean tile and pool deck. Clean skimmer basket and pump strainer.

Step 2—Fill the pool to the very top, near the overflow point.

Step 3—Test the water. If convenient, take a water sample to your local pool supplier and have it analyzed. If you correct water imbalance before you close the pool, off-season maintenance will be simplified.

Step 4—Adjust pH to the 7.4 to 7.6 range. Bring alkalinity to between 80 and 100 ppm. Alkaline or acidic water can damage the pool shell and equipment while the pool is covered.

Step 5—Add 1 quart of stain preventative per 25,000 gallons of water. Stain preventative is available from pool suppliers.

Step 6—Add 1 quart of algae control per 25,000 gallons of water.

Step 7—Shock or superchlorinate pool. See page 124.

Step 8—Bring chlorine level to 1.5. Don't overchlorinate. Add more chlorine only when test shows chlorine level below 1.5. You can use certain types of floating chlorinators under the pool cover if they are set at the lowest feed rate. Continue to test during the off-season to make sure chlorine levels are sufficient.

Step 9—Cover pool and set filter to run 2 hours each day.

Step 10—Check chemical balance every few weeks.

Step 11—Pull back cover and inspect pool once a month. Brush pool to help prevent scale formation.

WINTERIZING IN COLD CLIMATES

Most pool builders and pool manufacturers recommend that water be left in the pool during the off-season. Freezing and thawing is more likely to damage pool walls if the pool has been drained. Follow pool manufacturer's instructions if they have been provided. Here are the guidelines for closing a pool in a cold climate:

Step 1—Follow step 1 in *Winterizing*

Pool cover is used to keep debris out of pool during off-season. This one uses water-filled bags to keep it in place. A sturdy cover is an essential item in winterizing your pool. *Photo courtesy of Cantar Corp., Carlstadt, NJ.*

Expect to spend 4 to 8 hours a week on basic cleaning and maintenance during the swimming season. Less than half that time will be necessary during the off-season. Maintenance time can be cut several hours a week by installing an automatic pool-cleaning system.

While maintenance may take less time than in the past, there is still no substitute for establishing a basic maintenance program. A routine schedule helps avoid more costly, time-consuming work that can be caused by neglect.

An inexpensive, hand operated vacuum cleaner and a few handtools will keep a pool clean. What additional equipment you choose is largely a matter of weighing cost against convenience. Many pool suppliers offer a variety of basic startup kits that include brushes, skimmers, a vacuum head, test kit and other pool-cleaning essentials.

Vacuum Cleaners—Several fully automatic, robot-like vacuum cleaners are on the market. They automatically patrol the bottom of the pool, picking up debris. There are models that will clean walls and steps. Some connect to the pool's filtration system, as described on page 56. Others are self-contained units that plug into an outside electrical outlet. They are lowered into the pool and collect debris in their own filter bags.

The two most common vacuum systems are operated manually. One is connected to a vacuum inlet that is built into the pool's filtration system, usually at the skimmer. This system is installed when the pool is built.

The second is called a *jet cleaner*. It utilizes water action from a standard garden hose connected to the domestic water supply. It operates independently of the filter system.

The vacuum connected to the filtration system includes a suction head, wheels to enable it to roll across the pool floor, a floating hose from the suction head to the vacuum fitting and a handle. Some models are equipped with nylon brushes for scrubbing.

This unit is pushed slowly around the floor of the pool to pick up dirt, leaves and other debris. Material is sucked into the filtration system. Leaves and larger objects are caught in the pump strainer basket pump and fine debris is trapped in the pool filter.

in *Mild Climates,* page 137.

Step 2—Backwash the filter or remove and clean cartridges. Never leave a dirty filter or store dirty cartridges. Deposits and scale may cake or harden during the winter, forcing filter repairs or cartridge replacement in the spring.

Step 3—Lower the water level in the pool to expose all return lines, usually 18 inches to 2 feet. This will permit water to be drained out of plumbing lines and support equipment.

Step 4—Turn off main power and gas supply and remove OFF and ON trippers from the time clock. Remove drain plugs from the pump strainer housing, filter tank and automatic chlorinator. If the equipment isn't enclosed or otherwise protected from the elements, components should be dismantled and stored in a dry, non-freezing place until spring. This is an expensive, time consuming procedure. All equipment in cold climates should be protected by an enclosure.

Step 5—Drain water from all return lines and plumbing. Install expandable-rubber winterizing plugs in return lines and skimmer line. You have the option of leaving the system dry or filling it with antifreeze. Pool-supply companies sell a special antifreeze for this purpose. Never use automobile antifreeze, which is toxic. It will contaminate pool water when the system is started up in the spring. For specific winterizing suggestions, consult owner's manuals for support equipment components.

Step 6—Follow steps 3 through 8 for conditioning pool water in *Winterizing In Mild Climates,* page 137.

Step 7—Some pool manufacturers recommend placing air pillows, plastic balls, plastic bottles or other non-corrosive floating objects in the water to absorb pressure of expanding ice.

Step 8—Cover the pool. Monitor water quality until surface freezes.

POOL MAINTENANCE TOOLS

The development of automatic chlorinators, automatic vacuums, professional water analysis and a number of special maintenance tools has greatly reduced the amount of time the average pool owner must spend on pool care.

Fully automatic vacuum roams bottom and sides of pool, collecting debris. Vacuum inlet is connected to support equipment so collected dirt gets trapped in filter. On and off times are governed by support-equipment timer. This model is manufactured by *Kreepy Krauly, U.S.A. Inc.*, Plantation, FL.

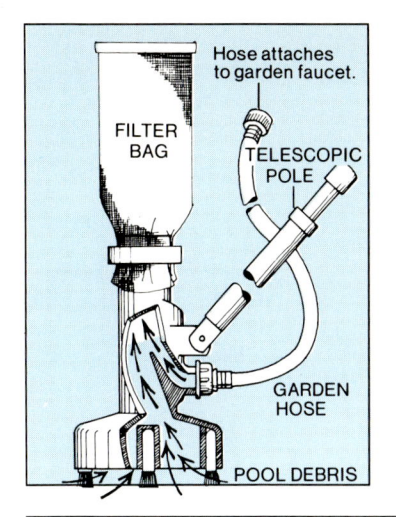

Self-contained vacuum operates using water pressure from garden hose. Other types connect to pool's filtration system.

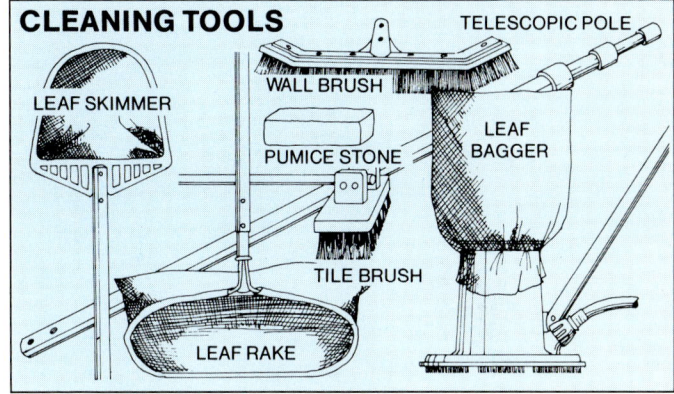

The jet cleaner uses a garden hose connected to a standard outdoor water faucet. Water flow creates the vacuum at the cleaner head. This pulls dirt off the pool bottom into a fine-mesh filter bag as the head is moved around the pool bottom. When the vacuuming is completed, the filter bag is emptied and washed out and is ready to be used again.

The jet cleaner is the fastest cleaning system. It picks up more debris than the type of vacuum integrated with the filtration system. However, jet cleaners won't filter fine material as effectively as a vacuum that directs dirt through a pool filter.

Agitators—The purpose of an agitator or *pool sweep* is to help keep the pool clean, but it does not pick up dirt and debris like a vacuum cleaner. The most common agitator is attached to the pool's water-inlet and floats on the pool surface. Two or more hoses are attached to the floating head and swirl around the top of the pool propelled by the force of the water entering the pool.

The agitator stirs up the water to keep debris and dirt particles suspended so they will be carried into the filtration system during the normal filtration cycle.

Another agitator system works with jet hoses built into the sides of the pool. When the system is turned on, the hoses automatically extend into the pool and snake their way around sides and bottom, propelled by water pumped through them. When the system is shut off, the hoses retract into the pool sidewalls.

A third type of system directs returning pool water through jets built into the pool bottom. This produces a current that directs dirt toward the main drain so it will be filtered out in the regular filtration cycle.

Leaf Skimmer—This is a net attached to a long handle. It is used to scoop leaves and other matter floating on the pool surface. There are several different sizes and styles available.

Leaf Rake—This is similar to a leaf skimmer, but with a wide, deep pocket that is drawn across the pool bottom to pick up leaves and other objects. Units are available that attach to the same handle used for the leaf skimmer.

Leaf Bagger—This unit operates in a similar way to the jet vacuum. It is used to pick up leaves from the pool bottom and collect them in a large bag on top of the unit. Pressure from water flow through a hose attached to the bagger creates a suction that pulls leaves into the filter bag.

Wall Brush—A sturdy brush with nylon bristles—usually about 18 inches wide—is used to brush pool walls and bottom. A nylon brush is adequate for painted, fiberglass and vinyl-lined pools. Plaster requires an additional stainless-steel brush for scrubbing stains, algae and dirt trapped in plaster pores.

Tile Brush—This is a plastic-bristle brush or a nylon scrubber used for cleaning tile and grout. Some brushes have long handles so cleaning can be done from a standing position.

Pumice Stone—A block of natural pumice can be used to remove stains and scale buildup on plaster. The block can also be used to remove stains and buildup on ceramic tile, but too frequent use can scratch the tile surface. Use only for stubborn stains.

Telescopic Pole—This is a long handle to use with pool-cleaning tools, designed to extend from 8 to 15 feet. A telescopic pole is easy to store and will reach all areas of the pool. A pole with a snap adapter makes it easy to change brushes and tools. A telescopic pole should not be used with a shepherd's crook, safety hook or other rescue device.

Pool Care & Repair 139

Lap pools are long and narrow, but they don't have to be rectangular. Jagged sides of this pool act as baffles to help prevent swimmer-created waves from washing up on deck. *Design: Walt Young, Landscape Architect, Northridge, CA.*

140 Swimming For Fitness

CHAPTER 10

Swimming for Fitness

Tiled lap pool complements geometry of modern home. Photo courtesy of American Olean Tile Company, Lansdale, PA.

The importance of regular exercise to maintain good physical and mental health is a commonly accepted fact. The questions are which forms of exercise offer the greatest benefits, and exactly how much exercise is the right amount.

Fitness experts have individual preferences, but they all place swimming at or near the top of the list of individual-participant sports. All agree that endurance sports with positive aerobic effects, including swimming, jogging, running, cycling and cross-country skiing, are the most beneficial. Why swimming is a favorite is easy to understand.

First, swimming laps is an effective *aerobic exercise,* as explained on page 144. Second, swimming is one of the few endurance activities that exercises all the important muscle groups in the body. Third, there is little risk of injury. Finally, you don't have to be an expert swimmer to derive positive conditioning benefits—and swimming can be a lifelong sport.

In addition to swimming, a pool can be used for flexibility and strength exercises. Conditioning through water exercises is popularly called *aqua dynamics.* One such series of exercises was compiled by the *President's Council on Physical Fitness and Sports.*

Strength and flexibility exercises are more easily performed in water because there is a lesser pull of gravity than on land. If you are immersed to your neck in water, you lose 90% of your weight. The feet and legs of someone who weighs 150 pounds need only support 15 pounds when the body is submerged.

In-water exercise is particularly beneficial for people with painful joints or weak leg and back muscles. They will find it possible to move and stretch more easily in water. Pool exercise offers an opportunity for older people who are unable to jog or exercise on land to improve their physical condition. Aqua dynamics classes are taught by local recreational and fitness centers. Also check the local YMCA to see if these classes are available.

LAP POOLS

Those who are serious about swimming for fitness can benefit several ways by installing their own *lap pool.* A lap pool is a long, narrow pool designed specifically for swimming measured distances. See photos at left and above. Other lap pools are shown on pages 142 and 144.

Swimming laps provides the sustained, vigorous exercise necessary to raise your heartbeat to a point where you achieve a positive aerobic effect. By swimming measured distances, it is easy to keep a record of distance, time and physical progress.

Swimmers who train at local public pools or health clubs must adjust their own schedules to fit the hours the pool is open for lap swimming. Even if a pool is relatively handy, getting there can be a minor inconvenience.

For the swimmer forced to juggle a work schedule, the convenience of having a lap pool available day or night is a luxury with great appeal.

Because conditioning is a year-round activity, a lap pool in a warm climate is ideal. But swimmers living in cold climates can use their lap pools much of the year. In the winter months, they may have to rely on commercial pools to continue training, but commercial indoor pools are usually less crowded in the off-season. Lap pools can also be enclosed to allow year-round swimming. A fully covered, all-season pool offers an ideal solution.

Lap pools built in cold climates can be covered with a greenhouse-type enclosure. The structure is a series of hoops running the length of the pool and covered with clear plastic or similar material.

Enclosed pools are easier to heat than open pools. The narrow width of

Swimming For Fitness 141

Primarily designed for lap swimming, this pool also allows other activities. It includes steps and shallow play area for children, built-in underwater seating, attached spa, fountain and slide. *Design: Loaring Construction Company Limited, Windsor, Ontario, Canada.*

a lap pool makes it possible to design a shelter that is smaller and much less expensive than an enclosure for a conventional rectangular pool.

If yard space is limited, a lap pool that fits into a narrow space may be more practical to install than a typical residential pool. Installing a pool in a restricted space may require a zoning variance. To determine local code restrictions, see page 8.

Multipurpose Pools—If other family members don't share your enthusiasm for vigorous exercise, a multipurpose pool designed to permit lap swimming can be as much a social center as any conventional pool. See photo above. The pool can be any shape you wish as long as it's designed with a clear lane for lap swimming and a flat-sided turn area at each end of the lane. If possible, the lane should be a standard lap distance.

If fitness isn't a primary consideration in deciding whether or not to install a private pool, the potential for serious swimming added to the social and family benefits could provide the extra bit of incentive to justify the whole project.

One advantage in designing a multipurpose pool is that it will have broader appeal to potential buyers if you should sell your home. A narrow lap pool may be perfect for you, but it may not please a buyer looking for a new home.

Consider the Cost—Although the shape of a lap pool may make it appear smaller than a standard pool, size may be an illusion. A lap pool won't necessarily be less expensive than a traditional pool. Many pool contractors base their cost estimates on perimeter feet. A standard 20x40' pool has 120 perimeter feet. A lap pool of a practical minimum size, 9 x 37-1/2', has 93 perimeter feet. But a 12x60' lap pool has 144 perimeter feet.

Lap pools with straight sides and standard depth are no more complicated to build than other in-ground pools. If you are considering a lap pool, discuss the project with pool builders who have installed these pools. When you look for a pool builder, follow all the basic steps and precautions for selecting one, discussed on pages 36-37.

To be functional, a lap pool has to be long enough to permit at least 8 to 10 strokes on each lap, otherwise the swimmer will spend most of the time in the water turning and pushing off.

Short-course, indoor pools designed for competition are usually a minimum of 25 yards, or 25 meters, in length. Long-course pools, both indoor and outdoor, are 50 meters, which permits competition in "Olympic" or metric distances. Competitive swimming is an international sport. Almost all new pools for serious competition are being built for metric distances. A satisfactory lap pool designed for personal use can be in yards or meters, it doesn't really matter. A personal lap pool should be a minimum of 12-1/2 yards or 15 meters.

When possible, choose a length divisible into a standard swimming distance. For example, a 60-foot pool requires five laps for 100 yards. A 20 meter pool requires five laps for 100 meters. It takes 88 laps to swim a mile in a 60-foot pool. From a technical point of view, there is no real limit as to how long a lap pool may be. The ground area available and your budget are the determining factors.

JET POOLS

Where space is limited, or the expense of a lap pool can't be justified, small pools with jets make it possible to swim in place against an artificially created current.

Most prefabricated jet pools are fiberglass with an acrylic finish. They can double as a spa or come with a spa attached. They are produced as complete units that include the support equipment necessary to filter and heat the water as well as a motor and pump to power the jets. They are available for in-ground installation. Some of the smaller models can be installed above ground with skirt and steps, similar to a portable spa, or can be built into a deck.

The largest models are up to 20 feet long and 10 feet wide. The minimum practical size is about 10 feet. Water jets are adjustable to vary swimming speeds.

Prefabricated jet pools are available with several different accessories, including underwater lights, foam insulation, solar covers and border tile.

Some pool builders offer custom-designed jet pools. These are usually sprayed concrete (gunite or shotcrete). The main advantage of a custom jet pool is that it can be designed to fit any space and to complement the surrounding landscape or architecture.

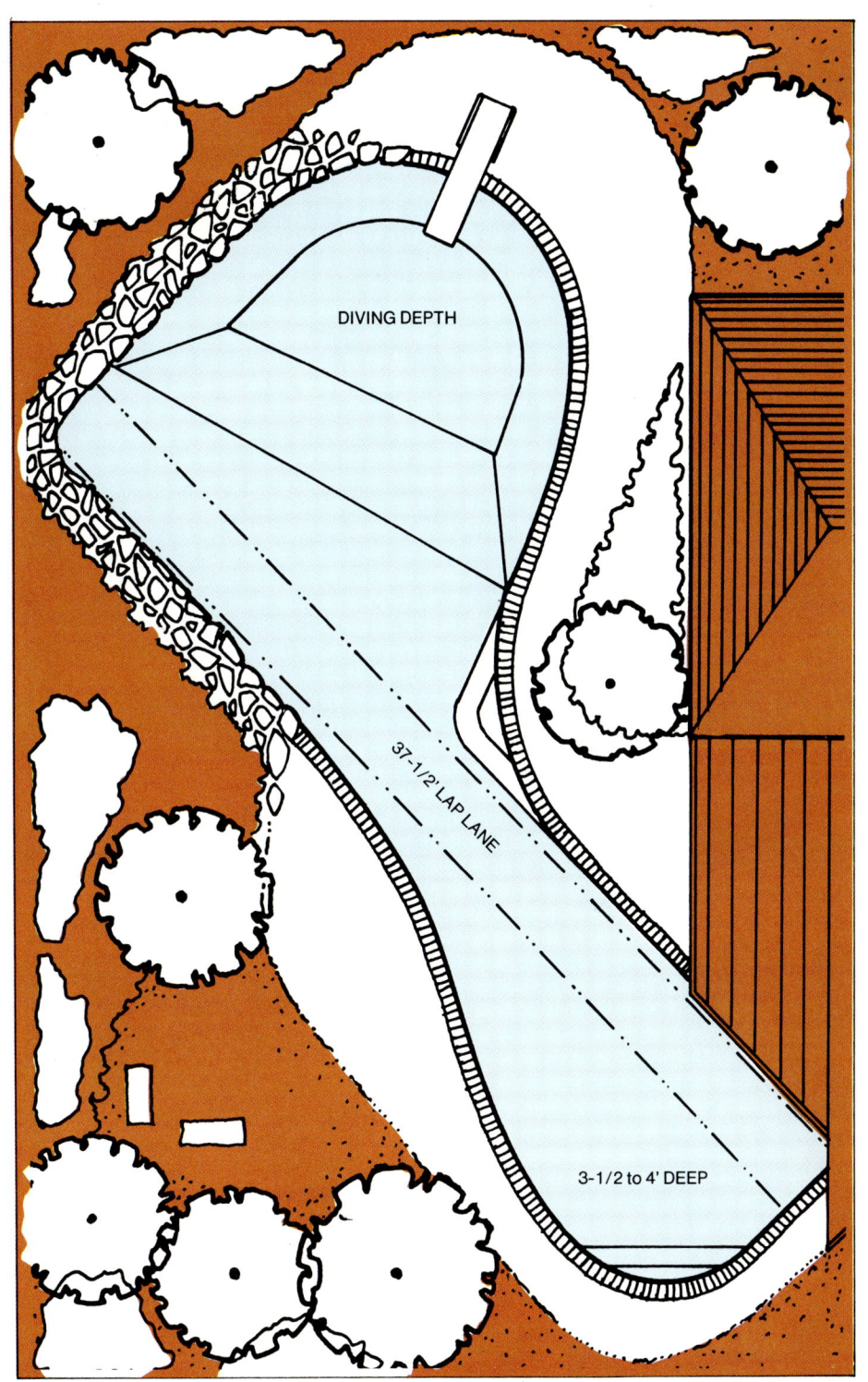

This is one of many possible designs for a multipurpose pool that allows lap swimming. It includes shallow play area and deep end for diving. Lap distance divides evenly into standard competition length.

Swimming For Fitness 143

Prefabricated lap pool is easily installed on hillside lot. Blue and white floats along pool sides help dissipate waves, serve as safety grabs. Lap pools are perfect for narrow spaces where conventional pools won't fit. *Design: Fastlane Pools, Santa Cruz, CA.*

SWIMMING FOR HEALTH

How physical conditioning and diet affect our physical and mental well-being is a complex area of study. Research is just beginning to produce sophisticated answers to questions about how exercise affects our overall health and longevity.

But the essential facts that support swimming as an ideal physical exercise are relatively simple.

Aerobic Exercise—Swimming offers positive *aerobic* benefits. The term *aerobic* has often been misused. It is often applied to exercises of questionable aerobic value. There is no specific aerobic exercise. Rather, aerobic exercises are physical activities requiring the use of an increased oxygen supply over a prolonged period of time. Aerobic exercise forces the body to improve its ability to use oxygen.

Aerobic exercise produces positive changes in the heart, lungs and vascular system. The body improves its ability to move air into and out of the lungs. This increases blood volume and improves the ability of the blood to move oxygen. As the heart is strengthened and the system becomes more efficient, the pulse rate drops and the vascular system functions more effectively.

A successful aerobic-exercise program involves adopting one or more endurance activities that can be pursued on a regular basis over an extended period of time. Most endurance forms of exercise, including swimming, must be continued for a minimum of 20 to 30 minutes at a time to achieve a positive training effect.

In swimming, covering distance at a steady, comfortable rate is of greater value than short bursts of intense swimming that are exhausting and can't be maintained for more than a few minutes.

Raising Heart Rate—A sufficiently high heart rate, or *pulse rate*, must be maintained during the exercise period to benefit the cardiovascular system. Pulse rate is the number of heartbeats per minute. There are several formulas being used to arrive at a minimum desirable pulse rate, but they all produce the same relative end numbers.

Men can determine their pulse-rate goal by subtracting 1/2 of their age from 205. Women should subtract their actual age from 220. Then both men and women should attempt to achieve a *target heart rate* of from 70 to 80% of that number. This is the heart rate that must be maintained during exercise to get a positive aerobic benefit.

As an example, a 40-year-old man should subtract 20 from 205 which is 185. Multiply 185 by 80% to get 148.

Because there is no simple way to determine your pulse rate while exercising, take your pulse rate at your wrist or heart *immediately* after your exercise. The pulse rate of individuals in good physical condition drops rapidly, so the rate must be

144 Swimming For Fitness

Jet pool has swim-in-place capability, takes up much less space than lap pool. This one is a custom-designed, sprayed-concrete pool. Prefabricated-fiberglass models are also available. With proper support equipment, a jet pool can double as a spa. Design: Patio Pools, Tucson, AZ.

determined within 15 to 20 seconds after completion of the exercise.

Count the number of beats in 10 seconds and multiply by 6, or determine your target heart rate for 10 seconds. Using the example of the 40-year-old man, 205 minus 20 equals 185. Or, 185 x 70% equals 129.5; 185 x 80% equals 148. Divide both answers by 6. The man's ideal heart-rate range is between 21 and 25 heartbeats in a 10-second period.

A Complete Exercise—One of the primary advantages swimming has over most other aerobic exercises is that it exercises both the lower and the upper body. Running, an effective aerobic exercise, is great exercise for the legs, but does little for the upper body. Of the basic exercises with strong aerobic value, only cross-country skiing is regarded as equal or superior to swimming. But cross-country skiing is seasonal and limited to those few regions of the country where snow is on the ground most of the winter. You are also more likely to injure yourself while skiing.

In addition to its physical benefits, swimming causes fewer exercise-related injuries than running, tennis, handball or basketball. Hard surfaces and sudden changes of direction place heavy stress on muscles and joints. Buoyancy and water resistance greatly reduce the chance of pulled muscles or damage to knees, hips and feet. Water resistance also makes a pool a practical place in which to practice non-aerobic strength and flexibility exercises. See *Aqua Dynamics,* page 146.

Swimming is specifically recommended as an exercise that can be continued to any age or adopted at any age. Many runners continue to put in their miles well into their 60s and 70s, but few take up the sport later in life nor are they encouraged to do so.

Unless you have been involved in some form of regular aerobic exercise, it makes sense to get a physical checkup before beginning a swimming program. This is particularly important if you are overweight or have had any other physical problems.

If you have not been exercising regularly, begin your lap swimming slowly, covering moderate distances. If you begin by swimming approximately 400 yards in 15 to 17 minutes four times a week, concentrate on reducing your time for 400 yards by about 2 minutes by the second week.

After two weeks, increase the distance by 100 yards and slightly increase the speed. At the end of 8 weeks, you should be swimming about 800 yards in under 23 minutes. No matter what starting distance you choose, use the same ratio to increase distances and shorten times.

If you are swimming to maintain a basic level of aerobic fitness, swimming 20 to 30 minutes four times a week at a pace of at least 40 yards per minute (800 yards in 20 minutes)

Swimming For Fitness **145**

should be about the minimum required to keep you in good physical condition. Fitness can be improved by swimming faster, longer distances or by adding a fifth day each week.

Competition—If you're interested in competitive swimming or are using swimming as part of a weight-control program, you will want to swim faster and increase distances. Competition, whether on a neighborhood, club, school or master's program level, can add excitement and dimension to a fitness program. Master's competition offers swimmers 25 years of age and older an opportunity to compete with swimmers in their own age groups.

One of the advantages of training is that the length of an exercise session is limited only by your physical condition, endurance and boredom threshold. Competition can provide a goal for conditioning and help relieve boredom.

For anyone in good physical condition, there is little danger of pulled muscles or the wear and tear on joints experienced by long-distance runners.

Once you have achieved a reasonable level of fitness, longer and more frequent exercise does increase fitness, but at a sharply less productive rate. If you increase your sessions from 1/2 hour to a full hour, you won't automatically double your level of fitness. It would improve only marginally. The key to a satisfactory program is establishing realistic goals and sticking to your program.

For anyone training for competition, any improvement in performance may justify longer and more intense workouts. Trimming 1/10 second off your 100-meter time might make swimming that extra mile or two worthwhile if you're after a medal. But it's comforting to know that the physical benefit from swimming a moderately paced half-mile is almost as great as for a competitor covering the same distance at a much faster rate. How quickly you cover the distance is not really important if the pace is rapid enough to maintain your target heart rate.

Losing Weight—For more than one reason, swimming is an ideal exercise for anyone wishing to lose weight. The obvious reason is that any regular exercise burns calories. But another important reason is that overweight swimmers run much less chance of injury than participants in sports that involve running. Water has a cushioning effect.

A weight-loss program that involves swimming should also include a modification of eating habits. Both diet and exercise are essential to an effective weight-loss program. The most effective diets include some form of regular exercise.

Although the number of calories burned through swimming will vary slightly from one individual to the next, someone who weighs about 150 pounds will burn about 200 calories swimming 1/2 mile in 1/2 hour. The added energy it takes to swim 4/5 mile in 1/2 hour can raise the calories burned to about 350.

The value of dieting while exercising can be noted through these basic examples. Swimming at the rate of about 30 yards per minute, it takes 16 minutes to use up the calories in one martini, 60 minutes to consume the calories in a 16-ounce vanilla ice cream soda or 8 minutes to reverse the effects of 10 jelly beans.

AQUA DYNAMICS

The term *aqua dynamics* refers to a series of flexibility and strength exercises developed by the *President's Council on Physical Fitness and Sports*. It is designed as an exercise program that anyone can perform in a swimming pool. These exercises can be completed in water with less gravitational pull than on land. The water itself provides a controlled resistance to movement.

A pool-exercise program can be designed for individuals of any age and any physical condition. Water exercises and swimming are commonly prescribed for the rehabilitation of injuries suffered in other sports.

Pool exercises are grouped under several different categories: water-standing drills, pool-side standing drills, gutter-holding drills, bobbing, treading water, and other exercises performed while floating in the water.

Using the series of exercises, it is possible to exercise all muscle groups or to concentrate on specific muscle areas. Programs range from light, 15-minute workouts to a full series of high-intensity exercises that take approximately 1 hour to complete.

The National Spa and Pool Institute funded the printing of the President's Council book of water exercise. Copies are available free of charge through most NSPI member pool dealers, or may be obtained by writing NSPI directly at 2111 Eisenhower Ave., Alexandria, VA 22314.

A cassette tape of the Aqua Dynamics program for playing at poolside is also available from the NSPI. One 30-minute side is an easy-to-moderate workout and the second side is a moderate-to-advanced workout. The tape includes a brief description of the exercises and the program is set to music to provide the right rhythm.

SWIMMING WHILE PREGNANT

Water bouyancy makes swimming an ideal physical activity for pregnant women. Being pregnant puts a greater demand on the heart and on abdominal and pelvic-floor muscles, which can be strengthened by swimming.

Regular swimming can improve aerobic fitness, strength and flexibility while avoiding the stress of on-land exercising. Maintaining fitness during pregnancy will speed post-birth recovery. Pregnant women should *always* consult with their physician before undertaking any strenuous exercise, including swimming.

FITNESS & FUN FOR CHILDREN

Teaching children to swim at an early age will encourage a child to maintain a high level of physical fitness while having fun. Swimming and pool games strengthen a child's muscles and develop physical coordination. When properly supervised, children are less likely to get injured swimming than in other physical activities.

In addition to fitness benefits, swimming should be taught to children as a essential safety precaution. See page 149.

Pool Games—There are many contests and games that can be used to entertain children and adults, and promote physical fitness. They can range from basic lap or relay races to paddling rubber rafts across the pool or diving for objects tossed into the pool. In all cases, games should be supervised by an adult. Children, no matter how well they swim, should not be permitted in the pool area without supervision. There are a number of manufactured pool games available through pool dealers and suppliers. A few of the more popular ones are shown in the photos at right.

POOL GAMES

There are many games manufactured especially for pool use. They're designed to provide safe fun for children and adults of all ages. Whether you buy pool games or devise your own, they should be played only under adult supervision. Follow instructions and precautions provided by game manufacturers. A few of the more popular games are shown here.

Weighted hoops test underwater swimming ability. Hoops should be placed so swimmer can navigate them without holding breath for excessive periods. *Photo courtesy of Aquality, Chatsworth, CA.*

Water-volleyball games are made by several manufacturers. They require more surface area than most other games. *Photo courtesy of Classic Pool & Patio, Indianapolis, IN.*

Ring toss can be played with any number of players. Children of any age can play, provided they can stand up in the water with arms exposed. *Photo courtesy of Aquality, Chatsworth, CA.*

Water basketball is another popular pool sport. This basket is free-floating. Another version has a basket attached to the side of the pool. *Photo courtesy of Aquality, Chatsworth, CA.*

Swimming For Fitness 147

A pool can be a fun, safe place to play if children learn a few basic safety rules. Life jacket is added precaution for children still learning to swim. It will keep child afloat if he or she wanders into pool's deep end. *Photo courtesy of Aquality, Chatsworth, CA.*

CHAPTER 11

Pool Safety

A swimming pool is a potential safety hazard if common safety rules are ignored. Most pool accidents are preventable. If you use common sense and observe a few basic rules, a pool can be a safe place for fun and exercise.

As a pool owner, you assume responsibility for the safety of anyone who uses the pool. Although no one likes to discourage poolside exuberance, you are obligated to make certain everyone using your pool understands and agrees to a few sensible safety rules. Emphasize these rules before the first toe is dipped into the water.

If you have children, they are probably the most enthusiastic about acquiring a family pool. Turn that enthusiasm into support for your safety rules and regulations.

The most important safety step is to teach all family members to swim. Even infants and toddlers can be made *watersafe*. Local YMCA or recreational centers offer swimming classes for all age groups either free or for a small charge.

If you have installed a new pool and have two or three family members who are non-swimmers, you can probably find a qualified instructor who will provide lessons in your pool or theirs. The YMCA, Red Cross or local recreation center should be able to provide leads. Teaching family members to swim can be fun, make the pool safer and increase the overall enjoyment of owning a pool.

Watersafing—Children under 1 year of age can be taught to be *watersafe*—capable of surviving an accidental fall into a pool. At age 2, they can be capable swimmers. The first steps in introducing children to water are described in the book, *How to Watersafe Infants & Toddlers,* by Lana Whitehead and Lindsay Curtis, M.D., published by HPBooks.

Older family members should complete a course in rescue methods and water safety, including *mouth-to-mouth resuscitation,* and *cardiopulmonary resuscitation (CPR).* CPR involves both chest compressions to circulate blood and restart a non-beating heart, and mouth-to-mouth breathing.

Children are capable of learning simple mouth-to-mouth resuscitation. The American Red Cross, YMCA, local recreational centers and hospitals offer water-safety and CPR courses free or with a minimal registration fee. Many of these organizations offer pamphlets on rescue and lifesaving techniques. Basic mouth-to-mouth resuscitation techniques are given on page 156.

CPR—The technique of *cardiopulmonary rescucitation* includes the basic steps of mouth-to-mouth resuscitation combined with regular chest compressions. The chest compressions let you act as the pump instead of the heart.

Chest compressions pump the blood out of the heart and through the blood vessels. In cases of cardiac arrest, where there is no pulse, mouth-to-mouth techniques do little good if the victim's heart has stopped beating and blood is not circulating.

CPR is the most useful technique to learn. The CPR course offered by the Red Cross can be taught in only two or three evening classes. A valuable guide to keep on hand for review of CPR techniques is HPBook's *How to Save a Life Using CPR,* by Lindsay Curtis.

The more thoroughly you and your family are prepared to deal with the unexpected, the greater peace of mind you will have. Once you have taken all the steps necessary to deal with emergencies, owning a pool can be a satisfying experience.

RULES OF SAFETY

There are several essential pool-safety rules a pool owner must put into practice if the pool is to be safe. The primary rule is: *Never swim unless another person is in the area.* A minor

Pool Safety 149

Polystyrene flotation device is modern version of traditional "water wings." It's used to assist learning swimmers and provide safety. *Photo courtesy of Aquality, Chatsworth, CA.*

accident can have serious consequences if there is no one to lend assistance or go for help.

Emergency telephone numbers for your family doctor, hospital, fire department, police department or local rescue unit should be posted by all outdoor-telephone extensions and by the indoor telephone closest to the pool. An outdoor-telephone jack is a good investment because it permits you to place and answer calls without leaving children unsupervised.

Pool Capacity—There is a limit to the number of people who can safely use a pool at one time. Each swimmer needs about 36 square feet of water surface. A diver needs about 100 square feet. To determine the comfortable and safe capacity of the pool, figure the pool's surface area in square feet and make your calculation based on the anticipated maximum number of individuals using the pool for swimming or diving. For details on how to figure pool surface areas, see page 44.

Swimming at Night—This practice is unsafe unless the pool has been designed and lighted specifically for night swimming. Adequate lighting would include underwater lights and lights around the pool's edge. If a midnight or moonlight dip is irresistible, swim with friends. For more information on pool lighting, see pages 112-113.

Eating Before Swimming—Warnings about swimming too soon after eating have been passed down from one generation to the next. However, recent studies have concluded that there is no evidence that a light meal or snack followed by a swim will cause stomach cramps.

Georgia Tech professor Fred Langue completed a survey involving 10,000 male swimmers. Not one swimmer interviewed ever had a stomach cramp. None of the 10,000 swimmers had ever seen another swimmer with a stomach cramp. Other studies that have reached similar conclusions suggest that swimmers who reportedly drowned from cramps may have suffered unrelated heart attacks.

Many swimmers may get general muscle cramps—usually from lack of blood in a muscle or muscle group—that last only briefly. Relief can usually be obtained quickly by changing strokes, or swimming to the shallow end and massaging the cramped muscle.

A vigorous swim immediately after a heavy meal makes little more sense than attempting a 6-mile run on a full stomach. The consequences may not be serious, but no one likes to be uncomfortable while exercising.

Alcohol—Drinking and swimming can create tragic results. Almost half of all drowning victims tested have been found with alcohol in their bloodstreams. Alcohol contributes to a false sense of security and impairs judgment.

Drinking in the pool area also introduces the potential danger of broken glass or scattered pull tabs that are a hazard to guests walking with bare feet. A pool is a social area and is used for entertaining. Keep social drinking and swimming separate.

Diving Boards—A diving board under the foot of an inexperienced diver can be a hazard. Many new pools are built without diving boards for two reasons.

One is the trend to shallower pools for the subsequent savings in water and energy. Shallow pools make diving boards impractical. See page 57.

The second is for safety reasons. Diving boards and slides are responsible for most poolside accidents. If your pool has a diving board, encourage guests to attempt only simple dives and restrict board use to one person at a time.

Attempt to identify *real divers*. People commonly overestimate their abilities and claim to be divers when they lack the skills to use a board safely. A diver is someone who has achieved minimum safe diving skills through proper instruction from a qualified teacher or from an experienced diver.

There are several basic precautions to take to become a safe diver:

- *Think Ahead.* Once you have started a dive, you don't have time to think. Test board for its spring. Determine the shape of the pool bottom and water depth before you dive and plan your entry path to avoid others in the water. If you're not familiar with the pool, slide into it and explore. Judging depth from above the water is difficult.
- *Steer Up.* As soon as you enter the water, steer toward the surface. Your arms *must* be extended over your head with hands flat and aiming up. Direct your body up and arch your back. Your body will help you steer up from the bottom.
- *Keep Head and Hands Up.* Serious neck and spinal injuries can occur if your head strikes the bottom. Always remember to keep your head and hands up as soon as you enter water.
- *Control Your Entry Path.* Divers sometimes lose control through improper use of hands and arms. Do not attempt "deep dives." Most home pools are not deep enough to do them safely. Dive straight ahead, not off the side of the board.
- *Watch Depth.* A well-trained diver can execute a dive in shallow water. For most swimmers, this risks serious injury. Never dive into the shallow end. Don't attempt diving in an above-ground pool. Most diving accidents happen in shallow water.
- *Don't Run and Dive.* A short run and dive can produce the same impact as a dive from a board. Don't dive across the narrow width of the pool unless you have a 25-foot clear path ahead of you.

Pool Slides—There are only two safe ways to use a slide. One is sitting and going down feet first. The second is lying flat on your stomach and entering head first. All other methods of using a slide are dangerous and risk injury.

Sliding into the water head first follows the same rules as diving head first. If you install a pool slide, make sure there is a landing area with adequate depth and clearance from the deck or pool edge.

There are many different sizes and styles of pool slides. Follow the slide manufacturer's specifications for installation, clearance and depth. For more information on installing pool slides, see page 57.

It takes no skill to use a pool slide. It does to swim. Guests using a slide at the deep end of the pool should know how to swim. Prohibit jumping or diving from a slide.

A smooth, non-slip deck surface is essential to safety. Concrete surfacing material shown here is also cool on bare feet. Photo courtesy of Mortex Mfg. Co., Tucson, AZ.

Jumping—An incorrect jump into shallow water can be dangerous and result in leg or foot injuries. Before jumping, know the depth of the water. Watch out for submerged objects or other swimmers.

Always jump directly forward from the edge of the pool. Make sure you have good footing. Teach children and beginning swimmers how to jump correctly into a pool. This should be included in water-safety instructions.

Outside the Pool—While the potential for the most serious accidents is *in* the pool, more minor injuries occur *out* of the water than in. Slips and falls are common. Cuts and stubbed toes have spoiled many swims.

The deck around your pool should be smooth enough to be comfortable under bare feet and rough enough to prevent slipping. Non-skid paints and a variety of masonry materials provide attractive and relatively skidproof deck surfaces. See pages 92-94.

Keep the deck clean and in good repair. Information on deck cleaning and deck repair are discussed on page 135.

Frequently check the diving board, slide, ladders and other pool equipment to make sure bolts are tight and equipment is in good condition.

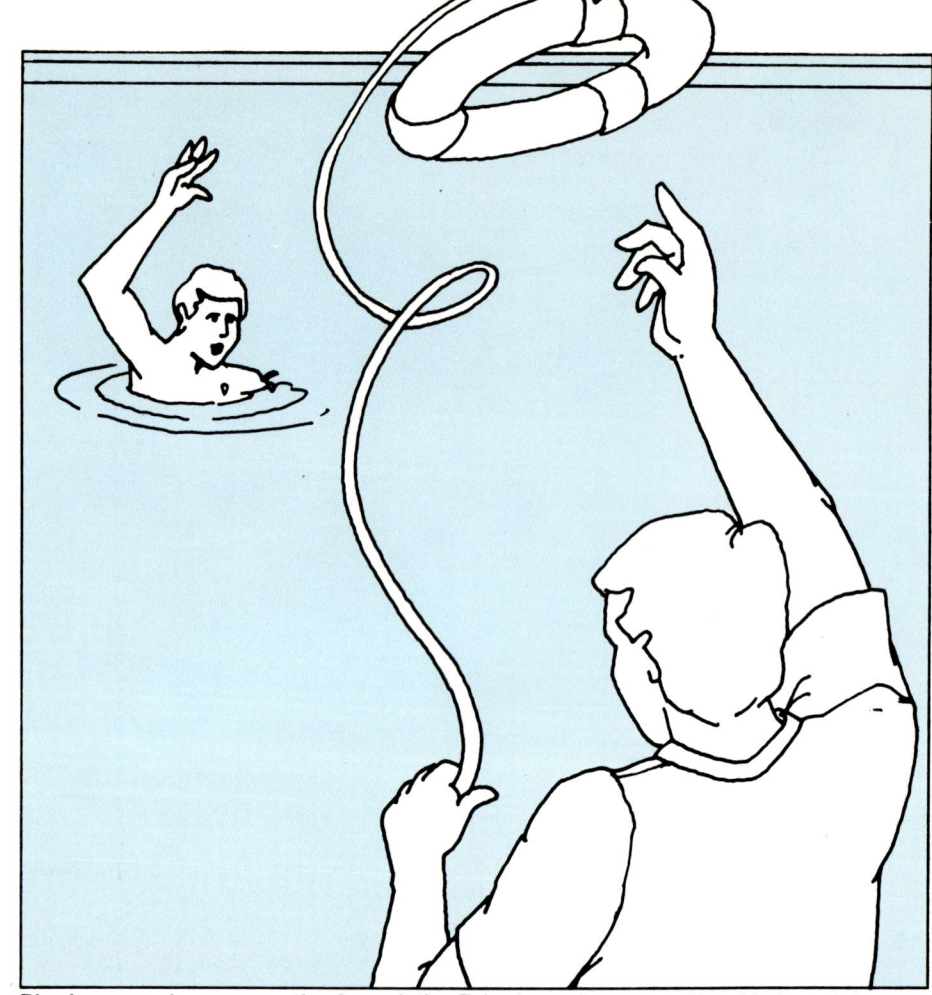

Ring buoy requires cooperation from victim. Faltering swimmer must be able to grab buoy.

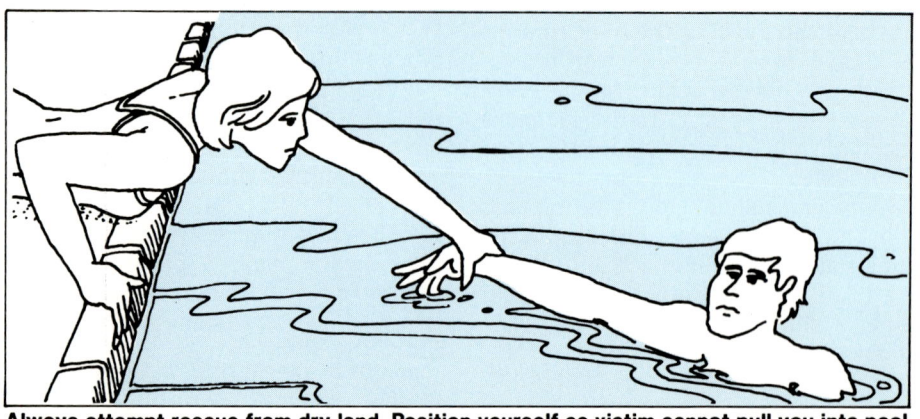

Always attempt rescue from dry land. Position yourself so victim cannot pull you into pool. If you can't reach victim, use shirt, branch, piece of pool furniture or other extension. *Never* jump in pool to attempt a swimming rescue.

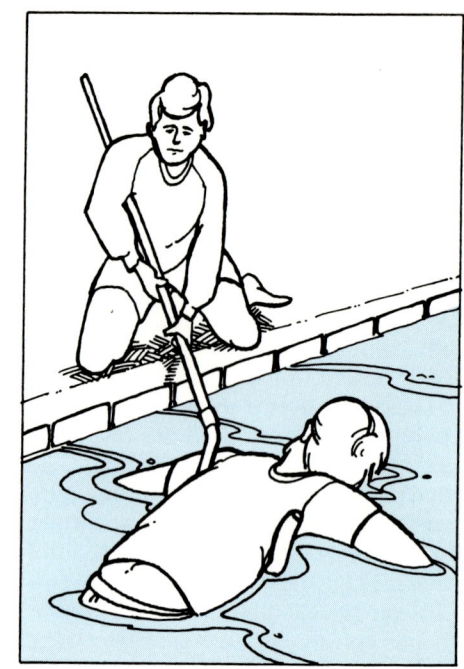

Rescue with shepherd's crook requires no cooperation from victim. Crook should be long enough to reach more than halfway across pool and to deepest part of pool.

There's an easy way to prevent broken glass either in the pool or around it: Never use breakable glassware, dishes or containers in the pool area. Use plastic dishes and glasses for pool service.

Keep plug-in electrical appliances and radios *away* from the pool's edge. Circuits for poolside appliances and pool-support equipment should be protected by ground-fault circuit interrupter (GFCI) breakers. Sudden power fluctuations will trip the breaker. This protection is required by most electrical codes covering pool installations. All outside electrical receptacles within 15 feet of the pool or attached spa require GFCI breakers or interrupters.

Pool chemicals should also be kept in a safe place so children won't be tempted to experiment. Specific instructions for safely using and storing pool chemicals are on page 121.

Water Quality—Although physical injuries are the first concern of most pool owners, illness due to poor water quality is another important consideration. Water quality is a function of correct pool maintenance. See pages 118-124. Also, swimmers with colds, flu, infected cuts, open sores, earaches and similar disorders should not be permitted in the pool—for their own sake and in the interest of fellow swimmers.

RESCUE EQUIPMENT AND TECHNIQUES

A first aid kit should be stored near the pool. Clearly mark its location so the kit can be quickly identified. The contents of the kit should be periodically checked to make sure outdated medications and missing items are replaced. Kits are available in many different sizes. Pool kits commonly include tape, disinfectants, scissors and other items to treat abrasions and cuts.

As a standard precaution, a rescue hook, called a *shepherd's crook*, should always be kept handy and visible. See drawing above. This is the single most important rescue tool. It can be used by a non-swimmer to pull a disabled person from the pool. A rescue doesn't require the cooperation of the swimmer in trouble. The shepherd's crook should have a lightweight, non-telescopic aluminum handle long enough to reach more than halfway

Safety fence discourages small children from entering pool area. See-through design allows view of pool from outside. Wrought iron is popular because it's attractive, unobtrusive and difficult to climb. *Design: Aqua-Rama of Atlanta, Marietta, GA.*

across the pool and to the deepest part of the pool.

Another rescue tool is a ring buoy on a line that can be tossed to a swimmer in trouble. The most common life-saving rings are 18 inches in diameter. Rings with proper flotation materials are approved by the U.S. Coast Guard.

The buoy has a serious purpose—it should never be used as a pool toy or float. Shepherd's crooks and ring buoys are available through most pool-equipment suppliers. Choose a buoy certified for rescue work, not an inflated toy of similar appearance.

How to Make a Rescue—If you have to rescue a faltering swimmer, always attempt the rescue from outside the pool. *Never leap into the water to attempt a swimming rescue.* A quick dive into the pool may be dramatic, but it can end tragically with two swimmers in trouble instead of one.

A successful swimming rescue is risky even for a swimmer trained in life-saving techniques. A faltering swimmer often panics and will pull the would-be rescuer underwater. The rescuer in a secure position has the greatest chance of a successful rescue.

If a floundering swimmer is within easy reach of the pool's edge, lie full length on the deck and reach out to grasp the swimmer. Don't try to pull a swimmer to the pool's edge while standing upright or leaning out over it. You may be toppled into the pool.

Always use the shepherd's crook to reach a swimmer more than an arm's length away. The hook can be used without the help of the swimmer. If the swimmer is alert or aware of the circumstances, tossing the ring buoy may be help enough.

If none of the conventional rescue implements are available, improvise. A branch, bamboo pole, shirt, pool net, broom or even a piece of pool furniture can be extended to the swimmer.

POOL ALARMS

There is no substitute for personal supervision of children using a pool. A pool alarm can sound a warning if a child, pet or any other heavy object falls into the pool. However, the alarm is only helpful if someone is nearby to hear it.

There are two common alarm systems. The first is a float in the pool that is activated and sounds a buzzer when a person or heavy object falls into the pool and disturbs the pool surface. The second is an electric eye system around the pool perimeter that sets off an alarm when the beam is broken.

Pool alarms can be useful supplements to personal supervision. The

Sturdy pool cover is capable of supporting adult's weight, helps prevent accidental falls into pool. *Photo courtesy of Loop Loc, Ltd., Deer Park, NY.*

major difficulty with pool alarms is that they can be set off in many ways other than a person falling into the pool.

An electronic eye can be set off by a bird or piece of paper blowing through the beam. A floating alarm can be set off by a sudden gust of wind that churns up the water. Frequent false alarms tend to reduce the awareness of anyone depending on the alarm for a warning.

POOL FENCES

Most state and local codes require fences around pools. The pool can be within a fenced yard or a fence can be erected around the pool itself.

Pool owners with small children in the family may elect to build a fence around the pool or between the pool and the house, even if the yard is sufficiently fenced. This reduces the chance of a young child straying too close to the water when unobserved. A fence rarely adds to the appearance of a pool, but the esthetic sacrifice is unimportant when balanced against safety.

Local codes usually require fences that can't easily be climbed by small children. Construction details are specified by codes.

Fences between the house and pool should be a see-through design, such as chain link, spaced slats, wire or similar materials. This permits a clear view of the pool from the house.

The decision to erect a fence should be made early in the planning stages so the fence can be incorporated in the design and your budget. Check local building codes and ordinances to determine if a fence is required. In some areas, it may be sufficient to have a fence around your yard.

Some areas may require a fence around the pool itself. Your local pool dealer should know the answer to that question.

For small children, a fence 4 to 4-1/2 feet tall is usually sufficient. It may take a fence 5 feet tall or more to keep older children out. The actual height required will be specified by code. The standard is 5 feet. Still, many pool owners have discovered that fence height is no obstacle to determined children.

Gates should be self-closing and self-latching with latches high enough off the ground so they can't be reached by small children.

POOL COVERS

Pool covers are used to keep unwanted swimmers out of the water and to prevent people from accidentally falling into the water. They come in a variety of materials and styles. They are commonly used to cover pools in the off-season or to protect the pool from blowing leaves, dirt and debris when the pool is not in use. Covers usually extend across the water from deck to deck and are anchored in place with ropes or *cover weights,* usually water-filled plastic bags.

Pool blankets and *solar pool covers* are used to insulate the pool when it isn't being used. Blankets float on top of the water and are not anchored in place.

An insulative pool blanket may discourage a child from entering the pool, but most are not designed to support weight. Most carry a warning to this effect. Only pool covers designed specifically to support weight should be used for safety purposes.

Insurance—Check with your insurance company to find out how a pool installation will affect your insurance rates. Ask how a pool cover, fence or other safety measures affect liability or premium rates. Most insurance companies have specific guidelines you must follow to qualify for various types of homeowner's policies.

LOOKING AFTER CHILDREN

Supervising children may require some diplomacy at times. Children should be expected to follow pool-use guidelines. Adults should be expected to set the example for the young.

Youthful enthusiasm can make children forget simple rules when playing in a pool. If you can convince young pool visitors to observe the no-running rule, you are an accomplished disciplinarian!

You will usually know the children using your pool and be familiar with their level of swimming ability. But you must observe the newcomers until you are confident they have the skills to use the pool safely.

If you have doubts, there is a simple test you can give your visitors to determine their basic ability. The following test need not be grim, but can be offered in the form of a game.

Swimming Test—A child should be able to pass these basic tests:
- Jump into deep water, rise to the surface, take air and swim to the edge of the pool.
- Float out from the pool edge on the stomach, turn over on the back and swim back to edge of pool.
- Swim in half-circle from the pool edge toward the center and back.
- Float on the back for 15 seconds.
- Bob or tread water for 30 seconds.

In addition, children can be taught how to use a shepherd's crook or toss a ring buoy to a swimmer in the water. Emphasize that life-saving devices are not for play.

The deep end of the pool should be

Safety precautions extend to the pool design itself. Pools with elevated walls, such as this one, should include a safety rope, ledge, railing, or other hand-hold along the raised-wall area. The rope or ledge can be positioned slightly below the waterline to make it less obtrusive. Design: Aquarius Pools, Sacramento, CA.

separated from the shallow end by a buoyed line. Swimmers of questionable ability should be restricted to the shallow end.

Supervising children also involves preventing too much exposure to the sun and too long a period of continuous play. Normally 30 to 45 minutes is long enough for young swimmers to be in the water at one time.

Trouble Signs—Signs indicating fatigue in young children are shivering, a bluish color in the lips, drawn or pinched faces or cold and clammy skin. Children who are having a good time may be reluctant to complain about discomfort or illness.

Children will invent games of their own. Contests to determine which child can hold his or her breath longest under water can be dangerous and should be discouraged. Use of flotation devices should be watched carefully. A child using an inflatable object for support in the water can easily cross into deep water. Inflatable toys are also deflatable toys. There are special flotation devices to keep learning swimmers afloat. See photos on pages 148 and 150.

In all cases, supervision should be continuous. If your friends or neighbors would like you to invite their children to use your pool, they should help with supervision.

Pool Safety 155

EMERGENCY TREATMENT

Mouth-to-mouth artificial respiration and cardiopulmonary resuscitation (CPR) are the most effective methods of emergency treatment for anyone who has stopped breathing for any reason.

They are valuable techniques to master for pool rescues. But they are also useful skills that can be used for any emergency treatment in or outside of the home.

CPR is more sophisticated than standard mouth-to-mouth artificial respiration and requires greater skill and physical strength. *It is the essential emergency treatment for a victim whose heart has stopped beating.* Most formal Red Cross classes for CPR are available to anyone 13 or over—or to youngsters who have completed the seventh grade.

Mouth-to-mouth respiration is still taught in Red Cross classes because it is an important part of CPR training. It can be taught to younger children and learned without the formal classroom training recommended by the Red Cross for CPR.

The ideal approach is to have adult family members take formal CPR training. Classes take only a few hours and the course can be completed in two or three sessions. Adults trained in CPR can instruct younger members of the family in mouth-to-mouth techniques. Post a card with the illustrated steps for mouth-to-mouth respiration by the pool.

Act Quickly—If oxygen supply has been cut off, the average person will die in 4 to 6 minutes. It is essential that artificial respiration or CPR be started as quickly as possible.

While you begin emergency treatment, have another member of the party call the fire department or local rescue unit. If there is nobody to assist you, do not delay treatment to phone for help. Shout for help even if no one is in sight. Treatment should be continued until the victim begins to breathe without aid or until a doctor or paramedics arrive to assume responsibility for the victim.

The Basic Steps—The technique for *mouth-to-mouth artificial respiration* is relatively simple and may be learned quickly, even by a child. The steps are as follows:

Step 1—Pull victim from the water as quickly as possible and rest victim flat on his back. Wipe any foreign matter from the victim's mouth. If possible, use a cloth wrapped around your fingers.

Step 2—Place one hand behind the victim's neck and lift while placing heel of the other hand on the victim's forehead to move the base of the tongue away from the back of the throat and to open the air passage. See drawing 1.

Step 3—Pinch the victim's nostrils shut with the thumb and index finger of your hand pressing on the victim's forehead. Open your mouth wide and place it tightly over the victim's mouth. Blow hard into the mouth, keeping your other hand behind the victim's neck. See drawing 2.

Step 4—Remove your mouth and turn your head to the side. Listen for exhaling. See drawing 3. Continue blowing air into the victim, once every 5 seconds for adults, or an average of 12 times per minute. Children normally take shallower breaths, so the rate should be about every 3 seconds, or 20 times per minute.

Step 5—Continue the blowing cycle, watching the victim's chest. Stop blowing when chest rises. Watch the chest to see that it falls, then repeat the cycle. Continue lifting behind the neck and holding the head tilted. If the victim is not getting an air exchange, check the head and jaw position and check to see if there is any obstruction in the back of the throat.

Step 6—If the victim is still not getting an air exchange, turn victim on his or her side and administer several sharp blows between the shoulder blades to dislodge any foreign material that may be preventing breathing.

Step 7—Some individuals who need artificial respiration never stop breathing completely, but gasp irregularly. Continue treatment until victim is breathing in a normal pattern.

These essential steps will help you provide emergency treatment for most victims of home pool accidents.

The essential steps of mouth-to-mouth respiration and CPR will help you provide emergency treatment for most victims who have stopped breathing. There are other methods of providing artificial respiration for victims remaining in the water. These are commonly used in lakes or large bodies of water where the victim cannot be returned easily or quickly to shore. These methods are also taught in most emergency rescue classes conducted by the Red Cross or YMCA.

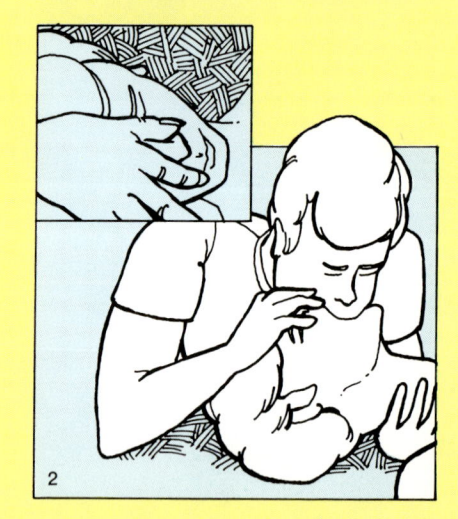

For individuals who have had their larynxes removed and breathe through an opening in the windpipe (a stoma), other techniques are necessary. These more sophisticated techniques are useful and are also included in rescue classes.

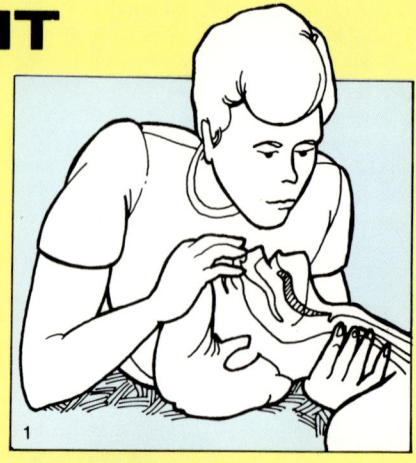

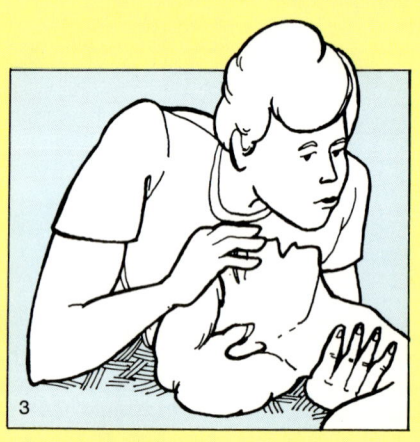

Design: Randy Garver, Creative Land Design, West Los Angeles, CA.

INDEX

A
Above-Ground pools, 7, 35, 96-103
　installing, 101-103
Accessories, 55-57, 100, 147
　above-ground pools, 100
　automatic chlorinators, 55
　automatic pool cleaners, 56
　diving boards, 56-57
　pool games, 147
　slides, 57
Acid, 120, 121, 126
Acid demand, 126
Active solar-heating systems, 61-66
Aerobic exercise, 141, 144
Agitators, 56, 139
Alarms, 153
Algae, 124-126
　brush, 125
　controlling, 124
Algaecides, 124-126
Alkali, 126
Alum, 126
Aqua dynamics, 146
Architects, 33, 37
Architect's drawings, 10
Architecture, fitting pool to, 22
Assessor's parcel maps, 9
Automatic pool cleaners, 56, 139
Automatic vacuums 56, 139

B
Backup heater for solar-heating system, 64
Backwashing, 49, 126, 130-131
　DE filters, 131
　high-rate sand filters 130
Bacteria, 126
Bicarbonate of soda (sodium bicarbonate), 121, 127
Bids, pool builders, 41
Black algae, 125
Blue-green water, 124
Boulders, 108-109
Break point, 126
Brick pool decks 18, 92, 93
British thermal units, (Btu's), 51
Bromine, 126
Brushes, pool, 125, 136, 139
　algae, 125
　tile, 139
　wall, 139
Builders, pool, 17, 35
Building codes, 8, 35, 43
Building department, 36
Building permits, 35
Buildings, pool, 31, 113-115

C
Cabanas, 114
Calcium carbonate, 126
Calcium hardness, 121-122, 126
Calcium hypochloride, 122-123, 126
Capacity, pool, 20, 44, 150
Cardiopulmonary resuscitation, (CPR), 149, 156
Cartridge filters, 48-50, 131
　cleaning, 131
Cash payments, 41
Centrifugal pumps, 46
Ceramic tile, 24-25, 112, 136
　cleaning, 136
Changing rooms, 31
Chemical safety, 121
Children, supervising, 154-155
　swimming test for, 154
Chloramines, 122-124, 126
Chlorinators, 55, 122-124
Chlorine, 55, 120, 122-126
　demand, 122, 126
　dispensers, 122-123
　gas, 122
　generators, 55, 122
　neutralizer, 126
　residual, 122, 126
Choosing a pool, 19-31

Choosing pumps, 44-47
Cleaning schedule, 136
Cleaning tools, 138-139
Closed-loop solar system, 61
Closed system, support equipment, 46
Closing pool for winter, 136
Cloudy water, 124
Coagulate, 126
Code requirements for support equipment, 43
Coil heaters, 52
Colored water, 124
Combined chlorine, 126
Competitive bids, 37-38
Competitive swimming, 146
Concrete decks, 30, 91-92
Concrete pools, 23-25, 75, 80-83
　installing, 80-83
Conditioner, water, 126
Contour lines, 10
Contractor, being your own, 35-36
Contractors, pool, 34-35
Contracts, 38-41
Contouring, 106
Copings, 91-92
Corrosion, 127
Costs, pool, 16, 20
Covenants, building, 8
Covers, 67,69-72, 154
Cracks in deck, 135
Cyanuric acid, 122, 127

D
DE filters, see *Diatomaceous-earth filters*.
DPD, 127
Dark-bottom pools, 67-68, 111
Dealers, pool, 34-35, 37
Decks and patios, 111-112
Decks, pool, 13, 30, 92, 100, 135
　repairing, 135
Deed maps, 9
Deed restrictions, 8
Depths, pool, 22
Design considerations, 21
Designing support system, 46
Diatomaceous-earth (DE) filters, 48-49, 131
　backwashing, 131
Diving, 22, 151
　safety rules, 151
Diving boards, 22, 31, 56-57, 151
Drainage, 13, 78
Drawings, 10-11
Drinking and swimming, 150
Dry acid, 127

E
Eating before swimming, 150
Electric heaters, 9, 50, 52
Electrolysis, 127
Emergency treatment, 155
Energy efficiency, pumps, 47
Equipment, see *Support Equipment*.
Estimates, 37
Excavating, 77-79, 81
Expansive soil, 79
Exposed-aggregate concrete, 30, 92-93

F
Fences, 12, 108, 110, 153-154
　code requirements, 110, 154
　decorative, 110
　wood, 110
　wrought-iron, 110, 153
Fiberglass pools, 6, 27-29, 36, 76, 88-91, 134
　fiberglass-sidewall pools, 28-29
　installing, 88-91
　one-piece shell, 88-89
　repair, 134
Fiberglass walls for vinyl-lined pools, 26-27
Filter sizes, 48
Filters, 48-50, 63, 73, 130-132
　cartridge, 49-50
　choosing, 48-50
　cleaning (backwashing), 130-132

DE, 49
　high-rate sand, 48-49, 130
Flagstone decks, 92, 111
Flat-plate solar collectors, 62-63
Flexible-plastic solar collectors, 62-63
Floc, 126-127
Flow rate, 45-46
Flowering plants, 106-107
Free chlorine, 127
Free-form pools, 20-22, 40
Front-loading skimmers, 53-54
Full-flow fittings, 46

G
Gas heaters, 9, 50-53, 132-133, 136
　choosing, 50-53
　servicing, 132-133
Gates, 12, 154
Gazebos, 31, 114-115
Glazed solar panels, 62
Grecian pools, 20
Green algae, 125
Greenhouses, 15
Grey-black water, 124
Gunite, 23-24, 75, 80-83

H
Hard water, treating, 121
Head loss, 45
Heat loss, preventing, 69-73
Heat pumps, 53
Heat-exchangers, 66
Heaters, 9, 50-53, 132-133, 136
　choosing, 50-53
　servicing, 132-133
　sizing, 50-51
　types, 52-53
Heating the pool, 72-73
Help, pool building, 36-37
High-rate sand filters, 48-49, 130
Hillside pools, 80, 98
Hot tubs, 51
Hydrostatic pressure, 79
Hydrostatic valve, 79

I
Impeller, pump, 45, 129
Indoor and enclosed pools, 15
Inorganic chlorine, 122
Insulated pools and equipment, 73
Insurance, 40, 154
Irregular pools, 44

J
Jet pool, 143, 145

K
Kidney-shaped pools, 20, 22
Kool Deck, 30-31, 92-93

L
L-shaped pools, 20
Ladders, pool, 101
Lanais, 31, 114-115
Landscape architects, 33-34
Landscaping, 16-17, 22, 105-115
Lap pools, 6, 21-22, 140-143
　sizes, 142-143
Lawns, 107
Lazy-L pools, 20
Leaf bagger, 139
Leaf rake, 139
Leaf skimmer, 139
Legal protection, pool contracts, 40
Life jacket, 148
Lighting, 29, 112-113, 150
　underwater, 29
Loans, 16
Locating pool, 11-12
Loose fill, 79

M
Maintenance, pool, 6, 117-139
　support equipment, 127-134
　tools, 138-139
　water, 117-126

Masonry-block pools, 24
Masonry walls for vinyl-lined pools, 27
Metal walls for vinyl-lined pools, 26-27
Micron, 127
Mineral balance, 118
Modified-rectangle pools, 20
Money-saving ideas, 16-17
Mosaic tile, 25
Motor, pump, 47, 128-130
Mouth-to-mouth resuscitation, 149, 156
Multilevel deck, 93
Multipurpose pools, 142-143
Muriatic acid, 120-121, 127

N
National Spa and Pool Institute (NSPI), 22, 37, 50, 57, 73, 92
Naturalistic pools, 21
Noise, controlling, 13

O
OTO, 127
Open-loop solar system, 61
Opening new pools, 134-136
Opening pool in spring, 134-136
Ordinances and zoning laws, 8
Organic chlorine, 122
Oval pools, 20, 44
Oxidizer, 127

P
PVC pipe, 46
Passive solar heating, 66
Patios, 111
Payment schedules, 38
pH, 119-122, 124-125, 127
    testing, 119
Phenol red, 127
Physical conditioning, 144-146
Pilot light, gas heater, 132
Planning the pool, 5-17
Plantings, 12, 107-108
    care, 108
    flowering plants, 107
    lawns, 107
    shrubs, 108
    trees, 108
    vines, 108
Plaster-finished pools, 125, 134
Plastic walls for vinyl-lined pools, 27
Polystyrene coping forms, 91
Pool budget, 16, 20
Pool buildings, 113
Pool chemicals, 117, 120
Pool contractors, 34
Pool covers, 67, 69-72, 154
Pool dealers, 34, 37
Pool-deck solar collectors, 65-66
Pool designers, 33-34
Pool enclosures, 15-16, 69-72
Pool games, 146-147
Pool houses, 113
Pool repair, 134
Pool shapes, 19-22
Pool sizes, 19-22
Pool sweeps, 56, 139
Pool-service companies, 117
Poured-concrete pools, 23-24
Prefabricated pools, 25-29, 144
    lap pool, 144
Pregnancy and swimming, 146
Pressure gage, filter, 49, 130
Priming a pump, 128
Privacy, 12, 98-99
Programmable timer, 54-55
Pumice stone, 125, 139
Pump, 44-47, 63, 73, 128-130
    choosing 44-47
    repairing, 128-130
    seal, replacing, 129
    sizing, 45-47

Q
Quarry tile, 94

R
Raising heart rate, 144-145
Reagents, 119, 127, 136
Rectangular pools, 20, 22, 44, 102
Reddish-brown water, 124
Repairing pool shell, 134
Rescue equipment, 152-153
Rescue techniques, 152-153
Ring buoy, 152
Rocks, 79, 108-109
Roof-mounted solar collectors, 64
Room addition for indoor pool, 15
Round pools, 20, 44, 101-102

S
Safety, 12, 121, 149-156
    handling chemicals, 121
Sand filters, 130
Sandy soil, 78
Scale, 127
Scale inhibitors, 121
Scaling, heaters, 133
Screens, privacy, 108, 111
Security fences, 12, 108, 110, 153-154
Self-priming pump, 47
Septa for DE filters, 49
Shallow play areas in pools, 21-22
Shallow pools, 7, 21-22, 67-68
Shapes, pool, 19-22
Shepherd's crook, 152
Shocking, 127
Shotcrete, 23
Shrubbery, 108
Site access for pool builder, 10, 38, 77
Site cleanup, 17, 38
Site plan, 10-11, 38-39, 105
Site preparation, 17, 76-79, 101
    above-ground pools, 101
Site selection, 9-13
Site surveys, 10
Sizes, pool, 19-22
Sizing support equipment, 44-51
    filter, 48
    heater, 50-51
    pump 45-46
Skimmer basket, 133
Skimmers, 53-54, 133
Skylights, 15
Slides, 31, 57, 151
    safety rules, 151
Small pools, 7, 16
Soda ash, 127
Sodium bicarbonate, 125, 127
Sodium bisulfate, 120, 127
Sodium carbonate, 120
Sodium dichlor, 123
Sodium hypochlorite, 122-123, 127
Soft water, treating, 121-122
Soil conditions, 78
Soil tests, 13
Solar-heating systems, 7, 9, 59-73
Solar covers, 71
Soluble salts, 120
Soot in pool heater, 133
Spalling plaster, 135
Spas, 13-15, 29, 42, 51
Sprayed-concrete pools, 18, 21, 23-25, 36, 75, 80-83, 135
    installing, 80-83
    repair, 135
Stabilized chlorine, 122
Stabilizer, 127
Stains on pool walls, 125
Standard distances for lap swimming, 143
Steppingstones, 112
Steps, pool, 29
Straight-wall oval pools, 20
Strainer basket, pump, 45-46, 128-129
Subcontractors, working with 35
Sun, orienting pool to, 11
Sunken barbecue center, 31
Superchlorination, 124, 127
Suppliers, pool, 36

Support equipment, 7, 16, 43-57, 95, 100, 127-134
    above-ground pools 100
    code requirements for, 43
    controls, 54
    designing the system, 46
    installing, 95
    maintenance, 127-134
    sheds, 31
Surface area of pool, calculating, 44
Swim-in-place pools, 143, 145
Swim-up snack bar, 31
Swimming for health, 144
Swimming pools, planning, 5-17
Swimming test for children, 154

T
Tank heaters, 53
Telescopic pole, 139
Test kits, 118, 136
Testing pool water, 118-121
    chlorine level, 119
    mineral balance, 119
    pH, 119
Tile, 136
Tile brush, 139
Tile decks, 94
Tiled pools, 24-25
Time clock, 54
Top-loading skimmers, 53-54
Total alkalinity, 120-121, 127
Total dynamic head, 45-46
Trees, 76, 108
    planting, 108
    removal, 76
Turnover rate, 45, 127
Two-speed pumps, 47
Types of pools, 23-29

U
Underwater lights, 29
Underwater solar collectors, 69
Utilities, 9

V
Vacuum cleaners, 55-56, 138-139
View, selecting site for, 12
Vines, 108
Vinyl-lined pools, 6, 25, 33-36, 75, 84-87, 134
    installing, 84-87
    repair, 134

W
Walks and paths, 111
Wall brush, 139
Walls, 108, 111
Warranties, 40
Water basketball, 147
Water column pressure, 52
Water conservation, 7, 22, 73
Water quality, 118-125
Water resistance in support system, 46
Water temperature, 50-51, 72-73
Water use, 9
Water volleyball, 147
Water-direction valve, 130
Water-flow gage, 49
Waterfalls, 42
Watersafing children, 149
Wet soil, 78
Wind control, 110
Wind patterns, 11-12
Winterizing in cold climates, 137
Winterizing in mild climates, 137
Wood decks, 94, 100, 112
Wood walls for vinyl-lined pools, 27
Work schedule for pool, 38

Z
Zoning laws, 8
Zoning variance, 8

Index 159

Acknowledgments

We would like to thank the following people and firms for their valuable assistance. The following list includes those who provided photographs and research materials, or otherwise shared their expertise to make this book possible. Photographs are indicated by page number.

Air Structures Inc., Sacramento, CA: 70 bottom.
American Olean Tile Company, Lansdale, PA: 141.
Aquality, Chatsworth, CA: 147, 148, 150.
Aqua-Rama of Atlanta, Marietta, GA: 8, 22, 25 bottom, 71, 99, 106 bottom, 153.
Aquarius Pools, Sacramento, CA: Title page, 40, 42, 106 top, 115 top right, 155.
Aquatic Pools, Sherman Oaks, CA: 93 bottom right.
Barnett-Hendricks Pools Inc., Cherry Hill, NJ: 4, 11, 15 top, 32, 68 top, 93 top right.
BioEnergy Systems, Ellenville, NY.
Boca Pool Lab. Inc., Boca Raton, FL: 94 bottom, 110 top and 110 bottom.
Cantar Corp., Carlstadt, NJ: 67, 70 top, 72, 101 top left, 138.
Chapman Pools, Old Lyme, CT: 60.
Classic Pool & Patio, Indianapolis, IN: 111, 147 top right.
Compool, Mountain View, CA: 54.
Mary Coventry, Sealed Air Corporation, Totowa, NJ
Engineering & Research Associates, Tucson, AZ: 59, 67 bottom.
Fastlane Pools, Santa Cruz, CA: 144.
Richard Fish, Photographer, Encino, CA: 14, 16, 25 top left, 31 bottom, 34, 58, 96, 109 bottom left, 113, 115 top left, 140, 157, back cover.
Hallmark Pools, Rolling Meadows, IL: 29, 90.
Heldor, Morristown, NJ: 17, 36, 39, 84-87, 110 center, 115 bottom left.
J&J Aquatech Pools, Shrewsbury, NJ: 13.
Jay Davis Pools Inc., San Antonio, TX: 114.
Loop Loc, Ltd., Deer Park, NY: 149, 154.
Mortex Mfg. Co., Tucson, AZ: 31, 91-92, 151.
Ken Nelson Aquatech Pools, Turlock, CA: 7, 18, 23, 107, 112 top right and bottom left.
Olympic Pools, Toledo, OH: 100, 101 right.
Ponderosa Pools, Tucson, AZ.
Carl, John and Mark Ragel, Patio Pools, Tucson, AZ: 35, 74-78, 81-83, 93 bottom, 105, 145.
Judy Ramminger, National Spa and Pool Institute, Alexandria, VA: 12, 15, 25, 93 top left, 94 top and center, 112 top left and bottom right, 113 top, 142.
Swim Factory, Marietta GA: 19, 27, 88.
Suzy Taylor, Wilson Pools, Tucson, AZ.
Teledyne Laars, North Hollywood, CA: 53.
20th Century Pools, Buena Park, CA: 6, 65, 68 bottom.
Whitaker Aquatech Pools, Tucson, AZ: 30.
Wildwood Pools, Fresno, CA: 21, 104, 109 top right and bottom right, 115 bottom right.
Carol Wright, San Pedro, CA.

Special thanks to our technical consultants for their many contributions to this book.

Bernard Burba, Baja Industries, Tucson, AZ.
Mary Coventry, Sealed Air Corporation, Totowa, NJ.
Dick Keabler, Imperial Pools, Albany, NY.
Mark Ragel, Patio Pools, Tucson, AZ.
Sharen Musgrove, Poolmaid, Tucson, AZ.
Bob Shearer, Aqua-Rama, Marietta, GA.
Jim Siebert, Bio-Lab Inc., Decatur, GA.
Joe Stecker, Hallmark Pools, Rolling Meadows, IL.

We would like to extend our gratitude to the **NATIONAL SPA AND POOL INSTITUTE** for their valuable cooperation and technical assistance in preparing this book.

Illustrations by Gary Barnard, Lakewood, CO.